COURT MASQUES

THE masque had a brief but splendid life as the dominant mode of entertainment at the early Stuart court, in which its extravagant fusion of dance, drama, music, and theatrical spectacle simultaneously served a number of different functions. At bottom a pretext for a costly (and sometimes disorderly) aristocratic knees-up, the masque displayed the magnificence of the court to itself and to the foreign ambassadors who competed for invitations. Writers and designers, however, attempted to imbue the transitory celebrations with moral and philosophical seriousness by translating the demands of the particular occasion, in Ben Jonson's words, into some 'more removed mystery' through complex and often arcane symbolism. At the same time, the occasional nature of the masque invited patrons, writers, and spectators to use it as the opportunity to comment in coded form upon specific issues of the time. In recent years the complexity of the negotiations masques frequently conducted with major political problems, from James I's desire to unite the realms of England and Scotland to Charles I's desperate attempts to find a path of political compromise on the eve of civil war, has been the object of a good deal of critical attention. In a wide variety of ways, then, the court masque offers a fascinating point of entry into the culture of the early Stuart court.

DAVID LINDLEY is a Senior Lecturer in the School of English at the University of Leeds. His publications include *Lyric* (1985), *Thomas Campion* (1986), and *The Trials of Frances Howard* (1993). He is editor of *The Court Masque* (1984) and *The Tempest* (forthcoming from The New Cambridge Shakespeare).

MICHAEL CORDNER is a Senior Lecturer in the Department of English and Related Literature at the University of York. He has edited editions of George Farquhar's *The Beaux' Stratagem*, the *Complete Plays* of Sir George Etherege, *Four Comedies* of Sir John Vanbrugh, and, for the World's Classics series, *Four Restoration Marriage Comedies*. He has also co-edited *English Comedy* (Cambridge, 1994) and is completing a book on *The Comedy of Marriage 1660–1737*.

PETER HOLLAND is Judith E. Wilson University Lecturer in Drama in the Faculty of English at the University of Cambridge.

MARTIN WIGGINS is a Fellow of the Shakespeare Institute and Lecturer in English at the University of Birmingham.

OXFORD DRAMA LIBRARY

J. M. Barrie
Peter Pan and Other Plays

Ben Jonson
The Alchemist and Other Plays

Christopher Marlowe
Doctor Faustus and Other Plays

Arthur Wing Pinero
Trelawny of the 'Wells' and Other Plays

J. M. Synge
The Playboy of the Western World and Other Plays

Oscar Wilde
The Importance of Being Earnest and Other Plays

Campion, Carew, Chapman, Daniel, Davenant, Jonson, Townshend
Court Masques

Chapman, Kyd, Middleton, Tourneur
Four Revenge Tragedies

Coyne, Fitzball, Jones, Lewes, Sims
The Lights o' London and Other Plays

Dryden, Lee, Otway, Southerne
Four Restoration Marriage Comedies

OXFORD DRAMA LIBRARY

━━

Court Masques
Jacobean and Caroline Entertainments
1605–1640

━━

Edited with an Introduction by
DAVID LINDLEY

General Editor
MICHAEL CORDNER

Associate General Editors
PETER HOLLAND   MARTIN WIGGINS

CLARENDON PRESS · OXFORD
1995

*This book has been printed digitally and produced in a standard design
in order to ensure its continuing availability*

OXFORD
UNIVERSITY PRESS

Great Clarendon Street, Oxford OX2 6DP

Oxford University Press is a department of the University of Oxford.
It furthers the University's objective of excellence in research, scholarship,
and education by publishing worldwide in

Oxford New York

Athens Auckland Bangkok Bogotá Buenos Aires Cape Town
Chennai Dar es Salaam Delhi Florence Hong Kong Istanbul Karachi
Kolkata Kuala Lumpur Madrid Melbourne Mexico City Mumbai Nairobi
Paris São Paulo Shanghai Singapore Taipei Tokyo Toronto Warsaw

with associated companies in Berlin Ibadan

Oxford is a registered trade mark of Oxford University Press
in the UK and in certain other countries

Published in the United States
by Oxford University Press Inc., New York

© David Lindley 1995

The moral rights of the author have been asserted
Database right Oxford University Press (maker)

Reprinted 2001

ISBN 0-19-812164-4

Jacket illustration by Bill Sanderson

CONTENTS

ACKNOWLEDGEMENTS

ANY editor owes much to the assistance of fellow scholars. Colleagues in the School of English at Leeds University have patiently endured lunchtime inquisition on many matters of detail; John Barnard, Paul Hammond, Joyce Hill, and Alistair Stead have all made valuable suggestions; Michael Brennan and Stephanie Wright have helped me in identifying a number of masquers. Richard Rastall of the Music Department at Leeds has assisted me with technical queries and John Peacock of Southampton University answered puzzling questions about scenic detail. Gordon McMullen of Newcastle University kindly allowed me to see the chapter of his D.Phil. thesis relevant to *The Coleorton Masque*, and Cedric Brown of Reading University has generously permitted me to make use of an unpublished paper on *Love's Welcome at Bolsover*. I am grateful also to Ken Rowe, for the enthusiasm with which he answered queries about classical mythology, and especially for his translation of most of the Latin material in the texts. My chief debt, however, is to my colleague Martin Butler, who has saved me from a number of howlers, and, more substantially, in conversation and by his writing has materially shaped my thinking about the genre.

Michael Cordner, Martin Wiggins, and Simon Leake have each examined drafts of the edition with exemplary scrupulousness, have made profitable suggestions, and prevented many errors. Needless to say, none of these people are to be held responsible for any mistakes and omissions which remain.

LIST OF ILLUSTRATIONS

(*Between pp.* 132 *and* 133)

INTRODUCTION

THE masques included in this selection run from Jonson's *Masque of Blackness* (1605), the second masque performed after the accession of James I, to Davenant's *Salmacida Spolia* (1640), the last court performance before the country slid into the Civil War. They not only span the period of the early Stuart monarchy, but also encapsulate virtually the whole history of the developed court masque in England. The form grew out of earlier entertainments, mummings, and disguisings, but as it was defined in Jonson's early masques, it centred on the arrival of aristocratic masquers, elaborately costumed, to perform their specially choreographed dances. After 1609 their entry was customarily preceded by an antimasque (also known as the 'antemasque' or 'antic masque'), performed by professional actors, and serving, as Jonson said, as a 'foil' to the main masque. In the later Caroline period these antimasques were much extended, though the basic pattern of comic or disruptive figures overthrown or contained by the final arrival of courtly aristocrats remained constant. At the end of the dramatic entertainment the world of the masque was dissolved, as the masquers took out partners from the audience to dance with them in the revels.

Masques were major political events, often inordinately costly, where the court displayed itself not only to itself, but also to foreign ambassadors and diplomats who eagerly sought invitation (and frequently caused problems in quarrels over precedence, or because of the refusal of an ambassador from one country to appear with another).

Theatre historians have long recognized the significance of the masque in the history of the aesthetics and mechanics of the stage. Inigo Jones, who was involved from the first to the last of these entertainments, and exercised an increasingly dominant role in their production, introduced perspective, illusionist setting to the English theatre, and developed ever-more ingenious stage machinery throughout his career. In the earlier masques scenes were changed by the *machina versatilis* or 'turning machine', but in later masques sophisticated series of flats slid in on shutters or dropped from flying galleries made complex scene changes possible. (See Fig. 11.) Musicologists, too, have charted in the masque the development of a musical style which, in projecting the words of songs in recitative and arioso setting, may have contributed to the rise of opera. But for literary critics, despite a thin trickle of major studies over the years, the court masque remains marginal to the study of the great age of English drama. The reasons are not difficult to find; the two major objections, then and now, can be summed up in two quotations.

Francis Bacon famously observed of court masques, that 'these things are but toys'.[1] It is hard not, at some level, to agree with him. The masques were performed as part of Christmas festivities or else to celebrate some particular event—the investiture of the Prince of Wales or an important marriage, for example. But at bottom the masques were always an elaborate frame for nothing more nor less than an aristocratic knees-up. For all the artistry that writers might exert in thematic exploitation of the structure of antimasque and masque, or the ingenuity of scene designers, it was the social dances of the revels and the feasting that followed that occupied the greater part of the evening.

In a second oft-quoted comment, a character in Beaumont and Fletcher's *The Maid's Tragedy* observes that masques are 'tied to rules of flattery'.[2] Again, the charge has to be in some measure conceded. Whether in the fulsome tributes to James's pacific wisdom or to the mutual love of Charles and Henrietta Maria, praise was obligatory, and often (as in *The Memorable Masque*, for example) the fulcrum upon which the action of the masque turned. Furthermore, praise of the monarch was often a kind of investment made by the noble sponsors or performers of masques in their own futures. Bacon, despite his low regard for masques, was prepared to spend over £2,000 in offering the Inns of Court *Masque of Flowers* at the marriage of the Earl of Somerset to Frances Howard, entirely, it would seem, to earn favour with the King and cement his connection with his favourite.

These charges against the masque have to be confronted. The starting-point for an answer to the first, Bacon's accusation of frivolity, has traditionally been Jonson's credo in the preface to *Hymenaei* (p. 10). There Jonson confronts the fact of the insubstantial transitoriness of the performance, and argues that it is by the

---

[1] Francis Bacon, *The Essays or Counsels*, ed. M. Kiernan (Oxford: Oxford University Press, 1985), 117.

[2] Francis Beaumont and John Fletcher, *The Maid's Tragedy*, ed. T. W. Craik, The Revels Plays (Manchester: Manchester University Press, 1988), I. i. 10–11.

intellectual seriousness of the programme underlying the text and its solid foundation of classical learning that it is able to reach transcendent truths. Though for Jonson the scenic display was merely part of the 'body' of the masque rather than the 'soul', his colleague Inigo Jones was equally convinced that the architecture of the scene and the iconographic detail of costumes, similarly founded upon research and the imitation of approved classical and foreign models, could lead the beholder to wisdom. Their stormy relationship came to an end after *Chloridia*, and Jonson delivered his last broadside against his erstwhile colleague in *Love's Welcome at Bolsover*. But, as D. J. Gordon long ago argued, their mutual antipathy derived from the way each of them was trying to occupy the same moral and philosophical ground.[3] As earnest of his serious intent Jonson provided learned footnotes to a number of his early masques (see Fig. 3) and, taking their cue from him, literary critics have explicated the richness and subtlety of the iconographic programmes of many of the entertainments.

Though it might seem that Bacon's charge is sufficiently rebutted by pointing to this intellectual ambition, it is too simple an answer to take the masque at the professed estimation of its writers. For if one considers the tone of the dedication of *The Masque of Queens* to Prince Henry, or the very overkill of Jonson's notes, which threaten to swamp the text they accompany, then the dominant feeling that emerges is one of anxiety. Jonson was only too aware that many in his audience would be incapable of recognizing what was going on. The same anxiety suffuses Chapman's preface to *The Memorable Masque* (p. 78–80), and is to be found in Campion's *The Lords' Masque* of 1613, for example. Though each of these poets manifests nothing but contempt for the inadequate understanding of some of their auditors, I would want to argue that this betokens a sense of insecurity about the status and effectiveness of the masque which is, paradoxically, one of the chief sources of its interest for the modern reader. The collision of the poets' ambition with their knowledge of the realities of their performance generates a tension which gives many of the masques their life.

One marker of this prevailing sense of precariousness is the way that so many masques take masquing itself as part of their subject.

[3] D. J. Gordon, 'Poet and Architect: The Intellectual Setting of the Quarrel between Ben Jonson and Inigo Jones', in Stephen Orgel (ed.), *The Renaissance Imagination* (Berkeley, Los Angeles, and London: University of California Press, 1975), 77–101.

Some of these discussions about the function and effect of the masque take place within the masque proper. In *Pleasure Reconciled to Virtue*, for example, the masquers are returned to the hill of virtue, and reminded of the struggle they must continually make to live up to the roles they have enacted. But it is most revealing that the issue is more frequently to be found in the antimasques. For the function of the antimasque was (to simplify somewhat) to represent the forces of disorder or dispute which the arrival of the aristocratic masquers dispels. What we see, then, in works like *Love Restored* or *Neptune's Triumph*, is the representation of anxiety about the status and efficacy of the genre displaced into the antimasque precisely in order that it may then seem to be overcome.

Something of the implications of this strategy can be seen in the deployment of a topos common to a number of antimasques, that of the difficulty of gaining entry to the performance. At one level this is no more than a representation of the real-life situation, where close checks were kept on those admitted to the masque, and it functions, therefore, as a confirmation to the courtly audience of its own exclusivity. But it is noticeable that those who are excluded are often representatives of the very people who had actually made the masque possible. Jonson may be joking at the beginning of *Love Restored*, when Masquerado observes that if the poet is not paid for his speeches 'it's no matter' (p. 66); but there is real bitterness in *Love's Welcome at Bolsover* when Philalethes claims 'Rhyme will undo you, and hinder your growth and reputation in court' (p. 198). Chapman may invite us to laugh at Capriccio in *The Memorable Masque*, but there is some sting in the way he is casually turned away without reward after providing the antimasque. In a masque not included in this volume, Shirley's *Triumph of Peace* (1633), a group irrupt into the work after the masque proper has well begun. They have almost all had some part in the making of costumes or sets, and claim thereby an equal right of entry. Suddenly the Tailor recognizes that he is being observed, and says: 'Tell us—hum? d'ye hear? Do not they laugh at us? What were we best to do? The Masquers will do no feats as long as we are here. Be ruled by me. Hark, everyone, 'tis our best course to dance a figary [figure] ourselves, and then they'll think it a piece of the plot, and we may go off again with the more credit.'[4] Such characters are signs, I suggest, both of the uncertainty that the writers

---

[4] T. J. B. Spencer and Stanley Wells (eds.), *A Book of Masques in Honour of Allardyce Nicoll* (Cambridge: Cambridge University Press, 1967), 302.

of masques had about their own relationship with the aristocratic audience they served, and of their awareness of larger questions concerning the function of the masque in court society.

Daniel's *Tethys' Festival* is a particularly interesting masque in this context, as it takes issue with Jonson's intellectual, Platonizing ambition, asserting that masques *are* nothing more nor less than transitory shadows. It is not that Daniel simply agrees with Bacon; rather, he turns the very evanescence of the masque into the lesson that it teaches (as Prospero does for Ferdinand and Miranda as he dissolves his betrothal masque for them in Shakespeare's *The Tempest* with the words: 'Our revels now are ended'). But Jonson himself, it would seem, had an ambiguous attitude to the genre he so championed. In his poem 'To Sir Robert Wroth' he complimented his addressee because he did not throng

> . . . when masquing is, to have a sight
> Of the short bravery of the night,
> To view the jewels, stuffs, the pains, the wit
> There wasted, some not paid for yet![5]

If even Jonson, the most pugnacious defender of the masque, had doubts—or at least was ready to write in other genres with less enthusiasm—about the masque, then we must surely recognize the problematic status of the genre.

If one turns to the charge of flattery, then there is again a standard defence of panegyric. The poet, it was argued, was not merely flattering the sovereign or nobleman, but presenting an ideal to which he or she should aspire; if they failed to live up to the ideal, then it was not a mark of the poet's insincerity but of their own moral failure. This is what Jonson claims in his poem 'To My Muse', when he writes:

> Who'er is raised
> For worth he hath not, he is taxed, not praised.[6]

Modern critics have customarily offered precisely the same defence for the sometimes grotesquely inflated praise that masques offer to successive monarchs. Praise was there to educate, we are frequently told. And it would be wrong for a modern cynicism entirely to reject the argument; we must suppose at the very least that James and Charles were also aware of the classical notions of education through

---

[5] Ian Donaldson (ed.), *Ben Jonson* (Oxford: Oxford University Press, 1985), 285.
[6] Ibid. 244.

praise, and that therefore they would have been *capable* of listening for a subtext of advice. But the problem of praise is complicated by the fact that it was not only the monarch who was celebrated, but the courtly masquers themselves, cast in their idealized roles. Performing before an audience who knew them well, the gap between real and ideal must have been only too obvious to many spectators. Jonson wrote in his 'Epistle to Master John Selden':

> I have too oft preferred
> Men past their terms, and praised some names too much;
> But 'twas with purpose to have made them such.[7]

Two years after this poem was written Jonson might well have recalled these lines when preparing his Folio of 1616. There he removed all mention of the participants in *Hymenaei*, written for the first marriage of Frances Howard, and *The Irish Masque* and *A Challenge at Tilt*, which had been presented at her remarriage to the Earl of Somerset, once the revelation of their part in the murder of Thomas Overbury precipitated their trial and imprisonment. *The Golden Age Restored*, indeed, represents Jonson's attempt to assuage his own, and the King's embarrassment, as he praises James for restoring justice to the world of the court. It is clear that, whatever the theory, Jonson was only too well aware of the practical consequences of praising the wrong courtier, and, as the quotation above demonstrates, was morally uneasy about the compromising of his integrity that panegyric threatened.

Though praise may be the goal to which every masque tends, it can be argued that the antimasque offered an opportunity to articulate problems and offer covert criticism of royal policy. Sometimes—as, for example, in the drunken revel of Comus's antimasque to *Pleasure Reconciled to Virtue* or Momus's parody of royal proclamations in *Coelum Britannicum*—these antimasques could dramatize abuses that the monarch might be encouraged to correct. It none the less has to be conceded that even if criticism is implied in an antimasque, the very structure of the masque suggests that such criticism is already contained by the benign royal power celebrated in the masque proper. This model of the functioning of the genre, stressing the 'containment' of any subversive energies, has indeed become the dominant frame for the reading of masques in many recent historicist accounts, but is itself open to question.

---

[7] Ibid. 331.

Perhaps the most important corrective to too simple a view of the functioning of panegyric is the fact that many works were presented *to* the monarch in the interests of the politics and ambition of the nobles who performed or commissioned them. Such masques might, therefore, embody a vision which might not square exactly with the policies of the King. Campion in *The Lord Hay's Masque*, for example, presents a rather qualified view of the Union of England and Scotland which the King so much desired, and many of his English subjects feared (and offers an ideal of temperance which must, at the very least, have made the court, which had recently participated in the notoriously drunken entertainment of Christian of Denmark, a little uneasy). This masque was probably paid for by the Earls of Salisbury and Suffolk, and so its muted anti-Scottishness might well represent something of their lack of enthusiasm for the King's pet project. *The Memorable Masque*, performed by the Inns of Court and probably influenced by Prince Henry, offered a view of Virginian exploration altogether more vigorous than James was inclined to adopt, even, it might be argued, going so far as to put the case of the imprisoned Raleigh, desperate to re-embark on his quest for gold in Guyana. In the Caroline masque it was perhaps more difficult to establish a sense of distance between the monarch and the message of the masque, since Charles and Henrietta Maria, unlike James, regularly performed themselves. But even here, in masques often assumed to be politically even more inert than those of the preceding reign, close attention to the political affiliation of those involved in the presentations suggests a more complex negotiation between court and sovereign than the text alone might indicate. The masques offered by Henrietta Maria to her husband, indeed, have a rather different agenda from those in which Charles performed; and the presence of masquers of very different persuasions performing together in *Salmacida Spolia* made it a highly charged political event.[8]

In a good deal of recent criticism the masque is characteristically represented as nothing more nor less than the voice of sovereign power endlessly reduplicated. But it is at least as useful a starting-point to suggest that for the writers and the audience of the original performances the masques were much less obviously univocal. Even if, in terms of their overall ideological position, they

[8] See Martin Butler, 'Politics and the Masque: *Salmacida Spolia*', in Thomas Healy and Jonathan Sawday (eds.), *Literature and the English Civil War* (Cambridge: Cambridge University Press, 1990), 59–74.

needs must present an 'illusion of power', careful attention to their detailed political context reveals that the apparently sycophantic panegyric may often be part of a work anxiously engaged in negotiation between court and king and between different political factions within the court itself. Furthermore, it always has to be remembered that, performed in a relatively small community, by representatives of itself, the audience was in a particularly 'knowing' relationship with the performers. It is not a straightforward matter to predict the potentially plural reaction of such an assembly.

For the modern reader, then, the court masque can profitably be studied, not simply as the mouthpiece of absolutist ideology, but as a stage where many of the contradictions of that ideology were consciously or unconsciously played out. They deserve our attention not because the charges laid against them by Bacon or Beaumont and Fletcher are untrue but, paradoxically, precisely because Jonson, Jones, and the rest were only too aware of their potential justice. The masque is not necessarily a complacent genre, however gloriously smooth its elaborate surface.

The selection of masques has been made with a number of criteria in mind. First, though Jonson is clearly the pre-eminent figure from 1605 until 1631, most of the other writers of masques are here represented. Their claims upon our attention have often been slighted in the past, but Campion, Chapman, and Carew in particular stand comparison simply as writers with Jonson. (And though I have stressed the political and ideological dimensions of the works, there is legitimate pleasure to be obtained from consideration of the artfulness of writers negotiating a highly stylized form with considerable learning and dexterity.)

Secondly, the selection registers something of the diversity of the genre. One strand of the heterogeneous ancestry of the form in mummings and disguisings is represented by *Christmas His Masque*. *Barriers at a Marriage* is included as a sample of a very different kind of courtly sport, the staged combat. Rather less popular perhaps in the Stuart court than in the time of Elizabeth, and not often surrounded with such elaborate texts as this, it yet demonstrates another way in which the masque writer might be called on to respond to and represent a political situation.

Most of the surviving Elizabethan entertainments were not performed at court, but were presented to the Queen on her progresses round the country. These entertainments were intimately engaged with the particular place of their performance and deployed material drawn from a rather different vocabulary from that of the masques at court. Their Stuart equivalents are represented here by Campion's *Caversham Entertainment* and Jonson's *Love's Welcome at Bolsover*. For their patrons, William Knollys and the Earl of Newcastle, these entertainments represented a major financial investment in securing the favour of the monarch, but yet in both cases the motive of self-advancement is wittily concealed by the writers' variations on the topos 'welcome to my humble home'.

Chapman's *Memorable Masque* is the one representative of the most elaborate sequence of masques and other entertainments in the whole period, the celebrations of the marriage of James's daughter Princess Elizabeth. It is interesting for its report on the procession through the streets of London, but more significant in that it was offered by two of the Inns of Court (whence came what is often claimed to be the first 'proper' masque, Francis Davison's *Proteus and the Adamantine Rock* in 1597). The Inns' position on the margins of court society permitted a rather different perspective to find voice (in Shirley's *Triumph of Peace* in 1633, indeed, we find some of the most pointed political criticism offered in any court entertainment).

Even further detached from the courtly centre is *The Coleorton Masque*, which represents the kind of domestic entertainments which must have been put on in large houses throughout the country. It is a pity that so very few examples of this sub-genre survive. It is a valuable reminder of the dangers of too exclusive a focus on the court, and suggests that many who had little to do with the court world (or, indeed, found themselves, as Essex did, in frequent opposition to it) were not thereby averse to the genre itself.[9] (It is worth remembering that the City Pageants, often articulating a distinct political and ideological position, deployed many of the same symbolic counters as the court masque.) It is important to stress the variety of the masque, and to insist on the ways in which its procedures, its iconology and symbolism, were not simply the efflorescence of a specifically monarchical way of thinking.

---

[9] See David Norbrook, 'The Reformation of the Masque', in David Lindley (ed.), *The Court Masque* (Manchester: Manchester University Press, 1984), 94–110.

NOTE ON THE TEXT

The Coleorton Masque survives in a single manuscript transcript, from which the present text is taken. The texts of masques by authors other than Jonson have been drawn from the earliest printed copies. Jonson carefully prepared the first Folio of 1616 for publication, and though the status of the posthumous 1640 Folio is somewhat more ambiguous, it has seemed right to base all the texts (with the single exception of the *Barriers*, for reasons explained in the notes) on these Folios. I have obviously been much aided by the labours of previous editors, and a list of those editions consulted can be found in the list of Abbreviations on p. 214.

Spelling has been modernized throughout. I have attempted to modernize punctuation in a way that aids the modern reader to follow the sense, but inevitably with compromises and inconsistencies. Elisions have not been indicated where the modern reader easily accepts them (in words like 'even' or 'heaven', for example); but every effort has been made to indicate where 'extra' syllables are required for the metre.

The annotation of masques poses particular problems. The allusiveness of the genre, both to the repertory of symbolic and mythological images and to the political circumstances of the time, demands a level of explication rather higher than the norm for this series. It is, furthermore, difficult to steer a course between annotation which is strictly explicatory and that which is interpretative and risks imposing a contentious reading on the reader. I hope I have found a satisfactory middle road.

SELECT BIBLIOGRAPHY

The court masque has commanded rather different kinds of interest during this century. After the surveys of the genre in the earlier part of the century, post-war critics focused chiefly on the handling of formal structure, and on detailed study of the iconology deployed in the texts. In the last fifteen years or so it has been the politics of the masque and its implication in the world of the court that has commanded interest. The student approaching the court masque for the first time would do well to start with Orgel's *Jonsonian Masque*, or Martin Butler's compact introduction in the *Cambridge Companion to English Renaissance Drama*, or my 'Introduction' to *The Court Masque*. After that it very much depends on where the student's interests lie.

If in the stagecraft, then Orgel and Strong's *Inigo Jones* is an essential point of departure, with John Peacock's articles (destined for publication in book form in the near future); if in the music, then Sabol provides the texts, but only Mary Chan's rather bland book offers a full-length study of the function of music in the masques. Students of dance have even less to work with—surely an area that would repay further research.

Though iconographic study has rather gone out of fashion, proper understanding of the handling of classical myth is an essential underpinning for any political analysis. D. J. Gordon's seminal essays are required reading, and Richard Peterson's more recent article on *Pleasure Reconciled* is an excellent example of such analysis.

The advent of New Historicism and Cultural Materialism has led to a rethinking of the relationships between literature and history. Strangely, perhaps, despite the (rather obscurely expressed) work of Jonathan Goldberg, most of the interesting recent books on the masque have operated from rather older historical principles. Whether in the slightly strained, but often stimulating, exegeses of Leah Marcus, or in the readings of Caroline masques by Altieri, Sharpe, Veevers, and Butler, much effort has gone into the precise elucidation of historical contexts for individual masques. Where these critics disagree, of course, is in their view of the history of the period—so a 'revisionist' like Sharpe slugs it out with a 'materialist' like Venuti. It all makes for vigorous debate, so that criticism of the masque is perhaps livelier now than at any time in the past.

Comprehensive bibliographies of masque criticism are to be found in David M. Bergeron (ed.), *Twentieth Century Criticism of English Masques, Pageants and Entertainments 1558–1642* (San Antonio: Trinity University Press, 1972) and Lindley, *The Court Masque*. The list which follows, therefore, concentrates on more recent work, and is divided into major general studies of the genre, particular studies of masques included in this volume, and studies of scene and music. It is necessarily highly selective.

A calendar of Jacobean masques by C. E. McGee and John C. Meagher is to be found in *Research Opportunities in Renaissance Drama*, 1984 (masques 1603–13) and 1988 (1613–25) bringing up to date the chronologies of Mary Susan Steele, *Plays and Masques at Court during the Reigns of Elizabeth, James and Charles* (Ithaca, NY: Cornell University Press; London: Oxford University Press, 1926) and G. E. Bentley, *The Jacobean and Caroline Stage*, 7 vols. (Oxford: Oxford University Press, 1941–68).

General Studies

ALTIERI, JOANNE, *The Theatre of Praise* (Newark: University of Delaware Press, London and Toronto: Associated University Presses, 1986).

BUTLER, MARTIN, 'Private and Occasional Drama', in A. R. Braunmuller and Michael Hattaway (eds.), *The Cambridge Companion to English Renaissance Drama* (Cambridge: Cambridge University Press, 1990).

—— 'Reform or Reverence: The Politics of the Caroline Masque', in J. R. Mulryne and Margaret Shewring (eds.), *Theatre and Government under the Early Stuarts* (Cambridge: Cambridge University Press, 1993).

GOLDBERG, JONATHAN, *James I and the Politics of Literature* (Baltimore and London: Johns Hopkins University Press, 1983).

GORDON, D. J., *The Renaissance Imagination*, ed. Stephen Orgel (Berkeley, Los Angeles, and London: University of California Press, 1975).

GOSSET, SUZANNE, ' "Man-Maid Begone!": Women in Masques', *English Literary Renaissance*, 18 (1988), 96–113.

KOGAN, STEPHEN, *The Hieroglyphic King* (Rutherford: Fairleigh Dickinson University Press; London and Toronto: Associated University Presses, 1986).

LEWALSKI, BARBARA KEIFER, *Writing Women in Jacobean England* (Cambridge, Mass., and London: Harvard University Press, 1993), 15–44.

LINDLEY, DAVID (ed.), *The Court Masque* (Manchester: Manchester University Press, 1984).

LOEWENSTEIN, JOSEPH, *Responsive Readings: Versions of Echo in Pastoral, Epic, and the Jonsonian Masque* (New Haven, Conn.: Yale University Press, 1984).

MARCUS, LEAH S., *The Politics of Mirth: Jonson, Herrick, Milton, Marvell and the Defense of Old Holiday Pastimes* (Chicago and London: University of Chicago Press, 1986).

ORGEL, STEPHEN, *The Illusion of Power* (Berkeley, Los Angeles, and London: University of California Press, 1975).

—— *The Jonsonian Masque* (Cambridge, Mass.: Harvard University Press, 1965).

—— and STRONG, ROY (eds.), *Inigo Jones: The Theatre of the Stuart Court*, 2 vols. (London, Berkeley, and Los Angeles: Sotheby Parke Bernet and University of California Press, 1973).

PARRY, GRAHAM, *The Golden Age Restor'd: The Culture of the Stuart Court* (Manchester: Manchester University Press, 1981).

PRESCOTT, ANNE LAKE, 'The Stuart Masque and Pantagruel's Dreams', *ELH* 51 (1984), 407–30.

REYHER, PAUL, *Les Masques anglais* (Paris: Hachette, 1909).

SHARPE, KEVIN, *Criticism and Compliment: The Politics of Literature in the England of Charles I* (Cambridge: Cambridge University Press, 1987).

STRONG, ROY, *Splendour at Court* (London: Weidenfeld and Nicolson, 1973), 2nd edition renamed *Art and Power: Renaissance Festivals, 1450–1650* (Woodbridge: Boydell, 1984).

VEEVERS, ERICA, *Images of Love and Religion: Queen Henrietta Maria and Court Entertainments* (Cambridge: Cambridge University Press, 1989).

VENUTI, LAWRENCE, *Our Halcyon Days: English Prerevolutionary Texts and Postmodern Culture* (Madison: University of Wisconsin Press, 1989).

WELSFORD, ENID, *The Court Masque* (Cambridge: Cambridge University Press, 1927).

YOUNG, ALAN, *Tudor and Jacobean Tournaments* (London: George Philip, 1987).

Campion

LINDLEY, DAVID, *Thomas Campion* (Leiden: E. J. Brill, 1986).

WILSON, CHRISTOPHER R., 'Some Musico-Poetic Aspects of Campion's Masques', in John Caldwell, Edward Olleson, and Susan Wollenberg (eds.), *The Well-Enchanting Skill* (Oxford: Oxford University Press, 1990), 91–105.

Chapman

GORDON, D. J. 'Chapman's *Memorable Masque*', in *The Renaissance Imagination*.

REESE, JACK E., 'Unity in Chapman's *Masque of the Middle Temple and Lincoln's Inn*', *Studies in English Literature*, 4 (1964), 291–305.

Coleorton Masque

FINKELPEARL, P. J., 'The Authorship of the Anonymous *Coleorton Masque* of 1618', *Notes and Queries*, 40 (1993), 224–6.

Daniel

PITCHER, JOHN, ' "In those figures which they seeme": Samuel Daniel's *Tethys Festival*', in Lindley, *The Court Masque*, 47–59.

Davenant

BUTLER, MARTIN, 'Politics and the Masque: *Salmacida Spolia*', in Thomas Healy and Jonathan Sawday (eds.), *Literature and the English Civil War* (Cambridge: Cambridge University Press, 1990), 59–74.

WEDGWOOD, C. V., 'The Last Masque', in *Truth and Opinion* (London: Collins, 1960).

Jonson

AASAND, HARDIN, 'To Blanch an Ethiop and Revive a Corse', *Studies in English Literature*, 32 (1992), 271–85.

ALLEN, DON CAMERON, 'Ben Jonson and the Hieroglyphics', *Philological Quarterly*, 18 (1939), 290–300.

BUTLER, MARTIN, 'Ben Jonson and the Limits of Courtly Panegyric', in Kevin Sharpe and Peter Lake (eds.), *Culture and Politics in Early Stuart England* (London: Macmillan, 1994), 91–115.

——and LINDLEY, DAVID, 'Restoring Astraea: Jonson's Masque for the Fall of Somerset', *ELH* (forthcoming).

FISCHER, JEFFREY, '*Love Restored*: A Defense of Masquing', *Renaissance Drama*, NS 8 (1977), 231–44.

GORDON, D. J., 'The Imagery of Ben Jonson's *Masques of Blacknesse and Beautie*' and '*Hymenaei*: Ben Jonson's Masque of Union', in *The Renaissance Imagination*.

KELLY, ANN CLINE, 'The Challenge of the Impossible: Ben Jonson's *Masque of Blackness*', *College Language Assoc. Journal*, 20 (1977), 341–55.

LINDLEY, DAVID, 'Embarrassing Ben: The Masques for Frances Howard', *English Literary Renaissance*, 16 (1986); repr. in Arthur F. Kinney and Dan S. Collins (eds.), *Renaissance Historicism* (Amherst: University of Massachusetts Press, 1987), 248–64.

LOEWENSTEIN, JOSEPH, 'Printing and "The Multitudinous Presse": The Contentious Texts of Jonson's Masques', in Jennifer Bardy and W. H. Herendeen (eds.), *Ben Jonson's 1616 Folio* (Newark: University of Delaware Press; London and Toronto: Associated University Presses, 1991).

MARCUS, LEAH S., 'City Metal and Country Mettle: The Occasion of Ben Jonson's *Golden Age Restored*', in David M. Bergeron (ed.), *Pageantry in the Shakespearean Theater* (Athens, Ga.: University of Georgia Press, 1985), 26–47.

MAURER, MARGARET, 'Reading Ben Jonson's *Queens*', in Sheila Fisher and Janet E. Halley (eds.), *Seeking the Woman in Late Medieval and Renaissance Writings: Essays in Feminist Contextual Criticism* (Lexington: University of Tennessee Press, 1989), 233–64.

MEAGHER, JOHN C., *Method and Meaning in Jonson's Masques* (Notre Dame, Ind.: University of Notre Dame Press, 1966).

ORGEL, STEPHEN, 'Jonson and the Amazons', in Elizabeth D. Harvey and Katharine Eisaman Maus (eds.), *Soliciting Interpretation, Literary Theory and Seventeenth-Century English Poetry* (Chicago and London: University of Chicago Press, 1991), 119–39.

PEARL, SARA, 'Sounding to Present Occasions: Jonson's Masques of 1620–5', in Lindley, *Court Masque*, 60–77.

PETERSON, RICHARD S., 'The Iconography of Jonson's *Pleasure Reconciled to Virtue*', *Journal of Medieval and Renaissance Studies*, 5 (1975), 123–54.

RIGGS, DAVID, *Ben Jonson: A Life* (Cambridge, Mass., and London: Harvard University Press, 1989).

Scene

CAMPBELL, LILY B., *Scenes and Machines on the English Stage* (Cambridge, Mass.: Harvard University Press, 1923).

NICOLL, ALLARDYCE, *Stuart Masques and the Renaissance Stage* (London: Harrap, 1937).

ORGEL, STEPHEN, 'The Renaissance Artist as Plagiarist', *ELH* 48 (1981), 476–95.

PEACOCK, JOHN, 'Inigo Jones's Stage Architecture and its Sources', *Art Bulletin*, 64 (1982), 193–216.

—— 'New Sources for the Masque Designs of Inigo Jones', *Apollo*, 107 (1978), 98–111.

—— 'The French Element in Inigo Jones's Masque Designs', in Lindley, *Court Masque*, 149–69.

—— 'Inigo Jones and the Florentine Court Theatre', *John Donne Journal*, 5 (1986), 201–34.

—— 'Ben Jonson's Masques and Italian Culture', in J. R. Mulryne and Margaret Shewring (eds.), *Theatre of the English and Italian Renaissance* (London: Macmillan, 1991), 70–91.

SOUTHERN, RICHARD, *Changeable Scenery* (London: Faber, 1952).

STURGESS, KEITH, *Jacobean Private Theatre* (London: Routledge and Kegan Paul, 1987).

Music and Dance

CHAN, MARY, *Music in the Theatre of Ben Jonson* (Oxford: Oxford University Press, 1980).

FULLER, DAVID, 'The Jonsonian Masque and its Music', *Music and Letters*, 54 (1973), 440–52 (corrections and additions by Peter Holman, ibid. 55 (1974), 250–2).

GOMBOSI, OTTO, 'Some Musical Aspects of the English Court Masque', *Journal of the American Musicological Society*, 1: 3 (1948), 3–19.

MEAGHER, JOHN C., 'The Dance and the Masque of Ben Jonson', *Journal of the Warburg and Courtauld Institutes*, 25 (1962), 258–77.

SABOL, ANDREW J., *Four Hundred Songs and Dances for the Stuart Masque* (Providence, RI: Brown University Press, 1978).

WARD, JOHN M., 'Newly Devis'd Measures for Jacobean Masques', *Acta Musicologica*, 60 (1988), 111–42.

SELECT CHRONOLOGY OF
STUART MASQUES

BEN JONSON

The Masque of Blackness

The Queen's Masques: the first
Of Blackness
Personated at the Court at Whitehall,
on the Twelfth Night, 1605.

The honour and splendour of these spectacles was such in the performance as, could those hours have lasted, this of mine now had been a most unprofitable work. But, when it is the fate even of the greatest and most absolute births to need and borrow a life of posterity, little had been done to the study of magnificence in   5
these,° if presently with the rage of the people, who, as a part of greatness, are privileged by custom to deface their carcasses,° the spirits had also perished. In duty, therefore, to that majesty who gave them their authority and grace, and no less than the most royal of predecessors deserves eminent celebration for these solemnities, I add   10
this later hand, to redeem them as well from Ignorance as Envy, two common evils, the one of censure, the other of oblivion.

Pliny, Solinus, Ptolemy, and of late Leo the African,° remember unto us a river in Ethiopia famous by the name of Niger,° of which the people were called *Nigritae*, now Negroes, and are the blackest   15
nation of the world. This river taketh spring out of a certain lake,° eastward, and after a long race, falleth into the western ocean. Hence (because it was her Majesty's will to have them blackamoors at first) the invention was derived by me, and presented thus.

First, for the scene, was drawn a Landtschap° *consisting of small woods,*   20
and here and there a void place filled with huntings; which falling,° an artificial sea was seen to shoot forth, as if it flowed to the land, raised with waves which seemed to move, and in some places the billow to break,° as imitating that orderly disorder, which is common in nature. In front of this sea were placed six tritons,° in moving and sprightly actions; their upper   25
parts human, save that their hairs were blue, as partaking of the sea-colour; their desinent parts fish, mounted above their heads, and all

1

*varied in disposition. From their backs were borne out certain light pieces
of taffeta, as if carried by the wind, and their music made out of wreathed
shells. Behind these, a pair of sea-maids, for song, were as conspicuously*   30
*seated; between which two great sea-horses, as big as the life, put forth
themselves; the one mounting aloft, and writhing his head from the other,
which seemed to sink forwards; so intended for variation, and that the
figure behind might come off better. Upon their backs Oceanus and Niger
were advanced.°*   35

*Oceanus, presented in a human form, the colour of his flesh blue, and
shadowed with a robe of sea green; his head grey and horned, as he is
described by the ancients; his beard of the like mixed colour. He was
garlanded with algae or sea-grass, and in his hand a trident.*

Niger, in form and colour of an Ethiop, his hair and rare beard curled,   40
*shadowed with a blue and bright mantle; his front, neck, and wrists
adorned with pearl; and crowned with an artificial wreath of cane and
paper-rush.*

*These induced the masquers, which were twelve nymphs, negroes, and
the daughters of Niger, attended by so many of the Oceaniae,° which were*   45
their light-bearers.

*The masquers were placed in a great concave shell, like mother of pearl,
curiously made to move on those waters, and rise with the billow; the top
thereof was stuck with a chevron of lights which, indented to the proportion
of the shell, struck a glorious beam upon them as they were seated one*   50
above another; so that they were all seen, but in an extravagant° order.

*On sides of the shell did swim six huge sea-monsters, varied in their
shapes and dispositions, bearing on their backs the twelve torch-bearers,
who were planted there in several greces, so as the backs of some were seen,
some in purfle (or side), others in face, and all having their lights burning*   55
out of whelks or murex shells.

*The attire of the masquers was alike in all, without difference; the
colours azure and silver, their hair thick, and curled upright in tresses, like
pyramids,° but returned on the top with a scroll and antique dressing of
feathers, and jewels interlaced with ropes of pearl. And for the front, ear,*   60
*neck and wrists, the ornament was of the most choice and orient pearl, best
setting off from the black.*

*For the light-bearers, sea-green, waved about the skirts with gold and
silver; their hair loose and flowing, garlanded with sea-grass, and that
stuck with branches of coral.*   65

*These thus presented, the scene behind seemed a vast sea (and united
with this that flowed forth)° from the termination or horizon of which
(being the level of the state,° which was placed in the upper end of the*

hall) was drawn, by the lines of perspective, the whole work, shooting
downwards from the eye; which decorum made it more conspicuous, 70
and caught the eye afar off with a wandering beauty. To which was
added an obscure and cloudy night piece,° that made the whole set off. So
much for the bodily part, which was of Master Inigo Jones his design and
act.

    By this, one of the tritons, with the two sea-maids, began to sing to the 75
others' loud music, their voices being a tenor and two trebles.

SONG

        Sound, sound aloud
        The welcome of the orient flood
        Into the west;
        Fair Niger, son to great Oceanus,° 80
        Now honoured thus
        With all his beauteous race,
        Who though but black in face,
        Yet are they bright,
        And full of life and light,° 85
        To prove that beauty best
        Which not the colour, but the feature
        Assures unto the creature.

OCEANUS Be silent, now the ceremony's done,
    And Niger, say, how comes it, lovely son, 90
    That thou, the Ethiop's river, so far east,
    Art seen to fall into th'extremest west
    Of me, the king of floods, Oceanus,
    And in mine empire's heart salute me thus?
    My ceaseless current now amazèd stands 95
    To see thy labour through so many lands
    Mix thy fresh billow with my brackish stream,°
    And in thy sweetness, stretch thy diademe°
    To these far distant and unequalled skies,
    This squarèd circle of celestial bodies.° 100
NIGER Divine Oceanus, 'tis not strange at all
    That, since the immortal souls of creatures mortal
    Mix with their bodies, yet reserve for ever
    A power of separation, I should sever
    My fresh streams from thy brackish, like things fixed, 105
    Though with thy powerful saltness thus far mixed.

'Virtue though chained to earth, will still live free;
And hell it self must yield to industry.'°
OCEANUS But what's the end of thy Herculean labours,
Extended to these calm and blessèd shores?   110
NIGER To do a kind and careful father's part,
In satisfying every pensive heart
Of these my daughters, my most lovèd birth;
Who, though they were the first formed dames of earth,°
And in whose sparkling and refulgent eyes   115
The glorious sun did still delight to rise,
Though he (the best judge, and most formal cause°
Of all dames' beauties) in their firm hues draws
Signs of his fervent'st love, and thereby shows
That in their black the perfect'st beauty grows,   120
Since the fixed colour of their curlèd hair
(Which is the highest grace of dames most fair)
No cares, no age can change, or there display
The fearful tincture of abhorrèd grey,
Since Death herself (herself being pale and blue)   125
Can never alter their most faithful hue;
All which are arguments to prove how far
Their beauties conquer in great beauty's war;
And more, how near divinity they be,
That stand from passion or decay so free.   130
Yet, since the fabulous voices of some few
Poor brain-sick men, styled poets here with you,
Have, with such envy of their graces, sung
The painted beauties other empires sprung,
Letting their loose and wingèd fictions fly   135
To infect all climates, yea, our purity;
As of one Phaëton, that fired the world,°
And that before his heedless flames were hurled
About the globe, the Ethiops were as fair
As other dames, now black with black despair,   140
And in respect of their complexions changed,
Are eachwhere, since, for luckless creatures ranged.
Which when my daughters heard (as women are
Most jealous of their beauties) fear and care
Possessed them whole; yea, and believing them,°   145
They wept such ceaseless tears into my stream
That it hath thus far overflowed his shore
To seek them patience; who have since e'ermore

4

As the sun riseth, charged his burning throne
With volleys of revilings, 'cause he shone°   150
On their scorched cheeks with such intemperate fires,
And other dames made queens of all desires.
To frustrate which strange error oft I sought,
Though most in vain against a settled thought
As women's are, till they confirmed at length   155
By miracle what I with so much strength
Of argument resisted; else they feigned:
For in the lake where their first spring they gained,
As they sat cooling their soft limbs one night,
Appeared a face all circumfused with light;   160
(And sure they saw't, for Ethiops never dream)°
Wherein they might decipher through the stream
These words:
    That they a land must forthwith seek,
    Whose termination (of the Greek)   165
    Sounds -*tania*; where bright Sol, that heat
    Their bloods, doth never rise or set,
    But in his journey passeth by,
    And leaves that climate of the sky
    To comfort of a greater light,°   170
    Who forms all beauty with his sight.
In search of this have we three princedoms past
That speak out -*tania* in their accents last:
Black Mauritania first, and secondly°
Swarth Lusitania, next we did descry°   175
Rich Aquitania, and yet cannot find°
The place unto these longing nymphs designed.°
Instruct and aid me, great Oceanus:
What land is this that now appears to us?
OCEANUS This land, that lifts into the temperate air   180
His snowy cliff, is Albion the fair,°
So called of Neptune's son, who ruleth here;°
For whose dear guard, myself four thousand year,
Since old Deucalion's days, have walked the round°
About his empire, proud to see him crowned   185
Above my waves.

*At this, the moon was discovered in the upper part of the house, triumphant
in a silver throne, made in figure of a* pyramis. *Her garments white and
silver, the dressing of her head antique, and crowned with a luminary or*

5

sphere of light, which striking on the clouds, and heightened with silver,   190
reflected as natural clouds do by the splendour of the moon. The heaven
about her was vaulted with blue silk, and set with stars of silver which
had in them their several lights burning. The sudden sight of which made
Niger to interrupt Oceanus with this present passion.°

NIGER   —O see, our silver star!   195
   Whose pure auspicious light greets us thus far!
   Great Æthiopia, goddess of our shore,°
   Since with particular worship we adore
   Thy general brightness, let particular grace
   Shine on my zealous daughters. Show the place   200
   Which long their longings urged their eyes to see.
   Beautify them, which long have deified thee.
ÆTHIOPIA Niger, be glad; resume thy native cheer.
   Thy daughters' labours have their period here,
   And so thy errors. I was that bright face   205
   Reflected by the lake, in which thy race
   Read mystic lines (which skill Pythagoras
   First taught to men by a reverberate glass).°
   This blessed isle doth with that *-tania* end
   Which there they saw inscribed, and shall extend   210
   Wished satisfaction to their best desires.
   Britannia, which the triple world admires,°
   This isle hath now recovered for her name;°
   Where reign those beauties that with so much fame
   The sacred Muses' sons have honourèd,   215
   And from bright Hesperus to Eos spread.°
   With that great name, Britannia, this blest isle
   Hath won her ancient dignity and style,
   A world divided from the world, and tried°
   The abstract of it in his general pride.°   220
   For were the world, with all his wealth, a ring,
   Britannia (whose new name makes all tongues sing)
   Might be a diamond worthy to enchase it,
   Ruled by a sun, that to this height doth grace it.
   Whose beams shine day and night, and are of force   225
   To blanch an Ethiop and revive a cor'se.°
   His light sciental is and (past mere nature)
   Can salve the rude defects of every creature.
     Call forth thy honoured daughters, then,
     And let them 'fore the Britain men   230

6

Indent the land with those pure traces°
They flow with in their native graces.
Invite them boldly to the shore,
Their beauties shall be scorched no more;
This sun is temperate, and refines   235
All things on which his radiance shines.

*Here the tritons sounded, and they danced on shore, every couple as they
advanced severally presenting their fans,° in one of which were inscribed
their mixed names, in the other a mute hieroglyphic, expressing their mixed
qualities. Which manner of symbol I rather chose than* imprese, *as well*   240
*for strangeness, as relishing of antiquity, and more applying to that
original doctrine of sculpture which the Egyptians are said first to have
brought from the Ethiopians.*

	The Names°	The Symbols	
The Queen	*Euphoris*	*A golden tree, laden with fruit*	245
Countess of Bedford	*Aglaia*		
Lady Herbert	*Diaphane*	*The figure icosahedron of crystal*	
Countess of Derby	*Eucampse*		
Lady Rich	*Ocyte*	*A pair of naked feet in a river*	
Countess of Suffolk	*Kathare*		250
Lady Bevill	*Notis*	*The salamander simple*	
Lady Effingham	*Pscychrote*		
Lady Elizabeth Howard	*Glycyte*	*A cloud full of rain dropping*	
Lady Susan Vere	*Malacia*		
Lady Wroth	*Baryte*	*An urn, sphered with wine*	255
Lady Walsingham	*Periphere*		

The names of the Oceaniae were

Doris	*Cydippe*	*Beroe*	*Ianthe*	
Petrae	*Glauce*	*Acaste*	*Lycoris*	
Ocyrhoe	*Tyche*	*Clytia*	*Plexaure*	260

*Their own single dance ended, as they were about to make choice of their
men, one from the sea was heard to call 'em with this charm, sung by a
tenor voice.*

SONG

Come away, come away,
We grow jealous of your stay.   265
If you do not stop your ear,

7

> We shall have more cause to fear
> Sirens of the land, than they
> To doubt the sirens of the sea.

Here they danced with their men several measures and corantos. All which 270
ended, they were again accited to sea, with a song of two trebles, whose
cadences were iterated by a double echo from several parts of the land.

SONG

	Daughters of the subtle flood,	
	Do not let earth longer entertain you;	
1st ECHO	Let earth longer entertain you	275
2nd ECHO	Longer entertain you	

	'Tis to them enough of good	
	That you give this little hope to gain you.	
1st ECHO	Give this little hope to gain you.	
2nd ECHO	Little hope to gain you.	280

	If they love	
	You shall quickly see;	
	For when to flight you move,	
	They'll follow you, the more you flee.	
1st ECHO	Follow you, the more you flee.	285
2nd ECHO	The more you flee.	

	If not, impute it each to other's matter;	
	They are but earth—	
1st ECHO	But earth,	
2nd ECHO	Earth—	290
	And what you vowed was water.	
1st ECHO	And what you vowed was water	
2nd ECHO	You vowed was water.	

ÆTHIOPIA Enough, bright nymphs, the night grows old,
And we are grieved we cannot hold 295
You longer light; but comfort take.
Your father only to the lake
Shall make return; yourselves, with feasts,
Must here remain the Ocean's guests.
Nor shall this veil the sun hath cast 300
Above your blood, more summers last.
For which, you shall observe these rites:

Thirteen times thrice, on thirteen nights
(So often as I fill my sphere
With glorious light, throughout the year)   305
You shall, when all things else do sleep
Save your chaste thoughts, with reverence steep
Your bodies in that purer brine
And wholesome dew, called rosmarine;
Then with that soft and gentler foam,   310
Of which the ocean yet yields some,
Whereof bright Venus, beauty's queen,
Is said to have begotten been,
You shall your gentler limbs o'er-lave,
And for your pains, perfection have.   315
So that, this night, the year gone round,°
You do again salute this ground;
And in the beams of yond' bright sun
Your faces dry, and all is done.

At which, in a dance they returned to the sea, where they took their shell,   320
and with this full song, went out.

SONG

Now Dian, with her burning face,°
    Declines apace:
        By which our waters know
        To ebb, that late did flow.   325
Back seas, back nymphs, but with a forward grace
    Keep still your reverence to the place,
And shout with joy of favour you have won,
    In sight of Albion, Neptune's son.

So ended the first masque;° which (besides the singular grace of music and   330
dances) had that success in the nobility of performance, as nothing needs
to the illustration but the memory by whom it was personated.

9

BEN JONSON
Barriers at a Marriage

It is a noble and just advantage that the things subjected to
understanding have of those which are objected to sense, that the one
sort are but momentary and merely taking, the other impressing and
lasting. Else the glory of all these solemnities had perished like a blaze
and gone out in the beholders' eyes. So short lived are the bodies of   5
all things in comparison of their souls. And though bodies oft-times
have the ill luck to be sensually preferred, they find afterwards the
good fortune, when souls live, to be utterly forgotten. This it is hath
made the most royal princes and greatest persons (who are commonly
the personators of these actions) not only studious of riches and   10
magnificence in the outward celebration or show (which rightly
becomes them) but curious after the most high and hearty inventions
to furnish the inward parts, and those grounded upon antiquity and
solid learnings; which, though their voice be taught to sound to
present occasions, their sense or doth or° should always lay hold on   15
more removed mysteries. And howsoever some may squeamishly cry
out that all endeavour of learning, and sharpness in these transitory
devices especially, where it steps beyond their little or (let me not
wrong 'em) no brain at all, is superfluous, I am contented these
fastidious stomachs should leave my full tables and enjoy at home   20
their clean empty trenchers, fittest for such airy tastes; where perhaps
a few Italian herbs picked up and made into a salad may find sweeter
acceptance than all the most nourishing and sound meats of the world.
   For these men's palates let me not answer, O muses. It is not my
fault if I fill them out nectar and they run to metheglin.   25

   Vaticana bibant, si delectentur.°
   All the courtesy I can do them is to cry again,
   Praetereant, si quid non facit ad stomachum.°
   As I will, from the thought of them to my better subject.

[The masque of *Hymenaei*—here omitted—then follows]

On the next night, whose solemnity was of barriers (all mention of the   30
former being utterly removed and taken away) there appeared at the lower

10

end of the hall a mist made of delicate perfumes, out of which (a battle°
being sounded under the stage) did seem to break forth two ladies, the one
representing Truth, the other Opinion, but both so like attired as they could
by no note be distinguished. The colour of their garments were blue, their 35
socks white; they were crowned with wreaths of palm,° and in their hands
each of them sustained a palm bough. These, after the mist was vanished,
began to examine each other curiously with their eyes, and, approaching
the state, the one expostulated the other in this manner.

TRUTH Who art thou thus that imitat'st my grace   40
    In steps, in habit and resembled face?
OPINION Grave time and industry my parents are;°
    My name is Truth, who through these sounds of war,
    Which figure the wise mind's discursive fight,°
    In mists by nature wrapped, salute the light.   45
TRUTH I am that Truth, thou some illusive sprite,
    Whom to my likeness the black sorceress Night
    Hath of these dry and empty fumes created.
OPINION Best herald of thine own birth, well related:°
    Put me and mine to proof of words and facts   50
    In any question this fair hour exacts.
TRUTH I challenge thee, and fit this time of love
    With this position, which Truth comes to prove:°
    That the most honoured state of man and wife
    Doth far exceed th'insociate virgin life.   55
OPINION I take the adverse part; and she that best
    Defends her side, be Truth by all confessed.
TRUTH It is confirmed. With what an equal brow
    To Truth, Opinion's confident! And how°
    Like Truth her habit shows to sensual eyes!   60
    But whosoe'er thou be in this disguise,
    Clear Truth anon shall strip thee to the heart,
    And show how mere fantastical thou art.
     Know then, the first production of things
    Requirèd two; from mere one nothing springs.   65
    Without that knot, the theme thou gloriest in
    (Th'unprofitable virgin) had not been.
    The golden tree of marrïage began
    In paradise, and bore the fruit of man,
    On whose sweet branches angels sat and sung,   70
    And from whose firm root all society sprung.
    Love (whose strong virtue wrapped heaven's soul in earth,

And made a woman glory in his birth)°
In marriage opens his inflamèd breast;
And lest in him nature should stifled rest, 75
His genial fire about the world he darts,
Which lips with lips combines, and hearts with hearts.
Marriage Love's object is; at whose bright eyes
He lights his torches, and calls them his skies.
For her he wings his shoulders, and doth fly 80
To her white bosom, as his sanctuary,
In which no lustful finger can profane him,
Nor any earth with black eclipses wane him.
She makes him smile in sorrows, and doth stand
'Twixt him and all wants with her silver hand. 85
In her soft locks his tender feet are tied,
And in his fetters he takes worthy pride.
And as geometricians have approved
That lines and superficies are not moved°
By their own forces, but do follow still 90
Their bodies' motions, so the self-loved will
Of man or woman should not rule in them,
But each with other wear the anadem.
Mirrors, though decked with diamonds, are nought worth
If the like forms of things they set not forth; 95
So men or women are worth nothing neither,
If either's eyes and hearts present not either.
OPINION Untouched virginity, laugh out to see
Freedom in fetters placed, and urged 'gainst thee.
What griefs lie groaning on the nuptial bed? 100
What dull satiety? In what sheets of lead°
Tumble and toss the restless married pair,
Each oft offended with the other's air?
From whence springs all-devouring avarice
But from the cares which out of wedlock rise? 105
And where there is in life's best-tempered fires
An end set in itself to all desires,
A settled quiet, freedom never checked;
How far are married lives from this effect?
Euripus, that bears ships in all their pride° 110
'Gainst roughest winds, with violence of his tide,
And ebbs and flows seven times in every day,
Toils not more turbulent or fierce than they.
And then, what rules husbands prescribe their wives!

In their eyes' circles they must bound their lives. 115
The moon when farthest from the sun she shines
Is most refulgent, nearest most declines:°
But your poor wives far off must never roam,
But waste their beauties near their lords at home;
And when their lords range out, at home must hide 120
(Like to begged monopòlies) all their pride.°
When their lords list to feed a serious fit,
They must be serious; when to show their wit
In jests and laughter, they must laugh and jest;
When they wake, wake; and when they rest, must rest. 125
And to their wives men give such narrow scopes,
As if they meant to make them walk on ropes.
No tumblers bide more peril of their necks
In all their tricks, than wives in husbands' checks;
Where virgins in their sweet and peaceful state 130
Have all things perfect, spin their own free fate,
Depend on no proud second, are their own
Centre and circle, now and always one.
To whose example we do still hear named
One god, one nature, and but one world framed, 135
One sun, one moon, one element of fire,
So, of the rest; one king that doth inspire
Soul to all bodies in this royal sphere—
TRUTH And where is marriage more declared than there?
Is there a band more strict than that doth tie 140
The soul and body in such unity?
Subjects to sovereigns? doth one mind display
In th'one's obedience and the other's sway?°
Believe it, marriage suffers no compare
When both estates are valued as they are. 145
The virgin were a strange and stubborn thing
Would longer stay a virgin than to bring
Herself fit use and profit in a make.
OPINION How she doth err, and the whole heaven mistake!
Look how a flower that close in closes grows,° 150
Hid from rude cattle, bruisèd with no ploughs,
Which th'air doth stroke, sun strengthen, showers shoot higher,
It many youths and many maids desire;
The same when cropped by cruel hand is withered,
No youths at all, no maidens have desired:° 155
So a virgin, while untouched she doth remain,

13

Is dear to hers; but when with body's stain
Her chaster flower is lost, she leaves to appear
Or sweet to young men, or to maidens dear.
That conquest then may crown me in this war.   160
Virgins, O virgins, fly from Hymen far.°
TRUTH Virgins, O virgins, to sweet Hymen yield;
For as a lone vine in a naked field
Never extols her branches, never bears
Ripe grapes, but with a headlong heaviness wears   165
Her tender body, and her highest sprout
Is quickly levelled with her fading root,
By whom no husbandmen, no youths will dwell;
But if by fortune she be married well
To th'elm, her husband, many husbandmen°   170
And many youths inhabit by her then:
So whilst a virgin doth, untouched, abide
All unmanured, she grows old with her pride;°
But when to equal wedlock, in fit time,
Her fortune and endeavour lets her climb,   175
Dear to her love and parents she is held.
Virgins, O virgins, to sweet Hymen yield.
OPINION These are but words; hast thou a knight will try
By stroke of arms the simple verity?
TRUTH To that high proof I would have darèd thee.   180
I'll straight fetch champions for the bride and me.
OPINION The like will I do for Virginity.

*Here they both descended the hall, where at the lower end, a march being
sounded with drums and fifes, there entered (led forth by the Earl of
Nottingham, who was Lord High Constable for that night, and the Earl   185
of Worcester, Earl Marshal) sixteen knights armed with pikes and swords,
their plumes and colours carnation and white, all richly accoutred; and
making their honours to the state as they marched by in pairs, were all
ranked on one side of the hall. They placed,° sixteen others like accoutred
for riches and arms, only that their colours were varied to watchet and   190
white, were by the same earls led up, and passing in like manner by the
state, placed on the opposite side. Whose names (as they were given to me,
both in order and orthography) were these:*

TRUTH	OPINION
Duke of Lennox	*Earl of Sussex*
Lord Effingham	*Lord Willoughby* 195

Lord Walden	*Lord Gerrard*
Lord Mounteagle	*Sir Robert Carey*
Sir Thomas Somerset	*Sir Oliver Cromwell*
Sir Charles Howard	*Sir William Herbert*
Sir John Gray	*Sir Robert Drury*
Sir Thomas Monson	*Sir William Woodhouse*
Sir John Leigh	*Sir Carey Reynolds*
Sir Robert Maunsell	*Sir Richard Houghton*
Sir Edward Howard	*Sir William Constable*
Sir Henry Goodyere	*Sir Thomas Gerrard*
Sir Roger Dalison	*Sir Robert Killigrew*
Sir Francis Howard	*Sir Thomas Badger*
Sir Lewis Maunsell	*Sir Thomas Dutton*
Mr Gunteret	*Mr Digby*°

200

205

By this time, the bar° being brought up, Truth proceeded.   210

TRUTH Now join; and if this varied trial fail°
  To make my truth in wedlock's praise prevail,
  I will retire, and in more power appear,
  To cease this strife and make our question clear.

Whereat Opinion, insulting, followed her with this speech.   215

OPINION Aye, do; it were not safe thou shouldst abide:
  This speaks thy name, with shame to quit thy side.

*Here the champions on both sides addressed themselves for fight, first
single, after three to three; and performed it with that alacrity and vigour
as if Mars himself had been to triumph before Venus and invented a new   220
music.° When on a sudden (the last six having scarcely ended) a striking
light seemed to fill all the hall, and out of it an angel or messenger of glory
appearing.*

ANGEL Princes, attend a tale of height and wonder.
  Truth is descended in a second thunder,   225
  And now will greet you with judicial state,
  To grace the nuptial part in this debate,
  And end with reconcilèd hands these wars.
    Upon her head she wears a crown of stars
  Through which her orient hair waves to her waist,   230
  By which believing mortals hold her fast,
  And in those golden cords are carried even,
  Till with her breath she blows them up to heaven.

She wears a robe enchased with eagles' eyes
To signify her sight in mysteries;   235
Upon each shoulder sits a milk-white dove,
And at her feet do witty serpents move;°
Her spacious arms do reach from east to west,
And you may see her heart shine through her breast.
Her right hand holds a sun with burning rays,   240
Her left a curious bunch of golden keys,°
With which heaven gates she locketh and displays.
A crystal mirror hangeth at her breast,
By which men's consciences are searched and dressed;
On her coach wheels Hypocrisy lies racked;   245
And squint-eyed Slander, with Vainglory backed,
Her bright eyes burn to dust, in which shines fate.
An angel ushers her triumphant gait,
Whilst with her fingers fans of stars she twists
And with them beats back Error, clad in mists.   250
Eternal Unity behind her shines,
That fire and water, earth and air combines.
Her voice is like a trumpet, loud and shrill,
Which bids all sounds in earth and heaven be still.
And see! descended from her chariot now,   255
In this related pomp she visits you.°
TRUTH Honour to all that honour nuptials,
To whose fair lot, in justice, now it falls
That this my counterfeit be here disclosed,°
Who for virginity hath herself opposed.   260
Nor, though my brightness do undo her charms,
Let these her knights think that their equal arms
Are wronged therein: *for valour wins applause*
That dares but to maintain the weaker cause.

[*Opinion's disguise is removed*]°   265

And princes, see, 'tis mere Opinion,
That in Truth's forcèd robe for Truth hath gone!
Her gaudy colours, pieced with many folds,
Show what uncertainties she ever holds:
Vanish, adulterate Truth, and never dare   270
With proud maids' praise to press where nuptials are.
And champions, since you see the truth I held,
To sacred Hymen, reconcilèd yield;

Nor so to yield think it the least despite:
It is a conquest to submit to right. 275
   This royal judge of our contention
Will prop, I know, what I have undergone;
To whose right sacred highness I resign
Low at his feet, this starry crown of mine,
To show his rule and judgement is divine; 280
These doves to him I consecrate withal
To note his innocence, without spot or gall;
These serpents, for his wisdom, and these rays
To show his piercing splendour; these bright keys
Designing power to ope the ported skies, 285
And speak their glories to his subjects' eyes.
Lastly this heart, with which all hearts be true:
And truth in him make treason ever rue.

With this they were led forth hand in hand, reconciled, as in triumph; and
thus the solemnities ended. 290

     Vivite concordes, et nostrum discite munus.°

THOMAS CAMPION

The Lord Hay's Masque

To the most puissant and
Gracious JAMES, King of Great Britain°

The disunited Scythians, when they sought°
To gather strength by parties, and combine
That perfect league of friends, which once being wrought   5
No turn of time or fortune could untwine,
This rite they held: a massy bowl was brought,
And every right arm shot his several blood
Into the mazer till 'twas fully fraught;
Then, having stirred it to an equal flood,°   10
They quaffed to th'union, which till death should last,
In spite of private foe, or foreign fear.
And this blood sacrament being known t'have passed,
Their names grew dreadful to all far and near.
O then, great Monarch, with how wise a care   15
Do you these bloods divided mix in one,
And with like consanguinities prepare
The high and everliving Union
   'Tween Scots and English. Who can wonder then
   If he that marries kingdoms, marries men?°   20

An Epigram°

Merlin, the great King Arthur being slain,
Foretold that he should come to life again,
And long time after wield great Britain's state
More powerful ten-fold, and more fortunate.   25
   Prophet, 'tis true, and well we find the same,
   Save only that thou didst mistake the name.

Ad Invictissimum, Serenissimumque
JACOBUM Magnae Britanniae Regem

Angliae, et unanimis Scotiae pater, anne maritus   30
   Sis dubito, an neuter (Rex) vel uterque simul.

18

Uxores pariter binas sibi iungat ut unus,
   Credimus hoc ipso te prohibente nephas.
Atque maritali natas violare parentem
   Complexu, quis non cogitat esse scelus?   35
At tibi divinis successibus utraque nubit,
   Una tamen coniunx, coniugis unus amor.
Connubium O mirum! binas qui ducere, et unam
   Possis! tu solus sic Jacobe potes:
Divisas leviter terras componis in unam,   40
   Atque unam aeternum nomine, reque facis:
Natisque, et nuptis, pater et vir factus utrisque es,
   Unitis coniunx vere, et amore parens.°

> To the Right Noble and Virtuous
> Theophilus Howard, Lord of Walden,   45
> son and heir to the right Honourable
> the Earl of Suffolk

If to be sprung of high and princely blood,
If to inherit virtue, honour, grace,
If to be great in all things, and yet good,   50
If to be facile, yet t'have power and place,
   If to be just and bountiful may get
   The love of men, your right may challenge it.

The course of foreign manners far and wide,
The courts, the countries, cities, towns and state,   55
The blossom of your springing youth hath tried,
Honoured in every place and fortunate,
   Which now grown fairer doth adorn our court
   With princely revelling, and timely sport.

But if th'admirèd virtues of your youth   60
Breed such despairing to my daunted muse,
That it can scarcely utter naked truth,
How shall it mount, as ravished spirits use,
   Under the burden of your riper days,
   Or hope to reach the so far distant bays?°   65

My slender muse shall yet my love express,
And by the fair Thames' side of you she'll sing;
The double streams shall bear her willing verse
Far hence with murmur of their ebb and spring.

But if you favour her light tunes, ere long 70
She'll strive to raise you with a loftier song.

To the Right Virtuous, and Honourable,
The Lord and Lady HAYES°

Should I presume to separate you now,
That were so lately joined by holy vow, 75
For whom this golden dream which I report
Begot so many waking eyes at court,
And for whose grace so many nobles changed,
Their names and habits from themselves estranged?°
Accept together, and together view 80
This little work which all belongs to you,
And live together many blessèd days,
To propagate the honoured name of HAYES.

Epigramma

Haeredem (ut spes est) pariet nova nupta Scot' Anglum; 85
   Quem gignet post hac ille, Britannus erit,
Sic nova posteritas ex regnis orta duobus
   Utrinque egregios nobilitabit avos.°

The Description of a Masque
presented before the King's Majesty at Whitehall, 90
on Twelfth Night last,
in honour of the Lord HAYES, and his Bride,
daughter and heir to the Honourable the Lord DENNY,
their marriage having been the same day at court solemnized.

As in battles, so in all other actions that are to be reported, the first and 95
most necessary part is the description of the place, with his opportunities
and properties, whether they be natural or artificial. The great hall°
(wherein the masque was presented) received this division and order: the
upper part, where the cloth and chair of state were placed, had scaffolds
and seats on either side continued to the screen;° right before it was made 100
a partition for the dancing place, on the right hand whereof were consorted

ten musicians with bass and mean lutes,° a bandora, a double sackbut, and an harpsichord, with two treble violins. On the other side, somewhat nearer the screen, were placed nine violins and three lutes; and, to answer both the consorts (as it were in a triangle) six cornetts and six Chapel voices° were seated almost right against them, in a place raised higher in respect of the piercing sound of those instruments. Eighteen foot from the screen another stage was raised higher by a yard than that which was prepared for dancing. This higher stage was all enclosed with a double veil,° so artificially painted that it seemed as if dark clouds had hung before it. Within that shroud was concealed a green valley, with green trees round about it, and in the midst of them nine golden trees of fifteen foot high, with arms and branches very glorious to behold. From the which grove toward the state was made a broad descent to the dancing place, just in the midst of it. On either hand were two ascents, like the sides of two hills, dressed with shrubs and trees: that on the right hand leading to the bower of Flora, the other to the house of Night; which bower and house were placed opposite at either end of the screen; and between them both was raised a hill, hanging like a cliff over the grove below, and on the top of it a goodly large tree was set, supposed to be the tree of Diana; behind the which toward the window° was a small descent, with another spreading hill that climbed up to the top of the window, with many trees on the height of it, whereby those that played on the hoboys at the King's entrance into the hall were shadowed. The bower of Flora was very spacious, garnished with all kind of flowers and flowery branches with lights in them; the house of Night ample and stately, with black pillars, whereon many stars of gold were fixed. Within it, when it was empty, appeared nothing but clouds and stars, and on the top of it stood three turrets underpropped with small black starred pillars, the middlemost being highest and greatest, the other two of equal proportion. About it were placed on wire artificial bats and owls, continually moving, with many other inventions, the which for brevity sake I pass by with silence.

Thus much for the place; and now from thence let us come to the persons. The masquers' names were these, whom both for order and honour I mention in the first place:

1 Lord Walden
2 Sir Thomas Howard
3 Sir Henry Carey, Master of the Jewel House
4 Sir Richard Preston
5 Sir John Ashley
6 Sir Thomas Jarret, Pensioner

7 *Sir John Digby, one of the King's Carvers*
8 *Sir Thomas Badger, Master of the King's Harriers*
9 *Master Goring*

Their number nine,° the best and amplest of numbers; for as in music 145
*seven notes contain all variety, the eighth being in nature the same with
the first, so in numbering after the ninth we begin again, the tenth being
as it were the diapason in arithmetic. The number of nine is famed by the
muses, and worthies,° and it is of all the most apt for change and diversity
of proportion. The chief habit which the masquers did use is set forth to* 150
*your view in the first leaf.° They presented in their feigned persons the
Knights of Apollo, who is the father of heat and youth,° and consequently
of amorous affections.*

The speakers were in number four

FLORA,° the Queen of Flowers, attired in a changeable taffeta° gown, 155
*with a large veil embroidered with flowers, a crown of flowers, and white
buskins painted with flowers.*

*ZEPHYRUS,° in a white° loose robe of sky-coloured taffeta, with a
mantle of white silk propped with wire, still waving behind him as he
moved. On his head he wore a wreath of palm decked with primroses and* 160
*violets; the hair of his head and beard were flaxen, and his buskins white
and painted with flowers.*

*NIGHT, in a close robe of black silk and gold, a black mantle
embroidered with stars, a crown of stars on her head, her hair black and
spangled with gold, her face black, her buskins black, and painted with* 165
stars; in her hand she bore a black wand, wreathed with gold.

*HESPERUS,° in a close robe of a deep crimson taffeta mingled with
sky colour, and over that a large loose robe of a lighter crimson taffeta;
on his head he wore a wreathed band of gold, with a star in the front
thereof; his hair and beard red, and buskins yellow.* 170

*These are the principal persons that bear sway in this invention; others
that are but seconders to these I will describe in their proper places,
discoursing the masque in order as it was performed.*

*As soon as the King was entered the great hall, the hoboys (out of the
wood on the top of the hill) entertained the time till his Majesty and his* 175
*train were placed; and then, after a little expectation, the consort of ten
began to play an air, at the sound whereof° the veil on the right hand
was withdrawn, and the ascent of the hill with the bower of Flora were
discovered, where Flora and Zephyrus were busily plucking flowers from*

the bower, and throwing them into two baskets, which two Sylvans° held, 180
who were attired in changeable taffeta, with wreaths of flowers on their
heads. As soon as the baskets were filled, they came down in this order:
first Zephyrus and Flora, then the two Sylvans with baskets; after them
four Sylvans in green taffeta and wreaths, two bearing mean lutes, the
third a bass lute, and the fourth a deep bandora. 185
   As soon as they came to the descent toward the dancing place, the consort
of ten ceased, and the four Sylvans played the same air, to which Zephyrus
and the two other Sylvans did sing these words in a bass, tenor, and treble
voice; and going up and down as they sung, they strewed flowers all about
the place. 190

SONG

   Now hath Flora robbed her bowers
   To befriend this place with flowers;
      Strew about, strew about,
   The sky rained never kindlier showers.°
   Flowers with bridals well agree, 195
   Fresh as brides and bridegrooms be;
      Strew about, strew about,
   And mix them with fit melody.
      Earth hath no princelier flowers
   Than roses white, and roses red, 200
   But they must still be minglèd.°
   And as a rose new plucked from Venus' thorn,
   So doth a bride her bridegroom's bed adorn.

   Divers divers flowers affect°
   For some private dear respect; 205
      Strew about, strew about,
   Let every one his own protect.
   But he's none of Flora's friend
   That will not the rose commend;
      Strew about, strew about, 210
   Let princes princely flowers defend.
      Roses, the garden's pride,
   Are flowers for love, and flowers for kings,
   In courts desirèd, and weddings.
   And as a rose in Venus' bosom worn, 215
   So doth a bridegroom his bride's bed adorn.

The music ceaseth, and Flora speaks.

FLORA Flowers and good wishes Flora doth present,
Sweet flowers, the ceremonious ornament
Of maiden marriage, beauty figuring,   220
And blooming youth; which though we careless fling
About this sacred place, let none profane
Think that these fruits from common hills are ta'en,
Or vulgar valleys which do subject lie
To winter's wrath, and cold mortality.   225
But these are hallowed and immortal flowers,
With Flora's hands gathered from Flora's bowers.
Such are her presents, endless as her love,
And such forever may this night's joy prove.
ZEPHYRUS Forever endless may this night's joy prove,   230
So echoes Zephyrus, the friend of love,
Whose aid Venus implores when she doth bring
Into the naked world the green-leaved spring,
When of the sun's warm beams the nets we weave
That can the stubborn'st heart with love deceive.   235
That queen of beauty and desire by me
Breathes gently forth this bridal prophecy:
Faithful and fruitful shall these bedmates prove,
Blest in their fortunes, honoured in their love.
FLORA All grace this night, and Sylvans so must you,   240
Offering your marriage song with changes new.

THE SONG IN FORM OF A DIALOGUE

CANTUS	Who is the happier of the two, A maid or wife?°	
TENOR	Which is more to be desirèd, Peace or strife?	245
CANTUS	What strife can be where two are one, Or what delight to pine alone?	
BASS	None such true friends, none so sweet life, As that between the man and wife.	
TENOR	A maid is free, a wife is tied.	250
CANTUS	No maid but fain would be a bride.	
TENOR	Why live so many single then? 'Tis not, I hope, for want of men?	
CANTUS	The bow and arrow both may fit, And yet 'tis hard the mark to hit.	255
BASS	He levels fair that by his side°	

Lays at night his lovely bride.
CHORUS   Sing Io, Hymen; Io, Io, Hymen.°

This song being ended, the whole veil is suddenly drawn; the grove and
trees of gold, and the hill with Diana's° tree are at once discovered.   260
   Night appears in her house with her nine Hours, apparelled in large
robes of black taffeta, painted thick with stars; their hairs long, black, and
spangled with gold; on their heads coronets of stars, and their faces
black. Every Hour bore in his hand a black torch, painted with stars
and lighted. Night, presently descending from her house, spake as   265
followeth:

NIGHT Vanish, dark veils, let Night in glory shine°
  As she doth burn in rage; come, leave our shrine
  You black-haired Hours, and guide us with your lights:
  Flora hath wakened wide our drowsy sprights.   270
  See where she triumphs, see her flowers are thrown,
  And all about the seeds of malice sown.
  Despiteful Flora, is't not enough of grief
  That Cynthia's robbed, but thou must grace the thief?°
  Or didst not hear Night's sovereign queen complain   275
  Hymen had stol'n a nymph out of her train
  And matched her here, plighted henceforth to be
  Love's friend, and stranger to virginity?
  And mak'st thou sport for this?
FLORA   Be mild, stern Night;
  Flora doth honour Cynthia, and her right.   280
  Virginity is a voluntary power,
  Free from constraint, even like an untouched flower
  Meet to be gathered when 'tis throughly blown.°
  The nymph was Cynthia's while she was her own,
  But now another claims in her a right,   285
  By fate reserved thereto, and wise foresight.
ZEPHYRUS Can Cynthia one kind virgin's loss bemoan?
  How if perhaps she brings her ten for one?
  Or can she miss one in so full a train?
  Your goddess doth of too much store complain.   290
  If all her nymphs would ask advice of me,
  There should be fewer virgins than there be.
  Nature ordained not men to live alone;
  Where there are two, a woman should be one.

NIGHT Thou breath'st sweet poison, wanton Zephyrus,   295
    But Cynthia must not be deluded thus.
    Her holy forests are by thieves profaned,°
    Her virgins frighted; and lo, where they stand
    That late were Phoebus' knights, turned now to trees°
    By Cynthia's vengement for their injuries   300
    In seeking to seduce her nymphs with love.
    Here they are fixed, and never may remove
    But by Diana's power that stuck them here.
    Apollo's love to them doth yet appear,
    In that his beams hath gilt them as they grow,°   305
    To make their misery yield the greater show.
    But they shall tremble when sad Night doth speak,
    And at her stormy words their boughs shall break.

Toward the end of this speech Hesperus begins to descend by the house
of Night, and by that time the speech was finished he was ready to 310
speak.

HESPERUS Hail, reverend angry Night, hail, Queen of Flowers,
    Mild-spirited Zephyrus, hail, Sylvans and Hours.
    Hesperus brings peace; cease then your needless jars
    Here in this little firmament of stars.   315
    Cynthia is now by Phoebus pacified,
    And well content her nymph is made a bride,
    Since the fair match was by that Phoebus graced
    Which in this happy western isle is placed
    As he in heaven, one lamp enlightening all   320
    That under his benign aspèct doth fall.
    Deep oracles he speaks, and he alone
    For arts and wisdom's meet for Phoebus' throne.
    The nymph is honoured, and Diana pleased.
    Night, be you then, and your black Hours, appeased, 325
    And friendly listen what your Queen by me
    Farther commands: let this my credence be,
    View it, and know it for the highest gem
    That hung on her imperial diadem.°
NIGHT I know, and honour it, lovely Hesperus.   330
    Speak then your message, both are welcome to us.
HESPERUS Your Sovereign, from the virtuous gem she sends
    Bids you take power to retransform the friends
    Of Phoebus, metamorphosed here to trees,

And give them straight the shapes which they did leese.°   335
This is her pleasure.
NIGHT   Hesperus, I obey;°
Night must needs yield when Phoebus gets the day.
FLORA Honoured be Cynthia for this generous deed.
ZEPHYRUS Pity grows only from celestial seed.
NIGHT If all seem glad, why should we only lour,   340
Since t'express gladness we have now most power?
Frolic, graced captives; we present you here
This glass, wherein your liberties appear.
Cynthia is pacified, and now blithe Night
Begins to shake off melancholy quite.   345
ZEPHYRUS Who should grace mirth and revels but the Night?
Next Love, she should be goddess of delight.°
NIGHT 'Tis now a time when, Zephyrus, all with dancing
Honour me, above day my state advancing.
I'll now be frolic, all is full of heart,   350
And even these trees for joy shall bear a part:
Zephyrus, they shall dance.
ZEPHYRUS   Dance, goddess? How?
NIGHT Seems that so full of strangeness to you now?
Did not the Thracian harp long since the same?°
And (if we rip the old records of fame),   355
Did not Amphion's lyre the deaf stones call,°
When they came dancing to the Theban wall?
Can music these enjoy? Joy mountains moves—°
And why not trees? Joy's powerful when it loves.
Could the religious oak speak oracle°   360
Like to the Gods, and the tree wounded tell
T'Aeneas his sad story? Have trees therefore°
The instruments of speech and hearing more
Than th'have of pacing? And to whom but Night
Belong enchantments? Who can more affright   365
The eye with magic wonders? Night alone
Is fit for miracles, and this shall be one
Apt for this nuptial dancing jollity.
Earth, then be soft and passable to free
These fettered roots. Joy, trees! the time draws near   370
When in your better forms you shall appear.
Dancing and music must prepare the way;
There's little tedious time in such delay.

This spoken, the four Sylvans played on their instruments the first strain
of this song following; and at the repetition thereof the voices fell in with 375
the instruments, which were thus divided: a treble and a bass were placed
near his Majesty, and another treble and bass near the grove, that the
words of the song might be heard of all, because° the trees of gold instantly
at the first sound of their voices began to move and dance according to the
measure of the time which the musicians kept in singing and the nature of 380
the words which they delivered.

SONG

Move now with measured sound
  You charmèd grove of gold;
Trace forth the sacred ground
  That shall your forms unfold. 385

Diana and the starry night for your Apollo's sake
Endue your sylvan shapes with power this strange delight to make.
Much joy must needs the place betide where trees for gladness
    move;
A fairer sight was ne'er beheld, or more expressing love.

  Yet nearer Phoebus' throne 390
    Mete on your winding ways;°
  Your bridal mirth make known
    In your high-gracèd Hayes.

Let Hymen lead your sliding rounds, and guide them with his light,
While we do *Io Hymen* sing in honour of this night. 395
Join three by three, for so the night by triple spell decrees
Now to release Apollo's knights from these enchanted trees.

This dancing song being ended, the golden trees stood in ranks three by
three, and Night ascended up to the grove and spake thus, touching the
first three severally with her wand: 400

NIGHT By virtue of this wand, and touch divine,
  These sylvan shadows back to earth resign.°
  Your native forms resume, with habit fair,
  While solemn music shall enchant the air.

Presently the Sylvans, with their four instruments and five voices, began 405
to play and sing together the song following, at the beginning whereof that
part of the stage whereon the first three trees stood began to yield,° and
the three foremost trees gently to sink, and this was effected by an engine

placed under the stage. When the trees had sunk a yard, they cleft in three
parts, and the masquers appeared out of the tops of them, the trees were   410
suddenly conveyed away, and the first three masquers were raised again
by the engine. They appeared then in a false habit,° yet very fair, and in
form not much unlike their principal and true robe. It was made of green
taffeta cut into leaves, and laid upon cloth of silver, and their hats were
suitable to the same.   415

SONG OF TRANSFORMATION

    Night and Diana charge,
       And th'earth obeys,
      Opening large
       Her secret ways,
    While Apollo's charmèd men   420
       Their forms receive again.
    Give gracious Phoebus honour then,
    And so fall down, and rest behind the train.
    Give gracious Phoebus honour then
    And so fall, etc.,   425

When those words were sung, the three masquers made an honour to the
King; and so falling back, the other six trees three by three came forward,
and when they were in their appointed places Night spake again thus:

NIGHT Thus can celestials work in human fate,
    Transform and form as they do love or hate.   430
    Like touch and change receive: the gods agree°
    The best of numbers is contained in three.°

THE SONG OF TRANSFORMATION AGAIN

    Night and Diana, etc.

Then Night touched the second three trees and the stage sunk with them
as before. And, in brief, the second three did in all points as the first. Then   435
Night spake again:

NIGHT The last, and third of nine, touch, magic wand,
    And give them back their forms at Night's command.

Night touched the third three trees, and the same charm of Night and
Diana was sung the third time; the last three trees were transformed, and   440
the masquers raised, when presently the first music° began his full chorus.

Again this song revive and sound it high:
Long live Apollo, Britain's glorious eye.

*This chorus was, in manner of an echo,° seconded by the cornetts, then by
the consort of ten, then by the consort of twelve, and by a double chorus* 445
*of voices standing on either side, the one against the other, bearing five
voices° apiece. And sometime every chorus was heard severally, sometime
mixed, but in the end altogether; which kind of harmony, so distinguished
by the place,° and by the several nature of instruments and changeable
conveyance of the song, and performed by so many excellent masters as* 450
*were actors in that music (their number in all amounting to forty-two°
voices and instruments) could not but yield great satisfaction to the hearers.*

*While this chorus was repeated twice over, the nine masquers in their
green habits solemnly descended to the dancing place in such order as they
were to begin their dance; and as soon as the chorus ended, the violins (or* 455
*consort of twelve) began to play the second new dance, which was taken
in form of an echo by the cornetts, and then catched in like manner by the
consort of ten; sometime they mingled two musics together, sometime played
all at once, which kind of echoing music rarely became° their sylvan attire,
and was so truly mixed together, that no dance could ever be better graced* 460
*than that, as (in such distraction° of music) it was performed by the
masquers. After this dance Night descended from the grove and addressed
her speech to the masquers, as followeth:*

NIGHT Phoebus is pleased, and all rejoice to see
        His servants from their golden prison free.   465
        But yet since Cynthia hath so friendly smiled,
        And to you tree-born knights is reconciled,
        First, ere you any more work undertake,
        About her tree solemn procession make,
        Diana's tree, the tree of Chastity,   470
        That placed alone on yonder hill you see.
        These green-leaved robes, wherein disguised you made
        Stealths to her nymphs through the thick forest's shade,
        There to the goddess offer thankfully,
        That she may not in vain appeasèd be.   475
        The Night shall guide you, and her Hours attend you,
        That no ill eyes or spirits shall offend you.

*At the end of this speech, Night began to lead the way alone, and after
her an Hour with his torch, and after the Hour a masquer; and so in order
one by one, a torch-bearer and a masquer, they march on towards Diana's* 480

*tree. When the masquers came by the house of Night, every one by his
Hour received his helmet, and had his false robe plucked off, and bearing
it in his hand, with a low honour offered it at the tree of Chastity, and so
in his glorious habit, with his Hour before him, marched to the bower of
Flora. The shape of their habit the picture before discovers. The stuff was* 485
*of carnation satin laid thick with broad silver lace, their helmets being
made of the same stuff. So through the bower of Flora they came, where
they joined, two torch-bearers and two masquers; and when they passed
down to the grove the Hours parted on either side, and made way between
them for the masquers, who descended to the dancing place in such order* 490
*as they were to begin their third new dance. All this time of procession the
six cornetts and six Chapel voices sung a solemn motet of six parts made
upon these words:*

> With spotless minds now mount we to the tree
> > Of single chastity. 495
> The root is temperance grounded deep,
> Which the cold-juiced earth doth steep:
> > Water it desires alone,
> > Other drink it thirsts for none:
> Therewith the sober branches it doth feed, 500
> > Which though they fruitless be,
> Yet comely leaves they breed
> > To beautify the tree.
> Cynthia protectress is, and for her sake
> We this grave procession make. 505
> Chaste eyes and ears, pure hearts and voices
> Are graces wherein Phoebe most rejoices.

*The motet being ended, the violins began the third new dance, which was
lively performed by the masquers; after which they took forth the ladies
and danced the measures with them; which being finished, the masquers* 510
*brought the ladies back again to their places, and Hesperus with the rest
descended from the grove into the dancing place, and spake to the masquers
as followeth:*

HESPERUS Knights of Apollo, proud of your new birth,
> Pursue your triumphs still with joy and mirth; 515
> Your changèd fortunes and redeemed estate
> Hesperus to your sovereign will relate.
> 'Tis now high time he were far hence retired,
> Th'old bridal friend, that ushers Night desired

Through the dim evening shades, then taking flight   520
Gives place and honour to the nuptial Night.
I, that wished evening star, must now make way
To Hymen's rights, much wronged by my delay.°
But on Night's princely state you ought t'attend,
And t'honour your new-reconcilèd friend.   525
NIGHT Hesperus, as you with concord came, ev'n so
'Tis meet that you with concord hence should go.
Then join you that in voice and art excel,
To give this star a musical farewell.

A DIALOGUE OF FOUR VOICES, TWO BASSES
AND TWO TREBLES

1 Of all the stars which is the kindest   530
    To a loving bride?
2 Hesperus, when in the west
    He doth the day from night divide.
1 What message can be more respected
    Than that which tells wished joys shall be effected?   535
2 Do not brides watch the evening star?
1 O, they can discern it far.
2 Love bridegrooms revels?
1   But for fashion.
2 And why?
1   They hinder wished occasion.
2 Longing hearts and new delights   540
    Love short days and long nights.
CHORUS Hesperus, since you all stars excel
    In bridal kindness, kindly farewell, farewell.

*While these words of the chorus ('kindly farewell, farewell') were in
singing often repeated, Hesperus took his leave severally of Night,*   545
*Flora and Zephyrus, the Hours and Sylvans; and so while the chorus
was sung over the second time, he was got up to the grove, where turning
again to the singers, and they to him, Hesperus took a second farewell
of them, and so passed away by the house of Night. Then Night spake
these two lines, and therewith all retired to the grove where they stood*   550
before.°

NIGHT Come Flora, let us now withdraw our train
    That th'eclipsed revels may shine forth again.

Now the masquers began their lighter dances, as corantos, lavoltas, and
galliards; wherein when they had spent as much time as they thought fit,   555
Night spake thus from the grove, and in her speech descended a little into
the dancing place.

NIGHT Here stay: Night leaden-eyed and sprighted grows,°
    And her late Hours begin to hang their brows.
    Hymen long since the bridal bed hath dressed,   560
    And longs to bring the turtles to their nest.°
    Then with one quick dance sound up your delight,
    And with one song we'll bid you all goodnight.

At the end of these words, the violins began the fourth new dance, which
was excellently discharged by the masquers, and it ended with a light   565
change of music and measure.° After the dance followed this dialogue of
two voices, a bass and tenor, sung by a Sylvan and an Hour.

Tenor SYLVAN	Tell me, gentle Hour of night
	Wherein dost thou most delight?
Bass HOUR	Not in sleep.
SYLVAN	Wherein then? 570
HOUR	In the frolic view of men.
SYLVAN	Lovest thou music?
HOUR	O, 'tis sweet.
SYLVAN	What's dancing?
HOUR	Ev'n the mirth of feet.
SYLVAN	Joy you in fairies and in elves?
HOUR	We are of that sort ourselves. 575
	But, Sylvan, say, why do you love
	Only to frequent the grove?
SYLVAN	Life is fullest of content
	Where delight is innocent.
HOUR	Pleasure must vary, not be long, 580
	Come then, let's close, and end our song.
CHORUS	Yet ere we vanish from this princely sight,
	Let us bid Phoebus and his states goodnight.

This chorus was performed with several echoes of music and voices, in
manner as the great chorus before. At the end whereof the masquers,   585
putting off their vizards and helmets, made a low honour to the King, and
attended his Majesty to the banqueting place.

To the Reader

Neither buskin now, nor bays°
  Challenge I; a lady's praise
Shall content my proudest hope;   590
  Their applause was all my scope,
    And to their shrines properly
    Revels dedicated be:
Whose soft ears none ought to pierce
  But with smooth and gentle verse.   595
    Let the tragic poem swell,
    Raising raging fiends from hell,
    And let epic dactyls range,
Swelling seas and countries strange.
    Little room small things contains,   600
    Easy praise quites easy pains.
Suffer them whose brows do sweat
  To gain honour by the great;°
    It's enough if men me name
    A retailer of such fame.   605

Epigramma

Quid tu te numeris immisces? anne medentem
  Metra cathedratum ludicra scripta decent
Musicus, et medicus, celebris quoque Phoebe poeta es
  Et lepor aegrotos arte rogante iuvat.
Crede mihi doctum qui carmen non sapit, idem   610
  Non habet ingenuum, nec genium medici.°

BEN JONSON
The Masque of Queens

The Masque of Queens,
Celebrated from the House of Fame.
By the most absolute in all state and titles:
Anne
Queen of Great Britain, etc.,
With her honourable ladies at Whitehall,
Feb. 2, 1609

It increasing now to the third time° of my being used in these services
to her majesty's personal presentations, with the ladies whom she
pleaseth to honour, it was my first and special regard to see that the
nobility of the invention should be answerable to the dignity of their
persons. For which reason I chose the argument to be a celebration   5
of honourable and true fame, bred out of virtue; observing that rule
of the best artist,° to suffer no object of delight to pass without his
mixture of profit and example.

And because her Majesty, best knowing that a principal part of life
in these spectacles lay in their variety, had commanded me to think   10
on some dance or show that might precede hers, and have the place
of a foil or false masque, I was careful to decline,° not only from
others', but mine own steps in that kind, since the last year I had an
antimasque of boys;° and therefore now devised that twelve women
in the habit of hags or witches, sustaining the persons of Ignorance,   15
Suspicion, Credulity, etc., the opposites to good Fame, should fill that
part, not as a masque but a spectacle of strangeness, producing
multiplicity of gesture, and not unaptly sorting with the current and
whole fall of the device.

His Majesty then being set, and the whole company in full expectation,   20
that which presented itself was an ugly hell, which, flaming beneath,
smoked unto the top of the roof. And in respect all evils are, morally, said
to come from hell (as also from that observation of Torrentius upon Horace
his Canidia, quae tot instructa venenis, ex Orci faucibus profecta
videri possit°) these witches, with a kind of hollow and infernal music,   25
came forth from thence. First one, then two, and three, and more, till their
number increased to eleven;° all differently attired, some with rats on their

35

heads, some on their shoulders; others with ointment pots at their girdles;
all with spindles, timbrels, rattles, or other venefical instruments making a
confused noise with strange gestures. The device of their attire was Master 30
Jones his, with the invention and architecture of the whole scene and
machine. Only I prescribed them their properties of vipers, snakes, bones,
herbs, roots, and other ensigns of their magic, out of the authority of
ancient and late writers. Wherein the faults are mine, if there be any
found, and for that cause I confess them. 35

These eleven witches beginning to dance (which is an usual ceremony at
their convents, or meetings, where sometimes also they are vizarded and
masked) on the sudden one of them missed their chief, and interrupted the
rest with this speech.

Sisters, stay; we want our Dame. 40
Call upon her by her name
And the charm we use to say,
That she quickly anoint, and come away.°

CHARM 1

Dame, Dame, the watch is set;
Quickly come, we all are met. 45
From the lakes and from the fens,
From the rocks and from the dens,
From the woods and from the caves,
From the church-yards, from the graves,
From the dungeon, from the tree 50
That they die on, here are we.°
   Comes she not yet?
   Strike another heat.°

CHARM 2

The weather is fair, the wind is good;
Up, dame, on your horse of wood;° 55
Or else tuck up your gray frock,
And saddle your goat or your green cock,°
And make his bridle a bottom of thread,°
To roll up how many miles you have rid.
   Quickly come away, 60
   For we all stay.
   Nor yet? Nay then,
   We'll try her again.

36

CHARM 3

The owl is abroad, the bat and the toad,
  And so is the cat-a-mountain;   65
The ant and the mole sit both in a hole,
  And frog peeps out o' the fountain;
The dogs they do bay, and the timbrels play,
  The spindle is now a-turning;°
The moon it is red, and the stars are fled,   70
  But all the sky is a-burning;
The ditch is made, and our nails the spade,
  With pictures full of wax and of wool,
  Their livers I stick with needles quick;°
There lacks but the blood to make up the flood.   75
  Quickly, Dame, then, bring your part in,
  Spur, spur upon little Martin,°
  Merrily, merrily make him sail,
  A worm in his mouth and a thorn in's tail,
  Fire above and fire below,   80
  With a whip i' your hand to make him go.
  O, now she's come!
  Let all be dumb.

At this the Dame° entered to them, naked-armed, barefooted, her frock
tucked, her hair knotted and folded with vipers; in her hand a torch made 85
of a dead man's arm, lighted; girded with a snake. To whom they all did
reverence, and she spake, uttering by way of question the end wherefore
they came; which if it had been done either before or otherwise, had not
been so natural. For to have made themselves their own decipherers and
each one to have told upon their entrance what they were, and whether 90
they would, had been a most piteous hearing and utterly unworthy any
quality of a poem, wherein a writer should always trust somewhat to the
capacity of the spectator, especially at these spectacles, where men, beside
enquiring eyes, are understood to bring quick ears, and not those sluggish
ones of porters and mechanics, that must be bored through at every act 95
with narrations.°

DAME Well done, my hags. And come we, fraught with spite,
  To overthrow the glory of this night?
  Holds our great purpose?
HAGS   Yes.
DAME   But wants there none

Of our just number?

HAGS   Call us one by one   100
And then our Dame shall see.

DAME   First then advance
My drowsy servant, stupid Ignorance,
Known by thy scaly vesture; and bring on
Thy fearful sister, wild Suspicïon,
Whose eyes do never sleep; let her knit hands   105
With quick Credulity, that next her stands,
Who hath but one ear, and that always ope;
Two-faced Falsehood follow in the rope,
And lead on Murmur, with the cheeks deep-hung;
She Malice, whetting of her forkèd tongue,   110
And Malice Impudence, whose forehead's lost;
Let Impudence lead Slander on, to boast
Her oblique look; and to her subtle side°
Thou, black-mouthed Execration, stand applied;
Draw to thee Bitterness, whose pores sweat gall,   115
She flame-eyed Rage, Rage Mischief.

HAGS   Here we are all.°

DAME Join now our hearts, we faithful opposites
To Fame and Glory. Let not these bright nights
Of honour blaze thus to offend our eyes.
Show ourselves truly envious, and let rise   120
Our wonted rages. Do what may beseem
Such names and natures. Virtue else will deem
Our powers decreased, and think us banished earth
No less than heaven. All her antique birth,
As Justice, Faith, she will restore, and, bold   125
Upon our sloth, retrieve her age of gold.°
We must not let our native manners thus
Corrupt with ease. Ill lives not but in us.
I hate to see these fruits of a soft peace,
And curse the piety gives it such increase.°   130
Let us disturb it then, and blast the light,
Mix hell with heaven, and make Nature fight
Within herself; loose the whole hinge of things,°
And cause the ends run back into their springs.

HAGS What our Dame bids us do   135
We are ready for.

DAME   Then fall to.

But first relate me what you have sought,
Where you have been, and what you have brought.
FIRST HAG I have been all day looking after
  A raven feeding upon a quarter;°   140
  And, soon as she turned her beak to the south,
  I snatched this morsel out of her mouth.
SECOND HAG I have been gathering wolves' hairs,
  The mad dog's foam, and the adder's ears;
  The spurging of a dead man's eyes,   145
  And all since the evening star did rise.
THIRD HAG I last night lay all alone
  O' the ground, to hear the mandrake groan,°
  And plucked him up, though he grew full low,
  And, as I had done, the cock did crow.   150
FOURTH HAG And I ha' been choosing out this skull
  From charnel-houses that were full;
  From private grots and public pits,°
  And frighted a sexton out of his wits.
FIFTH HAG Under a cradle I did creep   155
  By day, and when the child was asleep
  At night, I sucked the breath, and rose
  And plucked the nodding nurse by the nose.
SIXTH HAG I had a dagger; what did I with that?
  Killed an infant to have his fat.   160
  A piper it got at a church-ale°
  I bade him again blow wind i' the tail.°
SEVENTH HAG A murderer yonder was hung in chains,
  The sun and the wind had shrunk his veins;
  I bit off a sinew, I clipped his hair,   165
  I brought off his rags that danced i' the air.
EIGHTH HAG The screech-owl's eggs and the feathers black,
  The blood of the frog and the bone in his back,
  I have been getting; and made of his skin
  A purset to keep Sir Cranion in.°   170
NINTH HAG And I ha' been plucking plants among,
  Hemlock, henbane, adder's tongue,
  Nightshade, moon wort, leopard's bane,
  And twice by the dogs was like to be ta'en.
TENTH HAG I from the jaws of a gardener's bitch   175
  Did snatch these bones, and then leaped the ditch;
  Yet went I back to the house again,

Killed the black cat—and here's the brain.
ELEVENTH HAG I went to the toad breeds under the wall,
  I charmed him out, and he came at my call. 180
  I scratched out the eyes of the owl before,
  I tore the bat's wing; what would you have more?
DAME Yes, I have brought, to help our vows,
  Hornèd poppy, cypress boughs,
  The fig-tree wild, that grows on tombs, 185
  And juice that from the larch tree comes,
  The basilisk's blood and the viper's skin.°
  And now our orgies let's begin.

Here the Dame put her self into the midst of them and began her following
invocation, wherein she took occasion to boast all the power attributed to 190
witches by the ancients, of which every poet (or the most) doth give some:
Homer to Circe in the Odyssey; *Theocritus to Simatha in* Parmaceutria;
Virgil to Alphesiboeus in his;° Ovid to Dipsas in Amores, *to Medea and*
Circe in Metamorphoses; *Tibullus to Saga; Horace to Canidia, Sagana,*
Veia, Folia; Seneca to Medea and the Nurse in Hercules Oetaeus, 195
Petronius Arbiter to his Saga, in Fragmenta, *and Claudian to his*
Megæra, lib. i In Rufinum, *who takes the habit of a witch as these do,*
and supplies that historical part in the poem, beside her moral person of a
Fury, confirming the same drift in ours.

[DAME] You fiends and furies (if yet any be 200
  Worse than ourselves) you, that have quaked to see
  These knots untied, and shrunk when we have charmed;°
  You, that to arm us have yourselves disarmed,
  And to our powers resigned your whips and brands
  When we went forth, the scourge of men and lands; 205
  You, that have seen me ride when Hecatè°
  Durst not take chariot, when the boisterous sea
  Without a breath of wind hath knocked the sky,
  And that hath thundered, Jove not knowing why;
  When we have set the elements at wars, 210
  Made midnight see the sun, and day the stars;
  When the winged lightning in the course hath stayed,
  And swiftest rivers have run back, afraid
  To see the corn remove, the groves to range,
  Whole places alter and the seasons change; 215
  When the pale moon at the first voice down fell

Poisoned, and durst not stay the second spell.
You, that have oft been conscious of these sights,
And thou, three-formèd star, that on these nights
Art only powerful, to whose triple name   220
Thus we incline; Once, twice, and thrice-the-same:
If now with rites profane and foul enough
We do invoke thee, darken all this roof
With present fogs, exhale earth's rott'nest vapours,
And strike a blindness through these blazing tapers.   225
    Come, let a murmuring charm resound
    The whilst we bury all i' the ground.
    But first, see every foot be bare,
    And every knee.
HAGS   Yes, Dame, they are.

CHARM 4

Deep, O deep, we lay thee to sleep;°   230
We leave thee drink by, if thou chance to be dry,
Both milk and blood, the dew and the flood.
We breathe in thy bed, at the foot and the head;
We cover thee warm, that thou take no harm;
And when thou dost wake   235
    Dame Earth shall quake,
    And the houses shake,
    And her belly shall ache
    As her back were brake
    Such a birth to make,   240
    As is the blue drake,°
    Whose form thou shalt take.
DAME Never a star yet shot?
    Where be the ashes?
HAGS   Here i' the pot.
DAME Cast them up, and the flint stone   245
    Over the left shoulder bone
    Into the west.
HAGS   It will be best.°

CHARM 5

The sticks are a-cross, there can be no loss;
The sage is rotten, the sulphur is gotten
Up to the sky, that was i' the ground.   250

Follow it then with our rattles, round,
Under the bramble, over the briar,
A little more heat will set it on fire;
Put it in mind to do it kind,°
Flow water, and blow wind.   255
Rouncy is over, Robble is under,°
A flash of light, and a clap of thunder,
A storm of rain, another of hail,
We all must home i' the eggshell sail.
The mast is made of a great pin,   260
The tackle of cobweb, the sail as thin,
And if we go through, and not fall in—

DAME Stay! all our charms do nothing win°
Upon the night. Our labour dies!
Our magic-feature will not rise,   265
Nor yet the storm! We must repeat
More direful voices far, and beat
The ground with vipers till it sweat.

CHARM 6

Bark dogs, wolves howl,
Seas roar, woods roll,   270
Clouds crack, all be black
But the light our charms do make.

DAME Not yet? My rage begins to swell.
Darkness, devils, night and hell,
Do not thus delay my spell.   275
I call you once and I call you twice,
I beat you again if you stay me thrice.
Through these crannies where I peep
I'll let in the light, to see your sleep;
And all the secrets of your sway   280
Shall lie as open to the day
As unto me. Still are you deaf?
Reach me a bough that ne'er bare leaf
To strike the air, and aconite
To hurl upon this glaring light;   285
A rusty knife to wound mine arm,
And as it drops I'll speak a charm
Shall cleave the ground, as low as lies

Old shrunk-up Chaos; and let rise°
Once more his dark and reeking head,   290
To strike the world and nature dead,
Until my magic birth be bred.

CHARM 7

Black go in, and blacker come out;
At thy going down, we give thee a shout:
        Hoo!   295
At thy rising again thou shalt have two,
And if thou dost what we would have thee do,
Thou shalt have three, thou shalt have four,
Thou shalt have ten, thou shalt have a score.
        Hoo! Har! Har! Hoo!   300

CHARM 8

A cloud of pitch, a spur and a switch,
To haste him away, and a whirlwind play
Before, and after, with thunder for laughter,
And storms for joy of the roaring boy,
His head of a drake, his tail of a snake.   305

CHARM 9

About, about, and about,
Till the mist arise, and the lights fly out;
The images neither be seen nor felt;
The woollen burn and the waxen melt;
Sprinkle your liquors upon the ground,   310
And into the air; around, around.
Around, around,
Around, around,
Till a music sound,
And the pace be found   315
To which we may dance,
And our charms advance.

At which, with a strange and sudden music, they fell into a magical dance,
full of preposterous change and gesticulation, but most applying to their
property,° who, at their meetings do all things contrary to the custom of 320
men, dancing back to back, hip to hip, their hands joined, and making
their circles backward to the left hand, with strange fantastic motions of

*their heads and bodies. All which were excellently imitated by the maker
of the dance, Master Jerome Herne, whose right it is here to be named.*

In the heat of their dance, on the sudden, was heard a sound of loud 325
*music, as if many instruments had given one blast. With which not only
the hags themselves but the hell into which they ran quite vanished, and
the whole face of the scene altered, scarce suffering the memory of any such
thing. But in the place of it appeared a glorious and magnificent building,
figuring the House of Fame, in the top of which were discovered the twelve* 330
*masquers, sitting upon a throne triumphal, erected in form of a
pyramid,° and circled with all store of light. From whom a person, by this
time descended, in the furniture of Perseus, and expressing heroical and
masculine virtue, began to speak.*

HEROIC VIRTUE So should, at Fame's loud sound, and virtue's sight 335
   All poor and envious witchcraft fly the light.
   I did not borrow Hermes' wings, nor ask
   His crookèd sword, nor put on Pluto's casque,
   Nor on my arm advanced wise Pallas' shield
   (By which, my face aversed, in open field 340
   I slew the Gorgon) for an empty name.°
   When Virtue cut off Terror, he gat Fame.
   And if when Fame was gotten Terror died,
   What black Erinyes or more hellish pride°
   Durst arm these hags, now she is grown and great, 345
   To think they could her glories once defeat?
   I was her parent, and I am her strength.
   Heroic Virtue sinks not under length
   Of years or ages, but is still the same
   While he preserves, as when he got, Good Fame. 350
   My daughter, then, whose glorious house you see
   Built all of sounding brass, whose columns be°
   Men-making poets, and those well-made men
   Whose strife it was to have the happiest pen
   Renown them to an after-life, and not 355
   With pride to scorn the muse, and die forgot;
   She, that enquireth into all the world,
   And hath about her vaulted palace hurled
   All rumours and reports, or true or vain,
   What utmost lands or deepest seas contain 360
   (But only hangs great actions on her file);°
   She, to this lesser world and greatest isle

Tonight sounds honour, which she would have seen
In yond' bright bevy, each of them a queen.
Eleven of them are of times long gone: 365
Penthesilea, the brave Amazon,
Swift-foot Camilla, queen of Volscia,
Victorious Thomyris of Scythia,
Chaste Artemisia, the Carian dame,
And fair-haired Berenicè, Egypt's fame, 370
Hypsicratea, glory of Asïa,
Candacè, pride of Ethiopia,
The Briton honour, Voadicea,
The virtuous Palmyrene Zenobia,
The wise and warlike Goth, Amalasunta, 375
And bold Valasca of Bohemia.
These, in their lives, as fortunes, crowned the choice
Of woman-kind, and 'gainst all opposite voice
Made good to Time, had after death the claim°
To live eternized in the House of Fame. 380
Where hourly hearing (as what there is old?)
The glories of Bel-Anna so well told,°
Queen of the ocean; how that she alone
Possessed all virtues, for which, one by one,
They were so famed; and wanting then a head 385
To form that sweet and gracious pyramid
Wherein they sit, it being the sovereign place
Of all that palace, and reserved to grace
The worthiest queen; these, without envy, on her
In life desired that honour to confer 390
Which with their death, no other should enjoy.
She this embracing with a virtuous joy,°
Far from self-love, as humbling all her worth
To him that gave it, hath again brought forth
Their names to memory, and means this night 395
To make her, once more, visible to light;
And to that light from whence her truth of spirit
Confesseth all the lustre of her merit:
To you, most royal and most happy king,
Of whom Fame's house in every part doth ring 400
For every virtue, but can give no increase,
Not though her loudest trumpet blaze your peace;
To you, that cherish every great example

45

Contracted in yourself, and being so ample
A field of honour, cannot but embrace   405
A spectacle so full of love and grace
Unto your court, where every princely dame
Contends to be as bounteous of her fame
To others as her life was good to her.
For by their lives they only did confer   410
Good on themselves, but by their fame to yours
And every age the benefit endures.

Here the throne wherein they sat, being machina versatilis,° *suddenly
changed, and in the place of it appeared* Fama Bona *as she is described in*
Iconologia di Cesare Ripa,° *attired in white with white wings, having a*   415
*collar of gold about her neck and a heart hanging at it; which Orus Apollo
in his* Hieroglyphica° *interprets the note of a good fame. In her right hand
she bore a trumpet, in her left an olive branch; and for her state, it was
as Virgil describes her,° at the full, her feet on the ground and her head
in the clouds. She, after the music had done (which waited on the turning*   420
*of the machine) called from thence to Virtue and spake this following
speech.*

FAME Virtue, my father and my honour, thou
      That mad'st me good as great, and dar'st avow
      No fame for thine but what is perfect, aid   425
      Tonight the triumphs of thy white-winged maid.
      Do those renownèd queens all utmost rites
      Their states can ask. This is a night of nights.
      In mine own chariots let them crownèd ride,
      And mine own birds and beasts in gears applied°   430
      To draw them forth. Unto the first car tie
      Far-sighted eagles, to note Fame's sharp eye;
      Unto the second griffins, that design°
      Swiftness and strength, two other gifts of mine;
      Unto the last, our lions, that imply   435
      The top of graces, state and majesty.
      And let those hags be led as captives, bound
      Before their wheels, whilst I my trumpet sound.

*At which the loud music sounded as before, to give the masquers time of
descending.*   440
      And here we cannot but take the opportunity to make some more
particular description of the scene, as also of the persons they

presented; which, though they were disposed rather by chance than election,° yet is it my part to justify them all virtuous; and then the lady that will own her presentation may.   445

To follow, therefore, the rule of chronology, which I have observed in my verse: the most upward in time was Penthesilea. She was Queen of the Amazons, and succeeded Otrera (or, as some will, Orythyia). She lived and was present at the war of Troy, on their part against the Greeks, where (as Justin gives her testimony) *inter fortissimos viros,*   450 *magna eius virtutis documenta extitere.*° She is nowhere named but with the preface of Honour and Virtue, and is always advanced in the head of the worthiest women. Diodorus Siculus makes her the daughter of Mars. She was honoured in her death to have it the act of Achilles. Of which Propertius sings this triumph to her beauty: 455

> *Aurea cui postquam nudavit cassida frontem,*
> *Vicit victorem candida forma virum.*°

Next follows Camilla, Queen of the Volscians, celebrated by Virgil; than whose verses nothing can be imagined more exquisite, or more honouring the person they describe. They are these, where he reckons   460 up those that came on Turnus' part against Aeneas.

> *Hos super advenit Volsca de gente Camilla,*
> *Agmen agens equitum, et florenteis aere catervas,*
> *Bellatrix. Non illa colo, calathisve Minervae*
> *Femineas assueta manus, sed proelia virgo*   465
> *Dura pati, cursuque; pedum praevertere ventos.*
> *Illa vel intactae segetis per summa volaret*
> *Gramina, nec teneras cursu laesisset aristas:*
> *Vel mare per medium, fluctu suspensa tumenti,*
> *Ferret iter, celereis nec tingeret aequore plantas.*°   470

And afterward tells her attire and arms, with the admiration that the spectators had of her. All which if the poet created out of himself without Nature, he did but show how much so divine a soul could exceed her.

The third lived in the age of Cyrus, the great Persian monarch, and   475 made him leave to live: Thomyris, Queen of the Scythians, or Massagets. A heroine of a most invincible and unbroken fortitude, who, when Cyrus had invaded her, and taking her only son (rather by treachery than war, as she objected) had slain him, not touched with the grief of so great a loss, in the juster comfort she took of a greater   480 revenge, pursued not only the occasion and honour of conquering so

47

potent an enemy, with whom fell two hundred thousand soldiers, but (what was right memorable in her victory) left not a messenger surviving of his side to report the massacre. She is remembered both by Herodotus, and Justin, to the great renown and glory of her kind, 485 with this elogy. *Quod potentissimo Persarum monarchae bello congressa est, ipsumque et vita, et castris spoliavit, ad iuste ulciscendam filii eius indignissimam mortem.*°

The fourth was honoured to life in the time of Xerxes, and present at his great expedition into Greece; Artemisia,° the Queen of Caria, 490 whose virtue Herodotus, not without some wonder, records. That a woman, a queen, without a husband, her son a ward, and she administering the government, occasioned by no necessity but a mere excellence of spirit, should embark herself for such a war, and there so to behave her, as Xerxes, beholding her fight, should say: *Viri* 495 *quidem extiterunt mihi feminae, feminae autem viri.*° She is no less renowned for her chastity and love to her husband, Mausolus, whose bones, after he was dead, she preserved in ashes and drunk in wine, making herself his tomb, and yet built to his memory a monument deserving a place among the seven wonders of the world, which could 500 not be done by less than a wonder of women.

The fifth was the fair-haired daughter of Ptolomaeus Philadelphus, by the elder Arsinoë, who (married to her brother Ptolomaeus, surnamed Euergetes) was afterwards Queen of Egypt. I find her written both Beronice and Berenice. This lady, upon an expedition of 505 her new-wedded lord into Assyria, vowed to Venus, if he returned safe and conqueror, the offering of her hair; which vow of hers (exacted by the success) she afterward performed. But her father missing it, and therewith displeased, Conon, a mathematician who was then in household with Ptolemy and knew well to flatter him, 510 persuaded the king that it was taken up to heaven and made a constellation; shewing him those seven stars, *ad caudam leonis,*° which are since called *Coma Berenices.* Which story, then presently celebrated by Callimachus in a most elegant poem, Catullus more elegantly converted, wherein they call her 'the magnanimous, even 515 from° a virgin'; alluding, as Hyginus says, to a rescue she made of her father in his flight, and restoring the courage and honour of his army, even to a victory. The words are: *Cognoram a parva virgine magnanimam.*°

The sixth, that famous wife of Mithridates, and Queen of Pontus, 520 Hypsicratea, no less an example of virtue than the rest; who so loved her husband, as she was assistant to him in all labours and hazards of

48

the war in a masculine habit. For which cause, as Valerius Maximus observes, she departed with a chief ornament of her beauty. *Tonsis enim capillis, equo se et armis assuefecit, quo facilius laboribus, et periculis* 525 *eius interesset.°* And afterward, in his flight from Pompey, accompanied his misfortune with a mind and body equally unwearied. She is solemnly registered by that grave author as a notable president of marriage loyalty and love; virtues that might raise a mean person to equality with a queen, but a queen to the state and honour of a 530 deity.

The seventh, that renown of Ethiopia, Candace; from whose excellency the succeeding queens of that nation were ambitious to be called so. A woman of a most haughty spirit against enemies, and a singular affection to her subjects. I find her, celebrated by Dion and 535 Pliny, invading Egypt in the time of Augustus; who, though she were enforced to a peace by his lieutenant Petronius, doth not the less worthily hold her place here, when everywhere this elogy remains of her fame; that she was *maximi animi mulier, tantique in suos meriti, ut omnes deinceps Æthiopum reginae eius nomine fuerint appellatae.°* She 540 governed in Meroë.

The eighth, our own honour, Voadicea, or Boodicea; by some Bunduica and Bunduca; Queen of the Iceni, a people that inhabited that part of the island which was called East Anglia, and comprehended Suffolk, Norfolk, Cambridge, and Huntingdon shires. 545 Since she was born here at home, we will first honour her with a home-born testimony, from the grave and diligent Spenser:

> Bunduca Britoness,
> Bunduca, that victorious conqueress,
> That, lifting up her brave heroic thought 550
> 'Bove women's weakness, with the Romans fought;
> Fought, and in field against them thrice prevailed, etc.°

To which, see her orations in story, made by Tacitus and Dion, wherein is expressed all magnitude of a spirit, breathing to the liberty and redemption of her country. The latter of whom doth honest her 555 beside, with a particular description: *Bunduica, Britannica femina, orta stirpe regia, quae non solum eis cum magna dignitate praefuit, sed etiam bellum omne administravit, cuius animus virilis, potius quam muliebris erat*; and afterward, *Femina, forma honestissima, vultu severo, etc.,°* all which doth weigh the more to her true praise, in coming 560 from the mouths of Romans and enemies. She lived in the time of Nero.

49

The ninth in time, but equal in fame and (the cause of it) virtue, was the chaste Zenobia, Queen of the Palmyrenes; who, after the death of her husband Odenatus, had the name to be reckoned among 565 the thirty that usurped the Roman empire from Gallienus. She continued a long and brave war against several chiefs, and was at length triumphed on by Aurelian, but *ea specie, ut nihil pompabilius P. Rom. videretur.* Her chastity was such, *ut ne virum suum quidem sciret, nisi tentatis conceptionibus.*° She lived in a most royal manner, 570 and was adored to the custom of the Persians. When she made orations to her soldiers, she had always her casque on. A woman of a most divine spirit, and incredible beauty. In Trebellius Pollio, read the most noble description of a queen, and her, that can be uttered with the dignity of an historian. 575

The tenth succeeding was that learned and heroic Amalasunta, Queen of the Ostrogoths, daughter to Theodoric, that obtained the principality of Ravenna and almost all Italy. She drave the Burgundians and Almains out of Liguria, and appeared in her government rather an example than a second. She was the most 580 eloquent of her age, and cunning in all languages of any nation that had commerce with the Roman empire. It is recorded of her, that *sine veneratione eam viderit nemo, pro miraculo fuerit ipsam audire loquentem; Tantaque illi in decernendo gravitas, ut criminis convicti, cum plecterentur, nihil sibi acerbum pati viderentur.*° 585

The eleventh was that brave Bohemian queen, Valasca, who, for her courage, had the surname of Bold; that, to redeem herself and her sex from the tyranny of men, which they lived in under Primislaus, on a night, and at an hour appointed, led on the women to the slaughter of their barbarous husbands and lords; and possessing themselves of 590 their horses, arms, treasure, and places of strength, not only ruled the rest, but lived many years after with the liberty and fortitude of amazons. Celebrated (by Raphael Voleterranus, and in an elegant tract of an Italian's in Latin, who names himself Philalethes, Polyptopiensis Civis) *inter praestantissimas feminas.*° 595

The twelfth and worthy sovereign of all, I make Bel-Anna, royal Queen of the Ocean; of whose dignity and person the whole scope of the invention doth speak throughout; which to offer you again here might but prove offence to that sacred modesty, which hears any testimony of others iterated with more delight than her own praise; 600 she being placed above the need of such ceremony, and safe in her princely virtue against the good or ill of any witness. The name Bel-Anna I devised to honour hers proper° by, as adding to it the

attribute of Fair, and is kept by me in all my poems wherein I
mention her majesty with any shadow or figure. Of which some may 605
come forth with a longer destiny than this age commonly gives
the best births, if but helped to light by her gracious and ripening
favour.

But here I discern a possible objection arising against me, to which
I must turn, as: how can I bring persons of so different ages to appear 610
properly together? Or, why (which is more unnatural) with Virgil's
Mezentius,° I join the living with the dead? I answer to both these at
once: nothing is more proper, nothing more natural, for these all live,
and together, in their fame; and so I present them. Besides, if I would
fly to the all-daring power of poetry, where could I not take 615
sanctuary? Or in whose poem? For other objections, let the looks and
noses of judges hover thick, so they bring the brains; or if they do
not, I care not. When I suffered it to go abroad, I departed with my
right; and now so secure an interpreter I am of my chance that neither
praise nor dispraise shall affect me. 620

*There rests only that we give the description we promised of the scene,
which was the House of Fame. The structure and ornament of which (as
is professed before) was entirely Master Jones his invention and design.
First, for the lower columns he chose the statues of the most excellent poets,
as Homer, Virgil, Lucan, etc. as being the substantial supporters of Fame.* 625
*For the upper, Achilles, Aeneas, Caesar, and those great heroes which
those poets had celebrated. All which stood as in massy gold. Between the
pillars, underneath, were figured land battles, sea fights, triumphs, loves,
sacrifices, and all magnificent subjects of honour, in brass and heightened
with silver. In which he professed to follow that noble description made by* 630
*Chaucer° of the place. Above were sited the masquers, over whose heads
he devised two eminent figures of Honour and Virtue for the arch. The
friezes, both below and above, were filled with several-coloured lights,° like
emeralds, rubies, sapphires, carbuncles, etc. the reflex of which, with other
lights placed in the concave, upon the masquers' habits, was full of glory.* 635
*These habits had in them the excellency of all device and riches, and were
worthily varied by his invention to the nations whereof they were queens.
Nor are these alone his due, but diverse other accessions to the strangeness
and beauty of the spectacle, as the hell, the going about of the chariots,
the binding of the witches, the turning machine, with the presentation of* 640
*Fame. All which I willingly acknowledge for him, since it is a virtue
planted in good natures, that what respects they wish to obtain fruitfully
from others, they will give ingenuously themselves.*

51

By this time, imagine the masquers descended, and again mounted into three triumphant chariots, ready to come forth. The first four were drawn 645
with eagles (whereof I gave the reason, as of the rest, in Fame's speech) their four torchbearers attending on the chariot sides, and four of the hags bound before them. Then followed the second, drawn by griffins, with their torchbearers, and four other hags. Then the last, which was drawn by lions, and more eminent, wherein her majesty was, and had six 650
torchbearers more, peculiar to her, with the like number of hags. After which, a full triumphant music, singing this song, while they rode in state about the stage.

SONG

Help, help all tongues to celebrate this wonder;
The voice of Fame should be as loud as thunder. 655
    Her house is all of echo made,
        Where never dies the sound;
    And, as her brows the clouds invade,
        Her feet do strike the ground.
Sing then, Good Fame, that's out of Virtue born, 660
For who doth Fame neglect, doth virtue scorn.

Here they lighted from their chariots, and danced forth their first dance; then a second immediately following it; both right curious and full of subtle and excellent changes, and seemed performed with no less spirits than of those they personated. The first was to the cornetts, the second to the 665
violins. After which they took out the men° and danced the measures, entertaining the time almost to the space of an hour with singular variety. When, to give them rest, from the music which attended the chariots, by that most excellent tenor voice and exact singer, her majesty's servant, Master John Allin, this ditty was sung. 670

SONG

When all the ages of the earth
Were crowned but in this famous birth,
And that, when they would boast their store
Of worthy queens, they knew no more;
How happier is that age, can give 675
A queen, in whom all they do live!

After it succeeded their third dance; than which a more numerous° composition could not be seen, graphically disposed into letters, and honouring the name of the most sweet and ingenious Prince, Charles,°

Duke of York. Wherein, beside that principal grace of perspicuity, the 680
motions were so even and apt, and their expression so just, as if
mathematicians had lost proportion, they might there have found it. The
author was Master Thomas Giles. After this, they danced galliards and
corantos, and then their last dance, no less elegant in the place than the
rest; with which they took their chariots again, and triumphing about the 685
stage, had their return to the House of Fame celebrated with this last song,
whose notes (as the former) were the work and honour of my excellent
friend, Alfonso Ferrabosco.

SONG

Who, Virtue, can thy power forget,
That sees these live and triumph yet? 690
Th'Assyrian pomp, the Persian pride,
Greeks' glory and the Romans' died;
    And who yet imitate
Their noises, tarry the same fate.
    Force greatness all the glorious ways 695
      You can, it soon decays;
    But so Good Fame shall never;
Her triumphs, as their causes, are for ever.

To conclude which, I know no worthier way of Epilogue, than the
celebration of who were the celebrators. 700

The Queen's Majesty
Countess of Arundel
Countess of Derby
Countess of Huntingdon
Countess of Bedford 705
Countess of Essex
Countess of Montgomery
Lady Cranborne
Lady Elizabeth Guildford
Lady Anne Winter 710
Lady Windsor
Lady Anne Clifford.

SAMUEL DANIEL

Tethys' Festival

Tethys' Festival
or
The Queen's Wake°
Celebrated at Whitehall, the fifth day of June 1610

The Preface to the Reader

For so much as shows and spectacles of this nature are usually
registered among the memorable acts of the time, being complements
of state, both to show magnificence° and to celebrate the feasts to our
greatest respects, it is expected (according now to the custom) that I,
being employed in the business, should publish a description and
form of the late masque, wherewithal it pleased the Queen's most
excellent majesty to solemnize the creation of the high and mighty
Prince Henry, Prince of Wales, in regard to° preserve the memory
thereof, and to satisfy their desires who could have no other notice
but by others' report of what was done. Which I do not out of a desire
to be seen in pamphlets, or of forwardness to show my invention
therein; for I thank God, I labour not with that disease of ostentation,
nor affect to be known to be the man *digitoque monstrarier, hic est,*°
having my name already wider in this kind than I desire, and more
in the wind than I would. Neither do I seek in the divulging hereof
to give it other colours than those it wore, or to make an Apology of
what I have done; knowing, howsoever, it must pass the way of
censure, whereunto I see all publications, of what nature soever, are
liable. And my long experience of the world hath taught me this: that
never remonstrances nor apologies could ever get over the stream of
opinion to do good on the other side, where contrary affection and
conceit had to do,° but only served to entertain their own partialness
who were fore-persuaded, and so was a labour in vain. And it is
oftentimes an argument of pusillanimity and may make *ut iudicium
nostrum, metus videatur,*° and render a good cause suspected by too
much labouring to defend it, which might be the reason that some of
the late greatest princes of Christendom would never have their

54

undertakings made good by such courses, but with silence endured (and in a most witty age) the greatest battery of paper that could possibly be made, and never once recharged the least ordnance° of a pen against it, counting it their glory to do whilst others talked. And shall we who are the poor engineers for shadows° and frame only images of no result, think to oppress the rough censures of those who, notwithstanding all our labour, will like according to their taste, or seek to avoid them by flying to an army of authors° as idle as ourselves? Seeing there is nothing done or written but encounters with detraction and opposition, which is an excellent argument of all our imbecilities° and might allay our presumption, when we shall see our greatest knowledges not to be fixed, but roll according to the uncertain motion of opinion, and controllable by any surly show of reason, which we find is double-edged, and strikes every way alike. And therefore I do not see why any man should rate his own at that value, and set so low prices upon other men's abilities.° *L'homme vaut l'homme*, a man is worth a man, and none hath gotten so high a station of understanding, but he shall find others that are built on an equal floor with him, and have as far a prospect as he, which, when all is done, is but a region subject to all passions and imperfections.

And for these figures of mine, if they come not drawn in all proportions to the life of antiquity (from whose tyranny I see no reason why we may not emancipate our inventions, and be as free as they to use our own images) yet I know them such as were proper to the business, and discharged those parts for which they served with as good correspondency as our appointed limitations would permit.

But in these things wherein the only life consists in show, the art and invention of the architect gives the greatest grace, and is of most importance, ours the least part and of least note in the time of the performance thereof; and therefore have I interserted the description of the artificial part, which only speaks Master Inigo Jones.°

Tethys' Festival

Wherein Tethys,° Queen of the Ocean and wife of Neptune, attended with thirteen nymphs of several rivers, is represented in this manner:

    First the Queen's majesty in the figure of Tethys, the ladies in the shape of nymphs, presiding several rivers appropriate either to their dignity, signories, or places of birth.

1. Whereof the first was the Lady Elizabeth's grace, representing the nymph of Thames;

2. *The Lady Arabella the nymph of Trent;*
3. *The Countess of Arundel the nymph of Arun (a river that runs by Arundel Castle);*
4. *The Countess of Derby the nymph of Derwent (a river that runs through Derby);*
5. *The Countess of Essex the nymph of Lea (the river that bounds Essex);*
6. *The Countess of Dorset the nymph of Aire (a river that runs near Skipton where this lady was born);*
7. *The Countess of Montgomery the nymph of Severn (a river that rises in Montgomeryshire);*
8. *The Viscountess Haddington the nymph of Rother (a river in Sussex);*
9. *The Lady Elizabeth Grey the nymph of Medway (a river in Kent).*
These four rivers are in Monmouthshire:°
The Lady Elizabeth Guildford the nymph of Dulas;
The Lady Katharine Petre the nymph of Olway;
The Lady Winter the nymph of Wye;
The Lady Windsor the nymph of Usk.

The description of the first scene

On the traverse which served as a curtain for the first scene was figured a dark cloud interset° with certain sparkling stars, which at the sound of a loud music being instantly drawn, the scene was discovered with these adornments: first, on either side stood a great statue of twelve foot high representing Neptune and Nereus,° Neptune holding a trident with an anchor made to it, and this motto: His artibus, *that is,* regendo et retinendo,° *alluding to this verse of Virgil,* Hae tibi erunt artes, etc.;° *Nereus holding out a golden fish in a net, with this word* Industria, *the reason whereof is delivered after, in the speech uttered by Triton.° These sea-gods stood on pedestals and were all of gold. Behind them were two pilasters, on which hung compartments with other devices, and these bore up a rich frieze, wherein were figures of ten foot long of floods and nymphs, with a number of naked children dallying with a drapery, which they seemed to hold up that the scene might be seen, and the ends thereof fell down in folds by the pilasters. In the midst was a compartment with this inscription:* Tethyos Epinicia—*'Tethys's feasts of triumph'. This was supported with two winged boys, and all the work was done with that force and boldness on the gold and silver as the figures seemed round and not painted.*

The scene itself was a port or haven° with bulwarks at the entrance, and the figure of a castle commanding a fortified town. Within this port 105
were many ships, small and great, seeming to lie at anchor, some nearer, and some further off, according to perspective. Beyond all appeared the horizon or termination of the sea, which seemed to move with a gentle gale, and many sails, lying some to come into the port, and others passing out. From this scene issued Zephyrus° with eight° naiads, nymphs of fountains, 110
*and two tritons sent from Tethys to give notice of her intendment, which was the antemasque° or first show. The Duke of York° presented Zephyrus, in a short robe of green satin embroidered with golden flowers, with a round wing made of lawn on wires, and hung down in labels;°
behind his shoulders two silver wings; on his head a garland of flowers* 115
consisting of all colours, and on one arm, which was out bare, he wore a bracelet of gold set with rich stones. Eight little ladies near of his stature represented the naiads, and were attired in light robes adorned with flowers, their hair hanging down, and waving with garlands of water ornaments on their heads. 120
The tritons wore skin-coats of watchet taffeta lightened with silver, to show the muscles of their bodies. From the waist almost to the knee were fins of silver in the manner of bases; a mantle of sea-green, laced, and fringed with gold, tied with a knot upon one shoulder and falling down in folds behind, was fastened to the contrary side; on their heads garlands of 125
sedge, with trumpets of writhen shells in their hands; buskins of sea-green laid with silver lace. These persons thus attired entered with this song of four parts, and a music of twelve lutes.

Youth of the spring, mild Zephyrus, blow fair,
    And breathe the joyful air 130
Which Tethys wishes may attend this day;
      Who comes herself to pay
      The vows her heart presents
      To these fair complements.

Breathe out new flowers, which yet were never known 135
    Unto the spring, nor blown
Before this time to beautify the earth.
      And as this day gives birth
      Unto new types of state,°
      So let it bliss create. 140

Bear Tethys' message to the ocean King,
    Say how she joys to bring

Delight unto his islands and his seas;
And tell Meliades,°
The offspring of his blood,   145
How she applauds his good.

The song ended, Triton in the behalf of Zephyrus delivers Tethys' message
with her presents (which was a trident° to the King, and a rich sword°
and scarf to the Prince of Wales) in these words.

TRITON From that intelligence which moves the sphere°   150
  Of circling waves (the mighty Tethys, queen
  Of nymphs and rivers, who will straight appear,
  And in a human character be seen)
  We have in charge to say, that even as seas
  And lands are graced by men of worth and might,   155
  So they return their favours, and in these°
  Exalting of the good seem to delight.
  Which she, in glory lately visiting
  The sweet and pleasant shores of Cambria, found
  By an unusual and most forward spring   160
  Of comfort, wherewith all things did abound,
  For joy of the investiture at hand
  Of their new prince, whose rites, with acts renowned,
  Were here to be solèmnized on this strand;
  And therefore straight resolves t'adorn the day   165
  With her all-gracing presence, and the train
  Of some choice nymphs she pleased to call away
  From several rivers which they entertain.
    And first the lovely nymph of stately Thames,
  The darling of the ocean, summoned is;   170
  Then those of Trent and Arun's graceful streams,
  The Derwent next, with clear-waved worthiness;
  The beauteous nymph of crystal-streaming Lea
  Gives next attendance; then the nymph of Aire
  With modest motion makes her sweet repair.   175
  The nymph of Severn follows in degree
  With ample streams of grace; and next to her
  The cheerful nymph of Rother doth appear
  With comely Medway, th'ornament of Kent,
  And then four goodly nymphs that beautify   180

Camber's fair shores, and all that continent,
The graces of clear Usk, Olway, Dulas, Wye.
   All these within the goodly spacious bay
Of manifold inharbouring Milford meet,
The happy port of union, which gave way   185
To that great hero Henry and his fleet,
To make the blest conjunction that begat
A greater, and more glorious far than that.°
   From hence she sends her dear-loved Zephyrus
To breathe out her affection and her zeal   190
To you, great monarch of Oceanus,°
And to present this trident as the seal
And ensign of her love and of your right.
   And therewithal she wills him greet the Lord
And Prince of th'Isles (the hope and the delight°   195
Of all the northern nations) with this sword,
Which she unto Astraea sacred found,°
And not to be unsheathed but on just ground.
Herewith, says she, deliver him from me
This scarf, the zone of love and amity,   200
T'engird the same; wherein he may survey
Enfigured all the spacious empery
That he is born unto another day.°
Which, tell him, will be world enough to yield
All works of glory ever can be wrought.   205
Let him not pass the circle of that field,
But think Alcides' pillars are the knot;°
For there will be within the large extent
Of these my waves and watery government
More treasure, and more certain riches got   210
Than all the Indies to Iberus brought;°
For Nereus will by industry unfold
A chemic secret, and turn fish to gold.
   This charge she gave, and looks with such a cheer
As did her comfort and delight bewray,   215
Like clear Aurora when she doth appear°
In brightest robes, to make a glorious day.

*The speech ended, the naiads dance about Zephyrus, and then withdraw
them aside; when suddenly at the sound of a loud and fuller music, Tethys*

with her nymphs appears, with another scene, which I will likewise describe   220
in the language of the architector who contrived it, and speaks in his own
mestier to such as are understanders and lovers of that design.° First at
the opening of the heavens appeared three circles of lights and glasses one
within another, and came down in a straight motion five foot, and then
began to move circularly; which lights and motion so occupied the eye of   225
the spectators that the manner of altering the scene° was scarcely discerned;
for in a moment the whole face of it was changed, the port vanished, and
Tethys with her nymphs appeared in their several caverns gloriously
adorned. This scene was comparted into five niches, whereof that in the
midst had some slender pillars° of whole round, and were made of modern   230
architecture in regard of room.° These were of burnished gold, and bare
up the returns of an architrave, frieze, and cornice of the same work; on
which, upon either side, was a plinth directly over the pillars, and on them
were placed for finishings two dolphins of silver, with their tails wreathed
together, which supported oval vases of gold.   235

    Between the two pillars on either side were great ornaments of relievo;
the basement were two huge whales of silver. Above, in an action
mounting, were two sea-horses, and above them on each side of Tethys'
seat was placed a great trident. The seat or throne itself was raised six
steps, and all covered with such an artificial stuff as seemed richer by   240
candle than any cloth of gold. The rests for her arms were two cherubins
of gold; over her head was a great scallop of silver, from which hung the
folds of this rich drapery.

    Above the scallop, and round about the sides, was a resplendent frieze
of jewel glasses or lights, which showed like diamonds, rubies, sapphires,   245
emeralds, and such like.°

    The part which returned from the two plinths that bare up the dolphins
was circular, and made a hollowness over Tethys' head, and on this circle
were four great cartouches° of gold, which bore up a round bowl of silver
in manner of a fountain, with mask-heads of gold, out of which ran an   250
artificial water. On the midst of this was a triangular basement formed of
scrolls and leaves, and then a rich veil adorned with flutings and enchased
work, with a frieze of fishes and a battle of tritons, out of whose mouths
sprang water into the bowl underneath. On the top of this was a round
globe of gold, full of holes, out of which issued abundance of water, some   255
falling into the receipt below, some into the oval vase borne up by the
dolphins; and indeed there was no place in this great aquatic throne that
was not filled with the sprinkling of these two natural-seeming waters. The
niches wherein the ladies sat were four, with pilasters of gold mingled with

60

rustic stones showing like a mineral to make it more rock- and cavern-like, 260
varying from that of Tethys' throne. Equal with the heads of the pillars
was an architrave of the same work; above was a circular frontispiece,
which rose equal° with the bowl of the fountain fore-described. On the
rustic frontispiece lay two great figures in relief, which seemed to bear up
a garland of seaweeds, to which, from two antique candlesticks which stood 265
over the pilasters, were hanging labels of gold, and these were the finishings
of the top of the two niches next to that of Tethys.

In the space between the frontispiece and the architrave stood a great
concave shell,° wherein was the head of a sea-god, and on either side the
shell, to fill up the room, two great mask-heads in profile. The other two 270
niches which were outermost were likewise borne up with pilasters of gold,
and for variation had square frontispieces, and against the straight
architrave of the other was an arch. All these were mingled with rustic, as
before.

In the middle, between the frontispiece and the arch, was a bowl or 275
fountain made of four great scallops, borne up by a great mask-head which
had likewise four aspects, and lying upon this arch, to fill up the concaves,
were two figures turned half into fishes; these with their heads held up the
sides of this bowl. Above this were three great cherubins' heads spouting
water into the bowl. On the midst of the square frontispiece stood a great 280
vase adorned.

The rest of the ornaments consisted of mask-heads spouting water, swans,
festoons of maritime weeds, great shells and such like; and all this whole
scene was filled with the splendour of gold and silver; only some beautiful
colours behind to distinguish them and to set off the rest. 285

The whole work came into the form of a half round. There sat three
ladies in each niche, which made six of a side, the Queen in the midst, and
the Lady Elizabeth° at her feet.

Now concerning their habit: first, their head-tire was composed of shells
and coral, and from a great murex shell in form of the crest of an helm 290
hung a thin waving veil. Their upper garments had the bodice of
sky-coloured taffetas for lightness, all embroidered with maritime
invention;° then had they a kind of half-skirts of cloth of silver
embroidered with gold, all the ground work cut out for lightness, which
hung down full, and cut in points. Underneath that came bases (of the 295
same as was their bodice) beneath their knee. The long skirt was wrought
with lace, waved round about like a river, and on the banks sedge and
seaweeds all of gold. Their shoulders were all embroidered with the work
of° the short skirt of cloth of silver, and had cypress° spangled, ruffed out,

61

and fell in a ruff above the elbow. The under-sleeves were all embroidered   300
as the bodice; their shoes were of satin, richly embroidered, with the work
of the short skirt.

    In this habit they descended out of their caverns one after another, and
so marched up with winding meanders like a river, till they came to the
Tree of Victory, which was a bay° erected at the right side of the state,   305
upon a little mount there raised, where they offer their several flowers in
golden urns which they bare in their hands, whilst a soft music of twelve
lutes and twelve voices, which entertained the time, expressed as a chorus
their action in this manner.

Was ever hour brought more delight   310
   To mortal sight
Than this, wherein fair Tethys deigns to show
   Her and her nymphs a-row
   In glory bright?
See how they bring their flowers   315
   From out their watery bowers,
   To deck Apollo's tree,
   The Tree of Victory,
About whose verdant boughs
They sacrifice their vows,   320
   And wish an everlasting spring
   Of glory to the ocean's king.

This song and ceremony ended, they fall into their first dance, after which
Tethys withdraws and reposes her upon the mount under the Tree of
Victory, entertained with music and this song.   325

If joy had other figure
   Than sounds and words and motion
To intimate the measure
   And height of our devotion,
   This day it had been showed.   330
   But what it can, it doth perform,
Since nature hath bestowed
   No other letter
   To express it better
   Than in this form: 335
Our motions, sounds, and words,
   Tuned to accords,
Must show the well-set parts°
Of our affections and our hearts.

After this Tethys rises, and with her nymphs performs her second dance, 340
and then reposes her again upon the mount, entertained with another
song.°

Are they shadows that we see?
And can shadows pleasure give?
Pleasures only shadows be   345
Cast by bodies we conceive,
And are made the things we deem,
In those figures which they seem.
But these pleasures vanish fast,
Which by shadows are expressed.   350
Pleasures are not, if they last,
In their passing is their best.
Glory is most bright and gay
In a flash, and so away.
Feed apace then, greedy eyes,   355
On the wonder you behold.
Take it sudden as it flies,
Though you take it not to hold.
When your eyes have done their part,
Thought must length it in the heart.   360

After this song Tethys again arises, and with her nymphs taketh out the
lords to dance their measures, corantos, and galliards; which done, they
fall into their third and retiring dance, wherewith they return again into
their several caverns and suddenly vanish. When, to avoid the confusion
which usually attendeth the dissolve of these shows,° and when all was   365
thought to be finished, followed another entertainment, and was a third
show no less delightful than the rest, whose introduction was thus.

Zephyrus marching a certain space after Tethys and her nymphs,
attended with his tritons, a sudden flash of lightning causes them to stay,
and Triton delivereth this speech.   370

TRITON Behold, the post of heaven, bright Mercury,
Is sent to summon and recall again
Imperial Tethys with her company
Unto her watery mansion in the main,
And shift those forms wherein her power did deign   375
T'invest herself and hers, and to restore
Them to themselves whose beauteous shapes they wore.

And then bowing himself towards the state, craveth their stay, and
prepareth them to the expectation of a return of the Queen and her ladies
in their forms, with these words.   380

63

TRITON And now, bright star, the guidon of this state,
    And you great peers, the ornaments of power,
    With all these glittering troupes that have the fate
    To be spectators of this blessèd hour,
    Be pleased to sit awhile, and you shall see   385
    A transformation of far more delight
    And apter drawn to nature than can be
    Described in an imaginary sight.°

Triton having ended his speech, Mercury most artificially and in an
exquisite posture descends, and summons the Duke of York and six 390
young noblemen to attend him and bring back the Queen and her ladies in
their own form, directing him to the place where to find them with this
speech.

MERCURY Fair branch of power, in whose sweet feature here
    Mild Zephyrus a figure did present   395
    Of youth and of the springtime of the year,
    I summon you, and six of high descent
    T'attend on you (as hopeful worthies born
    To shield the honour and the clear renown
    Of ladies) that you presently return   400
    And bring back those in whose fair shapes were shown
    The late-seen nymphs in figures of their own;
    Whom you shall find hard by within a grove
    And garden of the spring addressed to Jove.

Hereupon the Duke of York with his attendants departing to perform this 405
service, the loud music sounds, and suddenly appears the Queen's majesty
in a most pleasant and artificial grove, which was the third scene, and
from thence they march up to the King, conducted by the Duke of York
and the noblemen, in very stately manner.

    And in all these shows this is to be noted, that there were none of inferior 410
sort° mixed amongst these great personages of state and honour (as usually
there have been) but all was performed by themselves with a due reservation
of their dignity. And for those two which did personate the tritons, they were
gentlemen known of good worth and respect. The introducing of pages with
torches might have added more splendour, but yet they would have pestered 415
the room, which the season would not well permit.

    And thus have I delivered the whole form of this show, and expose it to
the censure of those who make it their best show to seem to know, with this
postscript:

Pretulerim scriptor delirus inersque videri   420
Dum mea delectant mala me, vel denique fallant,
Quam sapere et ringi.°

BEN JONSON

Love Restored

In a Masque at Court,
by Gentlemen the King's Servants.°

MASQUERADO I would I could make 'em a show myself. In troth
ladies, I pity you all. You are here in expectation of a device
tonight, and I am afraid you can do little else but expect it.
Though I dare not show my face, I can speak truth under a
vizard.° Good faith, an't please your majesty, your masquers are 5
all at a stand; I cannot think your majesty will see any show
tonight, at least worth your patience. Some two hours since we
were in that forwardness, our dances learned, our masquing attire
on and attired.° A pretty fine speech was taken up o' the poet too,
which if he never be paid for now, it's no matter; his wit costs him 10
nothing.° Unless we should come in like a morris-dance,° and
whistle our ballad ourselves, I know not what we should do. We
ha' no other° musician to play our tunes but the wild music° here,
and the rogue play-boy that acts Cupid is got so hoarse, your
majesty cannot hear him half the breadth o' your chair. 15

[*Enter Plutus° disguised as Cupid*]

See, they ha' thrust him out at adventure. We humbly beseech
your majesty to bear with us. We had both hope and purpose it
should have been better; howsoever, we are lost in it.
PLUTUS What makes this light, feathered vanity here? Away, imper- 20
tinent folly! Infect not this assembly.
MASQUERADO How, boy!
PLUTUS Thou common corruption of all manners and places that
admit thee!
MASQUERADO Ha' you recovered your voice to rail at me? 25
PLUTUS No, vizarded impudence. I am neither player nor masquer,
but the god himself whose deity is here profaned by thee. Thou
and thy like think yourselves authorized in this place to all licence
of surquidry. But you shall find custom hath not so grafted you
here but you may be rent up and thrown out as unprofitable evils. 30

66

I tell thee, I will have no more masquing; I will not buy a false and
fleeting delight so dear. The merry madness of one hour shall not
cost me the repentance of an age.

[*Enter Robin Goodfellow*]°

ROBIN How! no masque, no masque?° I pray you say, are you sure   35
on't? No masque indeed? What do I here then? Can you tell?
MASQUERADO No, faith.
ROBIN 'Slight, I'll be gone again an there be no masque. There's a
jest. Pray you resolve me. Is there any? or no? A masque?
PLUTUS Who are you?   40
ROBIN Nay, I'll tell you that when I can. Does anybody know
themselves here, think you? I would fain know if there be a masque
or no.
PLUTUS There is none, nor shall be, sir. Does that satisfy you?
ROBIN 'Slight, a fine trick! A piece of *England's Joy*,° this. Are these   45
your court sports? Would I had kept me to my gambols o' the
country still, selling of fish, short service,° shoeing the wild mare,°
or roasting of robin redbreast. These were better than after all this
time no masque. You look at me. I have recovered myself now for
you.° I am the honest plain country spirit and harmless, Robin   50
Goodfellow, he that sweeps the hearth and the house clean (riddles
for the country maids°) and does all their other drudgery while
they are at hot cockles;° one that has discoursed with your court
spirits ere now, but was fain tonight to run a thousand hazards to
arrive at this place. Never poor goblin was so put to his shifts to   55
get in, to see nothing. So many thorny difficulties as I have passed
deserved the best masque, the whole shop of the revels.° I would
you would admit some of my feats,° but I ha' little hope o' that i'
faith, you let me in so hardly.
PLUTUS Sir, here's no place for them, nor you. Your rude° good   60
fellowship must seek some other sphere for your admitty.°
ROBIN Nay, so your stiff-necked porter told me at the gate, but not
in so good words. His staff spoke somewhat to that boisterous
sense. I am sure he concluded all in a non-entry, which made me
e'en climb over the wall and in by the wood-yard,° so to the   65
terrace, where when I came, I found the oaks of the guards more
unmoved, and one of 'em, upon whose arm I hung, shoved me off
o' the ladder and dropped me down like an acorn. 'Twas well there
was not a sow in the verge—I had been eaten up else. Then I heard
some talk o' the carpenters' way, and I attempted that; but there   70

the wooden rogues let a huge trap door fall o' my head. If I had
not been a spirit, I had been mazarded. Though I confess I am
none of those subtle ones that can creep through at a keyhole or
the cracked pane of a window. I must come in at a door; which
made me once think of a trunk, but that I would not imitate so   75
catholic a cockscomb as Coryat,° and make a case o' catsos.°
Therefore I took another course. I watched what kind of persons
the door most opened to, and one of their shapes I would belie to
get in with. First I came with authority, and said I was an engineer
and belonged to the motions.° They asked me if I were the fighting   80
bear of last year, and laughed me out of that, and said the motions
were ceased. Then I took another figure, of an old tirewoman, but
tired under that too, for none of the masquers would take note of
me; the mark was out of my mouth.° Then I pretended to be a
musician. Marry, I could not show mine instrument, and that bred   85
a discord. Now there was nothing left for me that I could presently
think on but a feather-maker of Blackfriars,° and in that shape I
told 'em, 'Surely I must come in, let it be opened unto me'; but
they all made as light of me as of my feathers, and wondered how
I could be a Puritan, being of so vain a vocation. I answered: 'We   90
all are masquers sometimes.' With which they knocked hypocrisy
o' the pate, and made room for a bombard-man that brought bouge
for a country lady or two, that fainted, he said, with fasting for the
fine sight since seven o'clock i' the morning. O how it grieved me
that I was prevented o' that shape, and had not touched on it in   95
time, it liked me so well. But I thought I would offer at it yet.
Marry, before I could procure my properties, alarum came that
some o' the whimlens had too much;° and one showed how
fruitfully they had watered his head as he stood under the greces;
and another came out complaining of a cataract shot into his eyes   100
by a planet as he was stargazing.° There was that device defeated.
By this time I saw a fine citizen's wife or two let in, and that figure
provoked me exceedingly to take it, which I had no sooner done
but one o' the Black Guard° had his hand in my vestry° and was
groping of me as nimbly as the Christmas cutpurse.° He thought   105
he might be bold with me because I had not a husband in sight to
squeak to. I was glad to forgo my form,° to be rid of his hot
steaming affection, it so smelt o' the boiling-house. Forty other
devices I had, of wiremen, and the chandry, and I know not what
else; but all succeeded alike. I offered money too, but that could   110
not be done so privately as it durst be taken, for the danger of an
example.° At last a troop of strangers came to the door, with whom

I made myself sure to enter; but before I could mix, they were all
let in, and I left alone without, for want of an interpreter. Which
when I was fain to be to myself, a colossus o' the company told 115
me I had English enough to carry me to bed; with which all the
other statues of flesh laughed. Never till then did I know the want
of a hook and a piece of beef, to have baited three or four o' those
goodly widemouths with. In this despair, when all invention, and
translation too, failed me, I e'en went back and stuck to this shape 120
you see me in, of mine own, with my broom and my candles, and
came on confidently, giving out I was a part of the device. At
which, though they had little to do with wit, yet because some on't
might be used here tonight contrary to their knowledge, they
thought it fit way should be made for me; and as it falls out, to 125
small purpose.

PLUTUS Just as much as you are fit for. Away, idle spirit; [*to
Masquerado*] and thou, the idle cause of his adventuring hither,
vanish with him. 'Tis thou that art not only the sower of vanities
in these high places, but the call of all other light follies to fall and 130
feed on them. I will endure thy prodigality nor riots no more; they
are the ruin of states.° Nor shall the tyranny of these nights
hereafter impose a necessity upon me of entertaining thee. Let 'em
embrace more frugal pastimes! Why should not the thrifty and
right worshipful game of post and pair content 'em? Or the witty 135
invention of noddy, for counters? Or 'God make them rich'° at the
tables? But masquing and revelling? Were not these ladies and
their gentlewomen more housewifely employed, a dozen of 'em to
a light, or twenty (the more the merrier) to save charges, i' their
chambers at home, and their old nightgowns, at draw-gloves, 140
riddles, dreams,° and other pretty purposes, rather than to wake
here in their flaunting wires and tires,° laced gowns, embroidered
petticoats, and other taken-up braveries?° Away! I will no more of
these superfluous excesses. They are these make me hear so ill,°
both in town and country, as I do; which if they continue, I shall 145
be the first shall leave 'em.

MASQUERADO Either I am very stupid, or this a reformed° Cupid.

ROBIN How? Does any take this for Cupid, the Love-in-Court?

MASQUERADO Yes, is't not he?

ROBIN Nay then, we spirits, I see, are subtler yet, and somewhat 150
better discoverers. No; it is not he, nor his brother Anti-Cupid,°
the Love of Virtue, though he pretend to it with his phrase and
face. 'Tis that impostor Plutus, the god of money, who has stolen
Love's ensigns, and in his belied figure reigns i' the world, making

friendships, contracts, marriages, and almost religion; begetting, 155
breeding, and holding the nearest respects of mankind, and
usurping all those offices in this age of gold which Love himself
performed in the Golden Age. 'Tis he that pretends to tie
kingdoms, maintain commerce, dispose of honours, make all places
and dignities arbitrary from him,° even to the very country, where 160
Love's name cannot be razed out, he has yet gained there upon
him, by a proverb insinuating his pre-eminence: *Not for love or
money.* There Love lives confined, by his tyranny, to a cold region,
wrapped up in furs like a Muscovite and almost frozen to death,
while he, in his enforced shape and with his ravished arms,° walks 165
as if he were to set bounds and give laws to destiny. 'Tis you,
mortals, that are fools, and worthy to be such, that worship him;
for if you had wisdom, he had no godhead. He should stink in the
grave with those wretches whose slave he was. Contemn him, and
he is one. Come, follow me. I'll bring you where you shall find 170
Love, and by the virtue of this majesty, who projecteth so powerful
beams of light and heat through this hemisphere, thaw his icy
fetters and scatter the darkness that obscures him. Then, in despite
of this insolent and barbarous Mammon, your sports may proceed,
and the solemnities of the night be complete without depending 175
on so earthy an idol.

PLUTUS Aye, do; attempt it! 'Tis like to find most necessary and
fortunate event, whatsoever is enterprised without my aids. Alas!
how bitterly the spirit of poverty spouts itself against my weal and
felicity! But I feel it not. I cherish and make much of myself, flow 180
forth in ease and delicacy, while that murmurs and starves.

Enter Cupid in his chariot, guarded with the masquers.

SONG

O how came Love, that is himself a fire,
    To be so cold?
Yes, tyrant money quencheth all desire, 185
    Or makes it old.
  But here are beauties will revive
  Love's youth and keep his heat alive;
  As often as his torch here dies,
  He needs but light it at fresh eyes. 190
Joy, joy the more; for in all courts
If Love be cold, so are his sports.

CUPID I have my spirits again, and feel my limbs.
    Away with this cold cloud that dims
    My light! Lie there, my furs and charms;   195
    Love feels a heat that inward warms,
    And guards him naked in these places,
    As at his birth, or 'mongst the Graces.
    [*To Plutus*] Impostor Mammon, come, resign
    This bow and quiver; they are mine.   200
    Thou hast too long usurped my rites,
    I now am lord o' mine own nights.
    Begone, whilst yet I give thee leave.
    When thus the world thou wilt deceive,
    Thou canst in youth and beauty shine,°   205
    Belie a godhead's form divine,
    Scatter thy gifts, and fly to those
    Where thine own humour may dispose;
    But when to good men thou art sent
    By Jove's direct commandement,°   210
    Thou then art agèd, lame and blind,
    And canst nor path nor persons find.
    [*To Robin*] Go, honest spirit, chase him hence
    T'his caves, and there let him dispense,
    For murders, treasons, rapes, his bribes   215
    Unto the discontented tribes;
    Where let his heaps grow daily less,
    And he and they still want success.
    The majesty that here doth move
    Shall triumph, more secured by love   220
    Than all his earth, and never crave
    His aids, but force him as a slave.°
    To those bright beams I owe my life,
    And I will pay it in the strife
    Of duty back. See, here are ten,   225
    The spirits of court and flower of men,
    Led on by me, with flamed intents,
    To figure the ten ornaments
    That do each courtly presence grace.
    Nor will they rudely strive for place,   230
    One to precede the other, but,
    As music them in form shall put,

So will they keep their measures true,
And make still their proportions new,
Till all become one harmony   235
Of honour and of courtesy,
True valour and urbanity,
Of confidence, alacrity,
Of promptness and of industry,
Hability, reality.   240
Nor shall those graces ever quit your court,
Or I be wanting to supply their sport.

Dances°

SONG

This motion was of love begot,
  It was so airy, light, and good,   245
His wings into their feet he shot,
  Or else himself into their blood.
But ask not how; the end will prove
That love's in them or they're in love.

SONG

Have men beheld the Graces dance,   250
  Or seen the upper orbs to move?
So did these turn, return, advance,
  Drawn back by doubt, put on by love.
And now, like earth, themselves they fix,
Till greater powers vouchsafe to mix   255
  Their motions with them. Do not fear,°
  You brighter planets of this sphere:
    Not one male heart you see
      But rather to his female eyes
        Would die a destined sacrifice   260
    Than live at home and free.

[*The Revels*]°

SONG

Give end unto thy pastimes, Love,
  Before they labours prove;
A little rest between   265
Will make thy next shows better seen.

72

Now let them close their eyes and see
    If they can dream of thee,
Since morning hastes to come in view,
And all the morning dreams are true.°   270

GEORGE CHAPMAN
The Memorable Masque

The Memorable Masque
of the two Honourable Houses or Inns of Court,
The Middle Temple, and Lincolns Inn;
As it was performed before the King, at White-Hall°
on Shrove Monday at night, being the 15 of February 1613.
With a description of their whole show,
in the manner of their march on horseback to the Court
from the Master of the Rolls° his house,
with all their right noble consorts, and most showful attendants.
Invented and fashioned, with the ground and special structure of
the whole work,
by our kingdom's most artful and ingenious
architect° Inigo Jones.
Supplied, applied, digested, and written
by Geo. Chapman°

To the most noble, and constant combiner of Honour and Virtue,
Sir Edward Philips, Knight, Master of the Rolls.

This noble and magnificent performance, renewing the ancient spirit
and honour of the Inns of Court, being especially furthered and
followed by your most laborious and honoured endeavours (for his   5
Majesty's service, and honour of the all-grace-deserving nuptials of
the thrice gracious Princess Elizabeth, his Highness' daughter) deserves especially to be in this sort consecrate to your worthy memory
and honour; Honour having never her fair hand more freely and nobly
given to Riches (being a fit particle of this invention) than by yours   10
at this nuptial solemnity. To which assisted and memorable ceremony
the joined hand and industry of the worthily honoured knight, Sir
H. Hobart, his Majesty's Attorney-General, deserving in good part a
joint memory with yours, I have submitted it freely to his noble
acceptance. The poor pains I added to this royal service, being wholly 15
chosen and commanded by your most constant and free favour, I hope

will now appear nothing neglective of their expected duties. Hearty will and care enough, I am assured, was employed in me; and the only ingenuous will° being first and principal step to virtue, I beseech you let it stand for the performing virtue itself. In which addition of your ever-honoured favours you shall ever bind all my future service to your most wished commandment. God send you long health, and your virtues will endue you with honour enough,

> By your free merits' ever-vowed honourer
> and most unfeignedly affectionate observant,
> Geo. Chapman

At the house of the most worthily honoured preferrer and gracer of all honourable actions and virtues, Sir Edward Philips, Knight, Master of the Rolls, all the performers and their assistants made their rendezvous, prepared to their performance, and thus set forth:°

Fifty gentlemen, richly attired and as gallantly mounted, with footmen particularly attending, made the noble vanguard of these nuptial forces. Next (a fit distance observed between them) marched a mock-masque of baboons,° attired like fantastical travellers° in Neapolitan suits and great ruffs, all horsed with asses and dwarf palfreys, with yellow foot-clothes, and casting cockle-demois about, in courtesy, by way of largesse; torches borne on either hand of them, lighting their state as ridiculously as the rest nobly. After them were sorted two cars triumphal, adorned with great mask-heads, festoons, scrolls, and antique leaves, every part enriched with silver and gold. These were through-varied with different invention,° and in them advanced the choice musicians° of our kingdom, six in each, attired like Virginian priests, by whom the sun is there adored° and therefore called the Phoebades.° Their robes were tucked up before, strange hoods of feathers° and scallops about their necks, and on their heads turbans, stuck with several coloured feathers, spotted with wings of flies of extraordinary bigness, like those of their country; and about them marched two ranks of torches.

Then rode the chief masquers in Indian habits, all of a resemblance: the groundcloth of silver, richly embroidered with golden suns, and about every sun ran a trail of gold, imitating Indian work; their bases of the same stuff and work, but betwixt every pane of embroidery went a row of white ostrich feathers mingled with sprigs of gold plate. Under their breasts they wore baldrics of gold embroidered high with purl, and about their necks ruffs of feathers spangled with pearl and silver; on their heads high sprigged feathers, compassed in coronets like the Virginian princes they presented. Betwixt every set of feathers, and about their brows in the under part of their coronets, shined suns of gold plate sprinkled with pearl, from whence sprung rays of the like plate that, mixing with the motion of the feathers, showed exceedingly delightful and gracious. Their legs were adorned with close long white silk stockings, curiously embroidered with gold to the mid-leg. And over these (being on horseback) they drew greaves 60 *or buskins embroidered with gold, and interlaced with rows of feathers, altogether estrangeful and Indian-like. In their hands (set in several postures as they rode) they brandished cane darts of the finest gold; their vizards of olive colour, but pleasingly visaged; their hair black and large, waving down to their shoulders.* 65

Their horse, for rich show, equalled the masquers themselves, all their caparisons being enchased with suns of gold and ornamental jewels, to every one of which was tacked a scarfing of silver that ran sinuously in works over the whole caparison, even to the dazzling of the admiring spectators; their heads no less gracefully and properly decked with the like 70 *light scarfing, that hung about their ears wantonly dangling. Every one of these horse had two Moors, attired like Indian slaves, that for state sided them, with swelling wreaths of gold and watchet on their heads, which arose in all to the number of a hundred.*

The torch-bearers' habits were likewise of the Indian garb, but more 75 *stravagant than those of the masquers, all showfully garnished with several-hued feathers. The humble variety whereof struck off the more amply the masquers' high beauties, shining in the habits of themselves,° and reflected in their kind a new and delightfully varied radiance on the beholders. All these sustained torches of virgin wax, whose staves were* 80 *great canes all over gilded; and these, as the rest, had every man his Moor, attending his horse.*

The masquers, riding single, had every masquer his torch-bearer mounted before him.

The last chariot, which was most of all adorned, had his whole frame 85 *filled with moulded work, mixed all with paintings and glittering scarfings of silver, over which was cast a canopy of gold, borne up with antic figures, and all composed* a la grotesca. *Before this, in the seat of it as the charioteer, was advanced a strange person, and as strangely habited, half French, half Swiss, his name Capriccio;° wearing on his head a pair of* 90 *golden bellows, a gilt spur in one hand, and with the other managing the reins of the four horses that drew it.*

On a seat of the same chariot, a little more elevate, sate Eunomia,° the virgin priest of the goddess Honour, together with Phemis,° her herald. The habit of her priest was a robe of white silk, gathered about the neck; 95 *a pentacle° of silvered stuff about her shoulders hanging foldedly down both before and behind; a vestal veil on her head of tiffany, striped with silver,*

*hanging with a train to the earth. The herald was attired in an antique
cuirass of silver stuff, with labels at the wings and bases; a short gown of
gold stuff, with wide sleeves cut in panes; a wreath of gold on his head,* 100
and a rod of gold in his hand.

*Highest of all, in the most eminent seat of the triumphal, sat, side to
side, the celestial goddess Honour, and the earthy deity Plutus,° or Riches.
His attire a short robe of gold, fringed; his wide sleeves turned up and
out-showed his naked arms; his head and beard sprinkled with showers of* 105
*gold; his buskins, clinquant, as his other attire. The ornaments of Honour
were these: a rich full robe of blue silk girt about her, a mantle of silver
worn over-thwart, full-gathered and descending in folds behind; a veil of
net lawn, embroidered with O's and spangled; her tresses in tucks, braided
with silver, the hinder part shadowing in waves her shoulders.* 110

*These, thus particularly and with propriety adorned, were strongly
attended with a full guard of two hundred halberdiers; two marshals
(being choice gentlemen of either House) commander-like attired, to and
fro coursing to keep all in their orders.*

A show at all parts so novel, conceitful, and glorious, as hath not in this 115
*land (to the proper use and object it had proposed) been ever before beheld.
Nor did those honourable Inns of Court at any time in that kind such
acceptable service to the sacred majesty of this kingdom, nor were returned
by many degrees with so thrice gracious and royal entertainment and
honour. But, as above said, all these so marching to the court at Whitehall,* 120
*the King, bride, and bridegroom, with all the lords of the most honoured
Privy Council and our chief nobility, stood in the gallery before the
tilt-yard to behold their arrival; who, for the more full satisfaction of his
Majesty's view, made one turn about the yard and dismounted; being then
honourably attended through the gallery to a chamber appointed, where* 125
they were to make ready for their performance in the hall, etc.

*The King being come forth, the masquers ascended, unseen, to their
scene. Then for the works.*

*First there appeared at the lower end of the hall an artificial rock, whose
top was near as high as the hall itself. This rock was in the undermost part* 130
*craggy and full of hollow places, in whose concaves were contrived two
winding pair of stairs, by whose greces the persons above might make their
descents, and all the way be seen. All this rock grew by degrees up into a
gold colour,° and was run quite through with veins of gold. On the one
side whereof, eminently raised on a fair hill, was erected a silver temple of* 135
*an octangle figure, whose pillars were of a composed order,° and bore up
an architrave, frieze, and cornice, over which stood a continued plinth,
whereon were advanced statues of silver. Above this was placed a bastard*

*order° of architecture, wherein were carved compartments, in one of which
was written in great gold capitals,* HONORIS FANUM.° *Above all was* 140
a cupola or type, which seemed to be scaled with silver plates.

*For finishing of all, upon a pedestal was fixed a round stone of silver
from which grew a pair of golden wings, both feigned to be Fortune's:° the
round stone (when her feet trod it) ever affirmed to be rolling, figuring her
inconstancy; the golden wings denoting those nimble powers that pompously* 145
*bear her about the world; on that temple (erected to her daughter Honour,
and figuring this kingdom°) put off by her and fixed,° for assured sign she
would never forsake it.*

*About this temple hung festoons wreathed with silver from one pillar's
head to another. Besides, the frieze was enriched with carvings, all showing* 150
greatness and magnificence.

*On the other side of the rock grew a grove, in whose utmost part
appeared a vast, withered, and hollow tree, being the bare receptacle of
the baboonery.*

These following° should in duty have had their proper places, after 155
*every fitted speech of the actors; but being prevented by the unexpected
haste of the printer, which he never let me know, and never sending me a
proof till he had past those speeches, I had no reason to imagine he could
have been so forward. His fault is therefore to be supplied by the
observation and reference of the reader, who will easily perceive where they* 160
were to be inserted.

*After the speech of Plutus (who, as you may see after, first entered) the
middle part of the rock began to move, and being come some five paces up
towards the King, it split in pieces with a great crack, and out brake
Capriccio, as before described. The pieces of the rock vanished, and he* 165
spake, as in his place.

*At the singing of the first song, full, which was sung by the Virginian
priests called the Phoebades to six lutes (being used as an Orphean virtue°
for the state of the mines opening) the upper part of the rock was suddenly
turned to a cloud, discovering a rich and refulgent mine of gold, in which* 170
*the twelve masquers were triumphantly seated, their torch-bearers
attending before them; all the lights being so ordered that, though none
were seen, yet had their lustre such virtue that by it the least spangle or
spark of the masquers' rich habits might with ease and clearness be
discerned as far off as the state.°* 175

*Over this golden mine, in an evening sky, the ruddy sun was seen ready
to set; and behind the tops of certain white cliffs by degrees descended,
casting up a bank of clouds in which a while he was hidden; but then
gloriously shining, gave that usually observed good omen of succeeding fair
weather.* 180

*Before he was fully set the Phoebades (showing the custom of the
Indians to adore the sun setting) began their observance with the song, to
whose place we must refer you for the manner and words. All the time they
were singing, the torch-bearers holding up their torches to the sun, to whom
the priests themselves and the rest did, as they sung, obeisance; which was
answered by other music and voices, at the commandment of Honour, with
all observances used to the King, etc. As in the following places.* 185

To answer certain insolent objections made against the length of my
speeches and narrations: being, for the probability of all accidents
rising from the invention of this masque, and their application to the 190
persons and places for whom and by whom it was presented, not
convenient, but necessary,° I am enforced to affirm this: that, as there
is no poem nor oration so general but hath his one particular
proposition, nor no river so extravagantly ample but hath his never-
so-narrow fountain, worthy to be named, so all these courtly and 195
honouring inventions (having poesy and oration in them, and a
fountain to be expressed, from whence their rivers flow) should
expressively arise out of the places and persons for and by whom they
are presented; without which limits they are luxurious and vain. But
what rules soever are set down to any art or act (though without their 200
observation no art nor act is true and worthy) yet are they nothing
the more followed, or those few that follow them credited. Every
vulgarly esteemed upstart dares break the dreadful dignity of ancient
and authentical poesy, and presume luciferously to proclaim in place
thereof repugnant precepts of their own spawn. Truth and worth have 205
no faces to enamour the licentious, but vainglory and humour. The
same body, the same beauty a thousand men seeing, only the man
whose blood is fitted hath that which he calls his soul enamoured.
And this out of infallible cause; for men understand not these of
Menander: 210

*est morbus opportunitas
Animae, quod ictus, vulnus accipit grave.*°

But the cause of some° men's being enamoured with Truth, and of
her slight respect in others, is the divine Freedom; one touching with
his apprehensive finger, the other passing. The Hill of the Muses 215
(which all men must climb in the regular way to Truth) is said of old
to be forked. And the two points of it, parting at the top, are *insania*
and *divinus furor.*° *Insania* is that which every rank-brained writer and
judge of poetical writing is rapt withal, when he presumes either to
write or censure the height of poesy, and that transports him with 220

humour, vainglory, and pride, most profane and sacrilegious; when *divinus furor* makes gentle and noble the never-so-truly inspired writer:

Emollit mores nec sinit esse feros°

And the mild beams of the most holy inflamer easily and sweetly 225 enter, with all understanding sharpness, the soft and sincerely humane. But with no time, no study, no means under heaven, any arrogant, all-occupation devourer (that will chandler-like set up with all wares, selling Poesy's nectar and ambrosia as well as mustard and vinegar) the chaste and restrained beams of humble truth will 230 ever enter, but only graze and glance at them, and the further fly them.

The Applicable Argument of the Masque

Honour is so much respected and adored that she hath a temple erected to her like a goddess, a virgin priest consecrated to her (which is Eunomia, or Law, since none should dare access to Honour but by virtue,° of which 235 Law being the rule must needs be a chief), and a Herald (called Phemis, or Fame) to proclaim her institutions and commandments. To amplify yet more the divine graces of this goddess, Plutus (or Riches), being by Aristophanes, Lucian, etc. presented naturally blind, deformed, and dull witted, is here by his love of Honour made see, made sightly, made 240 ingenious, made liberal. And all this converted and consecrate to the most worthy celebration of these sacred nuptials, all issuing (to conclude the necessary application) from an honourable temple, etc.

Non est certa fides, quam non iniuria versat.
Fallit portus et ipse fidem.° 245

The Names of the Speakers

Honour, A Goddess
Plutus (or Riches), a God
Eunomia (or Law), Priest of Honour
Phemis, Honour's Herald
Capriccio, a man of wit, etc. 250

The Presentment

Plutus appeared, surveying the work with this speech.

PLUTUS Rocks? Nothing but rocks in these masquing devices?° Is Invention so poor she must needs ever dwell amongst rocks? But it may worthily have chanced, being so often presented, that their vain custom is now become the necessary hand of heaven, trans- 255 forming into rocks some stony-hearted ladies courted in former masques,° for whose loves some of their repulsed servants have perished. Or perhaps some of my flinty-hearted usurers have been here metamorphosed, betwixt whom and ladies there is resem- blance enough: ladies using to take interest, besides their principal, 260 as much as usurers. See, it is so; and now is the time of restoring them to their natural shapes. It moves, opens. Excellent! This metamorphosis I intend to overhear.

A rock moving and breaking with a crack about Capriccio, he enters, with a pair of bellows on his head, a spur in one hand and a piece of gold ore 265 in the other, etc. He speaks, ut sequitur.°

CAPRICCIO How hard this world is to a man of wit! He must eat through main rocks for his food, or fast. A restless and tormenting stone his wit is to him; the very stone of Sisyphus° in hell, nay, the Philosopher's Stone° makes not a man more wretched. A man 270 must be a second Proteus,° and turn himself into all shapes (like Ulysses) to wind through the straits of this pinching vale of misery. I have turned myself into a tailor, a man, a gentleman, a nobleman, a worthy man; but never had the wit to turn myself into an alderman. There are many shapes to perish in, but one to live in, 275 and that's an alderman's. 'Tis not for a man of wit to take any rich figure upon him. Your bold, proud, ignorant, that's brave and clinquant, that finds crowns put into his shoes every morning by the fairies and will never tell, whose wit is humour, whose judgement is fashion, whose pride is emptiness, birth his full man, 280 that is in all things something, in sum total nothing: he shall live in the land of Spruce,° milk and honey flowing into his mouth sleeping.

PLUTUS This is no transformation,° but an intrusion into my golden mines. I will hear him further. 285

CAPRICCIO This breach of rocks I have made in needy pursuit of the blind deity, Riches, who is miraculously arrived here. For (accord- ing to our rare men of wit) heaven standing, and earth moving, her motion (being circular) hath brought one of the most remote parts of the world to touch at this all-exceeding Island, which a man of 290 wit would imagine must needs move circularly with the rest of the world, and so ever maintain an equal distance. But poets (our chief men of wit) answer that point directly, most ingeniously affirming that this isle is, for the excellency of it, divided from the world (*divisus ab orbe Britannus*)° and that, though the whole world 295 besides moves, yet this isle stands fixed on her own feet and defies the world's mutability, which this rare accident of the arrival of Riches in one of his furthest-off-situate dominions most demonstratively proves.

PLUTUS This is a man of wit indeed, and knows of all our arrivals. 300

CAPRICCIO With this dull deity Riches, a rich island lying in the South-sea, called Paeana, of the Paeans° (or songs) sung to the Sun whom they there adore (being for strength and riches called the navel of that South-sea) is by earth's round motion moved near this Britain shore. In which island, being yet in command of the 305 Virginian continent, a troop of the noblest Virginians inhabiting, attended hither the god of riches, all triumphantly shining in a mine of gold. For, hearing of the most royal solemnity of these sacred nuptials, they crossed the ocean in their honour and are here arrived. A poor snatch at some of the golden ore that the feet of 310 Riches have turned up as he trod here my poor hand hath purchased, and hope the remainder of a greater work will be shortly extant.°

PLUTUS You, sir, that are miching about my golden mines here!

CAPRICCIO What, can you see sir? You have heretofore been 315 presented blind, like your mother Fortune and your brother Love.

PLUTUS But now, sir, you see I see.

CAPRICCIO By what good means, I beseech you sir?

PLUTUS That means I may vouchsafe you hereafter; mean space, what are you? 320

CAPRICCIO I am, sir, a kind of man, a man of wit; with whom your worship has nothing to do, I think.

PLUTUS No sir, nor will have anything to do with him. A man of wit—what's that? A beggar!

CAPRICCIO And yet no devil, sir. 325

PLUTUS As I am, you mean?

CAPRICCIO Indeed sir, your kingdom is under the earth.

PLUTUS That's true, for Riches is the Atlas that holds it up; it would sink else.

CAPRICCIO 'Tis rather a wonder it sinks not with you sir, you're so 330 sinfully and damnably heavy.

PLUTUS Sinful and damnable? What, a Puritan? These bellows you
wear on your head show with what matter your brain is puffed up
sir. A religion-forger I see you are, and presume of inspiration
from these bellows, with which ye study to blow up the settled　335
governments of kingdoms.

CAPRICCIO Your worship knocks at a wrong door, sir; I dwell far
from the person you speak of.

PLUTUS What may you be then, being a man of wit? A buffoon, a jester?
Before I would take upon me the title of a man of wit, and be baffled　340
by every man of wisdom for a buffoon, I would turn bankrupt, or set
up a tobacco shop,° change cloaks with an alchemist, or serve a usurer,
be a watering-post for every groom, stand the push of every rascal
wit, enter lists of jests with trencher-fools° and be fooled down by
them, or (which is worse) put them down in fooling. Are these the　345
qualities a man of wit should run proud of?

CAPRICCIO Your worship, I see, has obtained wit with sight, which
I hope yet my poor wit will well be able to answer. For, touching
my jesting, I have heard of some courtiers that have run themselves out of their states with jousting, and why may not I then　350
raise my self in the state with jesting? An honest shoemaker° (in a
liberal king's time) was knighted for making a clean boot, and is it
impossible that I, for breaking a clean jest, should be advanced in
court or council, or at least served out for an ambassador to a dull
climate? Jests and merriments are but wild weeds in a rank soil,　355
which, being well manured, yield the wholesome crop of wisdom
and discretion at time o' th'year.

PLUTUS Nay, nay; I commend thy judgement for cutting thy coat so
just to the breadth of thy shoulders. He that cannot be a courser
in the field,° let him learn to play the jackanapes in the chamber;　360
he that cannot personate the wise man well amongst wizards,° let
him learn to play the fool well amongst dizzards.

CAPRICCIO 'Tis passing miraculous that your dull and blind worship
should so suddenly turn both sightful and witful.

PLUTUS The riddle of that miracle I may chance dissolve to you in　365
sequel; meantime, what name sustainest thou, and what toys are
these thou bearest so fantastically about thee?

CAPRICCIO These toys, sir, are the ensigns that discover my name
and quality, my name being Capriccio; and I wear these bellows
on my head to show I can puff up with glory all those that affect　370
me, and besides, bear this spur to show I can spur-gall even the
best that condemn me.

PLUTUS A dangerous fellow. But what makest thou, poor man of wit, at these pompous nuptials?

CAPRICCIO Sir, I come hither with a charge to do these nuptials, I   375
hope, very acceptable service. And my charge is a company of accomplished travellers that are excellent at antimasques, and will tender a taste of their quality, if your worship please.

PLUTUS Excellent well pleased. Of what virtue are they besides?

CAPRICCIO Passing grave, sir, yet exceeding acute; witty, yet not   380
ridiculous (never laugh at their own jests); laborious, yet not base, having cut out the skirts of the whole world in amorous quest of your gold and silver.

PLUTUS They shall have enough. Call them, I beseech thee, call them. How far hence abide they?   385

CAPRICCIO Sir, being by another eminent quality the admired soldiers of the world, in contempt of softness and delicacy they lie on the naturally hard boards of that naked tree. And will your worship assure them rewards fit for persons of their freight?

PLUTUS Dost thou doubt my reward, being pleased?   390

CAPRICCIO I know, sir, a man may sooner win your reward for pleasing you, than deserving you. But you great wise persons have a fetch of state—to employ with countenance and encouragement, but reward with austerity and disgrace;° save your purses, and lose your honours.   395

PLUTUS To assure thee of reward, I will now satisfy thee touching the miraculous cause both of my sight and wit, and which consequently moves me to humanity and bounty; and all is only this—my late being in love with the lovely goddess Honour.

CAPRICCIO If your worship love Honour, indeed, sir, you must   400
needs be bountiful. But where is the rare goddess you speak of to be seen?

PLUTUS In that rich temple, where Fortune fixed those her golden wings thou seest, and that rolling stone she used to tread upon, for sign she would never forsake this kingdom. There is adored the   405
worthy goddess Honour, the sweetness of whose voice, when I first heard her persuasions both to myself and the Virginian princes arrived here to do honour and homage to these heavenly nuptials, so most powerfully enamoured me that the fire of my love flew up to the sight of mine eyes, that have lighted within me a whole firmament of   410
bounty, which may securely assure thee thy reward is certain. And therefore call thy accomplished company to their antimasque.

CAPRICCIO See, sir, the time set for their appearance being expired, they appear to their service of themselves.

Enter the Baboons, after whose dance, being antic and delightful, they 415
returned to their tree, when Plutus spake to Capriccio.

PLUTUS Gramercy; now Capriccio, take thy men of complement and
travel with them to other marriages. My riches to thy wit, they will
get something somewhere.

CAPRICCIO What's this? 420

PLUTUS A strain of wit beyond a man of wit. I have employed you,
and the grace of that is reward enough. Hence, pack, with your
complemental fardel; the sight of an attendant for reward is
abominable in the eyes of a turn-served politician, and I fear will
strike me blind again. I cannot abide these bellows of thy head; 425
they and thy men of wit have melted my mines with them and
consumed me. Yet take thy life and be gone. Neptune let thy
predecessor Ulysses° live after all his slain companions, but to
make him die more miserably living, gave him up to shipwrecks,
enchantments. Men of wit are but enchanted, there is no such 430
thing as wit in this world. Go,° take a tree, inure thy soldiers to
hardness; 'tis honourable, though not clinquant.

CAPRICCIO Can this be possible?

PLUTUS Alas, poor man of wit, how want of reward daunts thy
virtue. But because I must send none away discontented from 435
these all-pleasing nuptials, take this wedge of gold, and wedge
thyself into the world with it, renouncing that loose wit of thine;
'twill spoil thy complexion.

CAPRICCIO Honour, and all Argus'° eyes, to earth's all-commanding
Riches. *Pluto etiam cedit Jupiter.*° 440

Exit Capriccio.

After this low induction, by these succeeding degrees the chief masquers
were advanced to their discovery.

Plutus calls to Eunomia.

PLUTUS These humble objects can no high eyes draw. 445
Eunomia (or the sacred power of Law)
Daughter of Jove and goddess Honour's priest,
Appear to Plutus, and his love assist.

Eunomia [appears] in the temple gates.

EUNOMIA What would the god of Riches?

PLUTUS   Join with Honour 450
In purposed grace of these great nuptials.
And since to Honour none should dare access,

85

But helped by Virtue's hand (thyself, chaste Law,°
Being Virtue's rule, and her directful light)
Help me to th'honour of her speech and sight. 455
EUNOMIA Thy will shall straight be honoured; all that seek
Access to Honour by clear Virtue's beam,
Her grace prevents their pains, and comes to them.

*Loud music, and Honour appears, descending with her herald, Phemis, and
Eunomia her priest before her. The music ceasing, Plutus spake.* 460

PLUTUS Crown of all merit, goddess, and my love,
'Tis now high time that th'end for which we come
Should be endeavoured in our utmost rite,
Done to the sweetness of this nuptial night.
HONOUR Plutus, the princes of the Virgin land, 465
Whom I made cross the Briton ocean
To this most famèd isle of all the world,
To do due homage to the sacred nuptials
Of Love and Beauty, celebrated here,
By this hour of the holy even I know 470
Are ready to perform the rites they owe
To setting Phoebus; which (for greater state
To their appearance) their first act advances,
And with songs ushers their succeeding dances.
Herald, give summons to the Virgin knights 475
No longer to delay their purposed rites.
HERALD Knights of the Virgin land, whom Beauty's lights
Would glorify with their inflaming sights,
Keep now obscured no more your fair intent
To add your beams to this night's ornament; 480
The golden-wingèd Hour strikes now a plain,°
And calls out all the pomp ye entertain;
The princely bridegroom and the bride's bright eyes
Sparkle with grace to your discoveries.

At these words the Phoebades (or Priests of the Sun) appeared first with 485
six lutes and six voices, and sung to the opening of the mine and masquers'
discovery this full song.

THE FIRST SONG

Ope, Earth, thy womb of gold,
Show, Heaven, thy cope of stars.

All glad aspects unfold,   490
  Shine out and clear our cares:
Kiss, heaven and earth, and so combine°
In all mixed joy our nuptial twine.

This song ended, a mount opened and spread like a sky, in which appeared
a sun setting; beneath which sat the twelve Masquers in a mine of gold, 495
twelve torch-bearers holding their torches before them; after which
Honour, etc.

HONOUR See now the setting sun casts up his bank,
  And shows his bright head at his sea's repair,
  For sign that all days future shall be fair.   500
PLUTUS May he that rules all nights and days confirm it.
HONOUR Behold the sun's fair priests, the Phoebades,
  Their evening service in an hymn address
  To Phoebus setting; which we now shall hear,
  And see the forms of their devotions there.   505

The Phoebades sing the first stance° of the second song, ut sequitur.

(One alone) 1
Descend, fair Sun, and sweetly rest
  In Tethys' crystal arms thy toil;°
Fall burning on her marble breast,
  And make with love her billows boil.   510

(Another alone) 2
Blow, blow, sweet winds, O blow away
  All vapours from the finèd air,
That to his golden head no ray
  May languish with the least impair.

Chorus
Dance, Tethys, and thy love's red beams   515
  Embrace with joy; he now descends,
Burns, burns with love to drink thy streams,
  And on him endless youth attends.

After this stance, Honour, etc.

HONOUR This superstitious hymn, sung to the Sun,   520
  Let us encounter with fit duties done
  To our clear Phoebus, whose true piety°
  Enjoys from heaven an earthly deity.°

Other music and voices, and this second stance was sung, directing their
observance to the King. 525

(One alone) 1

Rise, rise, O Phoebus, ever rise,
    Descend not to th'inconstant stream,
But grace with endless light our skies;
    To thee that Sun is but a beam.

(Another alone) 2

Dance, ladies, in our Sun's bright rays, 530
    In which the bride and bridegroom shine;
Clear sable night with your eyes' days,
    And set firm lights on Hymen's shrine.

Chorus

O may our Sun not set before
    He sees his endless seed arise, 535
And deck his triple-crownèd shore
    With springs of human deities.

This ended, the Phoebades sung the third stance.

1

Set, set, great Sun, our rising love
    Shall ever celebrate thy grace, 540
Whom, entering the high court of Jove,
    Each god greets, rising from his place.

2

When thou thy silver bow dost bend,
    All start aside and dread thy draughts;
How can we thee enough commend, 545
    Commanding all worlds with thy shafts?

Chorus

Blest was thy mother bearing thee,
    And Phoebe, that delights in darts.°
Thou artful songs dost set; and she°
    Winds horns, loves hounds, and high-palmed harts. 550

After this, Honour.

HONOUR Again our music, and conclude this song
    To him to whom all Phoebus' beams belong.

The other voices sung to other music the fourth stance.

1

Rise still, clear Sun, and never set,   555
   But be to earth her only light:
All other kings, in thy beams met,
   Are clouds and dark effects of night.

2

As when the rosy morn doth rise,
   Like mists, all give thy wisdom way;   560
A learnèd king is, as in skies,
   To poor dim stars, the flaming day.

Chorus

Blest was thy mother bearing thee,°
   Thee, only relic of her race,
Made by thy virtue's beams a tree   565
   Whose arms shall all the earth embrace.

This done, Eunomia spake to the masquers set yet above.

EUNOMIA Virginian princes, ye must now renounce
Your superstitious worship of these Suns,
Subject to cloudy darkenings and descents,   570
And of your fit devotions turn the events
To this our Briton Phoebus, whose bright sky,
Enlightened with a Christian piety,
Is never subject to black Error's night,
And hath already offered heaven's true light   575
To your dark region; which acknowledge now.°
Descend, and to him all your homage vow.

Loud music.° With this the torch-bearers descended, and performed
another antimasque, dancing with torches lighted at both ends; which
done, the masquers descended, and fell into their dances, two of which being 580
past, and others with the ladies, Honour spake.

HONOUR Music! your voices now tune sweet and high,
And sing the nuptial hymn of Love and Beauty.
Twins, as of one age, so to one desire°
May both their bloods give an unparted fire.   585
And as those twins that Fame gives all her prize
Combined their life's powers in such sympathies
That one being merry, mirth the other graced,
If one felt sorrow, th'other grief embraced,

If one were healthful, health the other pleased,   590
If one were sick the other was diseased,
And all ways joined in such a constant troth
That one like cause had like effect in both:
So may these nuptial twins their whole lives' store
Spend in such even parts, never grieving more   595
Than may the more set off their joys divine,
As after clouds the sun doth clearest shine.

This said, this song of Love and Beauty was sung, single.°

I

Bright Panthaea, born to Pan°
Of the noblest race of man,   600
  Her white hand to Eros giving,
With a kiss joined Heaven to Earth
And begot so fair a birth
  As yet never graced the living.

Chorus

A twin that all worlds did adorn,   605
For so were Love and Beauty born.

2

Both so loved they did contend
Which the other should transcend,
  Doing either grace and kindness.°
Love from Beauty did remove   610
Lightness, called her stain in love;
  Beauty took from Love his blindness.

Chorus

Love sparks made flame in Beauty's sky,
And Beauty blew up Love as high.

3

Virtue then commixed her fire,   615
To which Bounty did aspire,
  Innocence a crown conferring;
Mine and thine were then unused,
All things common, nought abused,
  Freely earth her fruitage bearing.   620

Chorus

Nought then was cared for that could fade,
And thus the golden world was made.°

This sung, the masquers danced again with the ladies, after which Honour.

HONOUR Now may the blessings of the golden age
    Swim in these nuptials, even to holy rage.°   625
    A hymn to sleep prefer, and all the joys
    That in his empire are of dearest choice,
    Betwixt his golden slumbers ever flow
    In these; and theirs in springs as endless grow.

This said, the last song was sung full.   630

THE LAST SONG.

    Now, sleep, bind fast the flood of air,
      Strike all things dumb and deaf,
    And to disturb our nuptial pair
      Let stir no aspen leaf.
    Send flocks of golden dreams   635
      That all true joys presage;
    Bring, in thy oily streams,
      The milk and honey age.
        Now close the world-round sphere of bliss,
        And fill it with a heavenly kiss.   640

After this, Plutus to the masquers.

PLUTUS Come, Virgin knights, the homage ye have done
    To Love and Beauty, and our Briton Sun,
    Kind Honour will requite with holy feasts
    In her fair temple; and her lovèd guests   645
    Gives me the grace t'invite, when she and I
    (Honour and Riches) will eternally
    A league in favour of this night combine,
    In which Love's second hallowed tapers shine;
    Whose joys may Heaven and Earth as highly please   650
    As those two nights that got great Hercules.°

The speech ended, they concluded with a dance that brought them off;
Plutus, with Honour and the rest, conducting them up to the Temple of
Honour.

THOMAS CAMPION

The Caversham Entertainment

A Relation of the Late Royal Entertainment
given by the Right Honourable the Lord Knollys
at Caversham House near Reading
to our most gracious Queen, Queen Anne,
in her Progress toward the Bath
upon the seven and eight and twenty days of April.
1613

For as much as this late entertainment hath been much desired in writing,
both of such as were present at the performance thereof, as also of many
which are yet strangers both to the business and place, it shall be
convenient in this general publication a little to touch at the description
and situation of Caversham° seat. The house is fairly built of brick,   5
mounted on the hillside of a park within view of Reading, they being
severed about the space of two miles. Before the park gate, directly opposite
to the house, a new passage was forced through arable land, that was lately
paled in, it being from the park about two flight-shots° in length, at the
further end whereof, upon the Queen's approach, a Cynic° appeared out   10
of a bower, dressed in a skin coat,° with bases, of green calico, set thick
with leaves and boughs, his nakedness being also artificially shadowed with
leaves; on his head he wore a false hair, black and disordered, stuck
carelessly with flowers.

The speech of the Cynic to the Queen and her train.   15

CYNIC Stay! Whether you human be or divine, here is no passage.
See you not the earth furrowed, the region solitary? Cities and
courts fit tumultuous multitudes: this is a place of silence. Here a
kingdom I enjoy without people; my self commands, my self
obeys; host, cook, and guest my self; I reap without sowing, owe   20
all to Nature, to none other beholding. My skin is my coat, my
ornaments these boughs and flowers, this bower my house, the
earth my bed, herbs my food, water my drink. I want no sleep nor
health. I envy none, nor am envied; neither fear I, nor hope, nor

joy, nor grieve. If this be happiness, I have it, which you all that   25
depend on others' service or command want. Will you be happy?
Be private: turn palaces to hermitages, noise to silence, outward
felicity to inward content.

A stranger on horseback was purposely thrust into the troop disguised,
and wrapped in a cloak that he might pass unknown, who at the con-   30
clusion of this speech began to discover himself as a fantastic traveller° in
a silken suit of strange chequer-work, made up after the Italian cut,
with an Italian hat, a band of gold and silk, answering the colours of
his suit, with a courtly feather, long gilt spurs, and all things
answerable.   35

The Traveller's speech on horseback.

TRAVELLER Whither travels thy tongue, ill-nurtured man? Thy
   manners show madness, thy nakedness poverty, thy resolution
   folly. Since none will undertake thy presumption, let me descend,
   that I may make thy ignorance know how much it hath injured   40
   sacred ears.

The Traveller then dismounts and gives his cloak and horse to his footman.
In the meantime the Cynic speaks.

CYNIC Naked I am, and so is truth; plain, and so is honesty. I fear
   no man's encounter, since my cause deserves neither excuse nor   45
   blame.
TRAVELLER Shall I now chide or pity thee? Thou art as miserable in
   life as foolish in thy opinion. Answer me: dost thou think that all
   happiness consists in solitariness?
CYNIC I do.   50
TRAVELLER And are they unhappy that abide in society?
CYNIC They are.
TRAVELLER Dost thou esteem it a good thing to live?
CYNIC The best of things.
TRAVELLER Hadst thou not a father and mother?   55
CYNIC Yes.
TRAVELLER Did they not live in society?
CYNIC They did.
TRAVELLER And wert not thou one of their society when they bred
   thee, instructing thee to go,° and speak?   60
CYNIC True.
TRAVELLER Thy birth then, and speech, in spite of thy spleen, make
   thee sociable. Go! thou art but a vainglorious counterfeit, and

wanting that which should make thee happy, contemnest the means. View but the heavens: is there not above us a sun and moon, giving and receiving light? Are there not millions of stars that participate their glorious beams? Is there any element simple? Is there not a mixture of all things? And wouldst thou only be singular? Action is the end of life, virtue the crown of action,° society the subject of virtue, friendship the band of society, solitariness the breach. Thou art yet young, and fair enough, wert thou not barbarous. Thy soul, poor wretch, is far out of tune; make it musical. Come follow me, and learn to live. 65

70

CYNIC I am conquered by reason, and humbly ask pardon for my error. Henceforth my heart shall honour greatness and love society. Lead now and I will follow, as good a fellow as the best. 75

The Traveller and Cynic instantly mount on horseback and hasten to the park gate, where they are received by two Keepers, formally attired in green perpetuana with jerkins and long hose, all things else being in colour suitable, having either of them a horn hanging formally at their backs; and on their heads they had green Monmouth-caps° with green feathers, the one of them in his hand bearing a hook-bill, and the other a long pike-staff, both painted green. With them stood two Robin-Hood-men in suits of green striped with black, dressed in doublets with great bellies and wide sleeves shaped farthingale-wise° at the shoulders, without wings. Their hose were round, with long green stockings; on their heads they wore broad flat caps with green feathers cross quite over them, carrying green bows in their hands, and green arrows by their sides. 80

85

In this space cornetts at sundry places entertain the time, till the Queen with her train is entered into the park; and then one of the Keepers presents her with this short speech. 90

KEEPER More than most welcome, renowned and gracious Queen; since your presence vouchsafes to beautify these woods whereof I am keeper, be it your pleasure to accept such rude entertainment as a rough woodman can yield. This is to us a high holy-day, and henceforth yearly shall be kept and celebrated with our country sports, in honour of so royal a guest. Come, friends and fellows, now prepare your voices, and present your joys in a silvan dance. 95

Here standing on a smooth green, and environed with the horsemen, they present a song of five parts, and withal a lively silvan dance of six persons. The Robin-Hood-men feign° two trebles, one of the Keepers with the Cynic sing two counter-tenors, the other Keeper the bass; but the 100

Traveller, being not able to sing, gapes in silence, and expresseth his
humour in antic gestures.   105

A SONG AND DANCE OF SIX:
Two Keepers, Two Robin-Hood-Men,
the Fantastic Traveller, and the Cynic

Dance now and sing; the joy and love we owe
Let cheerful voices and glad gestures show.
   The queen of grace is she whom we receive;
   Honour and state are her guides,
   Her presence they can never leave.   110
Then in a stately silvan form salute
   Her ever-flowing grace;
Fill all the woods with echoed welcomes,
   And strew with flowers this place;
Let every bough and plant fresh blossoms yield,   115
   And all the air refine;
Let pleasure strive to please our goddess,
   For she is all divine.

Yet once again, let us our measures move,
And with sweet notes record our joyful love.   120
   An object more divine none ever had.
   Beauty and heaven-born worth
   Mixed in perfection never fade.
Then with a dance triumphant let us sing
   Her high advancèd praise,   125
And even to heaven our gladsome welcomes
   With wings of music raise.
Welcome, O welcome, ever-honoured Queen,
   To this now-blessèd place;
That grove, that bower, that house is happy   130
   Which you vouchsafe to grace.

This song being sung and danced twice over, they fall instantly into a kind
of coranto, with these words following:

No longer delay her,
'Twere sin now to stay her   135
   From her ease with tedious sport.
Then welcome still crying,
And swiftly hence flying,
   Let us to our homes resort.

In the end whereof the two Keepers carry away the Cynic, and the 140
two Robin-Hood-men the Traveller; when presently cornetts begin again
to sound in several places, and so continue with variety while the
Queen passeth through a long, smooth, green way, set on each side with
trees in equal distance;° all this while her Majesty being carried in her*
caroche. 145

But because some wet had fallen that day in the forenoon (though the
garden-walks were made artificially smooth and dry) yet all her foot-way
was spread with broad cloth, and so soon as her Majesty with her train
were all entered into the lower garden, a Gardener with his man and boy
issued out of an arbour to give her Highness entertainment. The Gardener 150
was suited in grey with a jerkin double-jagged all about the wings and
skirts. He had a pair of great slops with a codpiece,° and buttoned
gamachios all of the same stuff; on his head he had a strawen hat,
piebaldly dressed with flowers, and in his hand a silvered spade. His man
was also suited in grey, with a great buttoned flap on his jerkin, having 155
large wings and skirts, with a pair of great slops and gamachios of the
same; on his head he had a strawen hat, and in his hand a silvered
mattock. The Gardener's boy was in a pretty suit of flowery stuff, with a
silvered rake in his hand. When they approached near the Queen, they all
vailed bonnet, and louting low, the Gardener began after his antique° 160
fashion this speech.

GARDENER Most magnificent and peerless deity, lo I, the surveyor of
Lady Flora's works, welcome your grace with fragrant phrases into
her bowers, beseeching your greatness to bear with the late wooden
entertainment of the woodmen; for woods are more full of weeds 165
than wits, but gardens are weeded and gardeners witty, as may
appear by me. I have flowers for all fancies: thyme for truth,
rosemary for remembrance, roses for love, heartsease for joy, and
thousands more, which all harmoniously rejoice at your presence.
But myself, with these my paradisians here, will make you such 170
music as the wild woodists shall be ashamed to hear the report of
it. Come, sirs, prune your pipes and tune your strings, and agree
together like birds of a feather.

A SONG OF A TREBLE AND BASS
Sung by the Gardener's Boy and Man, to Music of Instruments
that was Ready to Second them in the Arbour

Welcome to this flowery place,
Fair goddess and sole queen of grace. 175

All eyes triumph in your sight,
Which through all this empty space
Cast such glorious beams of light.

Paradise were meeter far
To entertain so bright a star.   180
  But why errs my folly so?
Paradise is where you are,
Heaven above, and heaven below.

Could our powers and wishes meet,
How well would they your graces greet.   185
  Yet accept of our desire:°
Roses, of all flowers most sweet,
Spring out of the silly briar.

After this song, the Gardener speaks again.

GARDENER Wonder not, great Goddess, at the sweetness of our   190
  garden air (though passing sweet it be). Flora hath perfumed it for
  you (Flora our mistress, and your servant) who invites you yet
  further into her paradise. She invisibly will lead your grace the
  way, and we, as our duty is, visibly stay behind.

From thence the Queen ascends by a few steps into the upper garden, at 195
the end whereof, near the house, this song was sung by an excellent
counter-tenor voice, with rare variety of division,° unto two unusual
instruments, all being concealed within the arbour.

O joys exceeding,
From love, from power of your wished sight proceeding.   200
  As a fair morn shines divinely,
  Such is your view, appearing more divinely.

Your steps ascending
Raise high our thoughts, for your content contending;
  All our hearts of this grace vaunting,   205
  Now leap as they were movèd by enchaunting.

So ended the entertainment without the house for that time; and the
Queen's pleasure being that night to sup privately, the King's violins
attended her with their solemnest music, as an excellent consort in like
manner did the next day at dinner.   210

Supper being ended, her Majesty, accompanied with many lords and
ladies, came into the hall, and rested herself in her chair of state, the

scaffolds of the hall being on all parts filled with beholders of worth.
Suddenly forth came the Traveller, Gardener, Cynic, with the rest of their
crew, and others furnished with their instruments, and in manner following   215
entertain the time.

TRAVELLER   A hall, a hall for men of moment, rationals and irrationals, but yet not all of one breeding. For I an academic am, refined by travel, that have learned what to courtship belongs, and so divine a presence as this. If we press past good manners, laugh at our   220
follies, for you cannot show us more favour than to laugh at us. If we prove ridiculous in your sights, we are gracious; and therefore we beseech you to laugh at us. For mine own part (I thank my stars for it), I have been laughed at in most parts of Christendom.

GARDENER   I can neither brag of my travels, nor yet am ashamed of   225
my profession. I make sweet walks for fair ladies; flowers I prepare to adorn them; close arbours I build wherein their loves unseen may court them—and who can do ladies better service, or more acceptable? When I was a child and lay in my cradle (a very pretty child) I remember well that Lady Venus appeared unto me, and   230
setting a silver spade and rake by my pillow, bade me prove a gardener. I told my mother of it (as became the duty of a good child) whereupon she provided straight for me two great platters full of pap;° which having dutifully devoured, I grew to this portraiture you see, sprung suddenly out of my cabin, and fell to   235
my profession.

TRAVELLER   Verily, by thy discourse thou has travelled° much, and I am ashamed of my self that I come so far behind thee, as not once to have yet mentioned Venus or Cupid or any other of the gods to have appeared to me. But I will henceforth boast truly that   240
I have now seen a deity as far beyond theirs as the beauty of light is beyond darkness, or this feast, whereof we have had our share, is beyond thy salads.

CYNIC   Sure I am, it hath stirred up strange thoughts in me. Never knew I the difference between wine and water before. Bacchus°   245
hath opened mine eyes. I now see bravery° and admire it, beauty and adore it. I find my arms naked, my discourse rude, but my heart soft as wax, ready to melt with the least beam of a fair eye, which, till this time, was as untractable as iron.

GARDENER   I much joy in thy conversion; thou hast long been a mad   250
fellow, and now provest a good fellow. Let us all therefore join together sociably in a song, to the honour of good fellowship.

CYNIC A very musical motion, and I agree to it.

TRAVELLER Sing that sing can; for my part I will only, while you
sing, keep time with my gestures, *à la mode de France.*° 255

A SONG OF THREE VOICES WITH DIVERSE INSTRUMENTS

Night as well as brightest day hath her delight
Let us then with mirth and music deck the night.
 Never did glad day such store
  Of joy to night bequeath.
 Her stars then adore, 260
  Both in heaven, and here beneath.

Love and beauty, mirth and music, yield true joys,
Though the Cynics in their folly count them toys.
 Raise your spirits ne'er so high,
  They will be apt to fall: 265
 None brave thoughts envy,
  Who had e'er brave thought at all.

Joy is the sweet friend of life, the nurse of blood,
Patron of all health, and fountain of all good.
 Never may joy hence depart, 270
  But all your thoughts attend;
 Nought can hurt the heart,
  That retains so sweet a friend.

At the end of this song enters Silvanus,° *shaped after the description of the
ancient writers; his lower parts like a goat, and his upper parts in an* 275
*antique habit of rich taffeta cut into leaves; and on his head he had a false
hair, with a wreath of long boughs and lilies, that hung dangling about
his neck; and in his hand a cypress branch, in memory of his love
Cyparissus.*° *The Gardener, espying him, speaks thus.*

GARDENER Silence, sirs, here comes Silvanus, god of these woods, 280
whose presence is rare, and imports some novelty.

TRAVELLER Let us give place, for this place is fitter for deities than
us.

*They all vanish, and leave Silvanus alone, who, coming nearer to the
state, and making a low congee, speaks.* 285

SILVANUS That health which harbours in the fresh-aired groves,
Those pleasures which green hill and valley moves,

Silvanus, the commander of them all,
Here offers to this state imperial,
Which as a homager he visits now, 290
And to a greater power his power doth bow.
With all, thus much his duty signifies:
That there are certain semi-deities
Belonging to his silvan walks who come,
Led with the music of a sprightly drum, 295
To keep the night awake and honour you,
Great Queen, to whom all honours they hold due.
So rest you full of joy and wished content,
Which, though it be not given, 'tis fairly meant.

At the end of this speech there is suddenly heard a great noise of drum and 300
fifes, and way being made, eight pages first enter, with green torches in
their hands lighted; their suits were of green satin, with cloaks and caps
of the same, richly and strangely set forth. Presently after them the eight
masquers came, in rich embroidered suits of green satin, with high hats of
the same, and all their accoutrements answerable to such noble and 305
princely personages as they concealed under their vizards.° And so they
instantly fell into a new dance, at the end whereof they took forth the
ladies and danced with them. And so well was the Queen pleased with her
entertainment that she vouchsafed to make her self the head of their revels,
and graciously to adorn the place with her personal dancing. Much of the 310
night being thus spent with variety of dances, the masquers made a
conclusion with a second new dance.

At the Queen's parting on Wednesday in the afternoon, the Gardener with
his man and boy and three handsome country maids, the one bearing a
rich bag with linen in it, the second a rich apron, and the third a rich 315
mantle, appear all out of an arbour in the lower garden, and, meeting the
Queen, the Gardener presents this speech.

GARDENER Stay, goddess, stay a little space,
Our poor country love to grace;
Since we dare not too long stay you, 320
Accept at our hands, we pray you,
These mean presents, to express°
Greater love than we profess,
Or can utter now for woe
Of your parting, hastened so. 325
Gifts these are, such as were wrought

By their hands that them have brought;
Home-bred things, which they presumed,
After I had them perfumed
With my flowery incantation,   330
To give you in presentation
At your parting. Come, feat lasses,
With fine curtsies and smooth faces,
Offer up your simple toys
To the mistress of our joys,   335
While we the sad time prolong
With a mournful parting song.

A SONG OF THREE VOICES
Continuing While the Presents are Delivered and Received

I

Can you, the author of our joy,
   So soon depart?
Will you revive and straight destroy,   340
New mirth to tears convert?
   O that ever cause of gladness
   Should so swiftly turn to sadness.

2

Now as we droop, so will these flowers,
   Barred of your sight;   345
Nothing avail them heavenly showers
Without your heavenly light.
   When the glorious sun forsakes us
   Winter quickly overtakes us.

3

Yet shall our prayers your ways attend   350
   When you are gone;
And we the tedious time will spend
Remembering you alone.
   Welcome here shall you hear ever,
   But the word of parting never.   355

*Thus ends this ample entertainment, which as it was most nobly performed
by the right honourable the Lord and Lady of the house, and fortunately
executed by all that any way were actors in it, so was it as graciously
received of her Majesty, and celebrated with her most royal applause.*

BEN JONSON

The Golden Age Restored

In a Masque at Court, 1616,
by the Lords, and Gentlemen the King's Servants.°

Loud music. Pallas° in her chariot descending. To a softer music:

[PALLAS]   Look, look! Rejoice and wonder!
    That you offending mortals are
    (For all your crimes) so much the care
Of him that bears the thunder!°   5

Jove can endure no longer
    Your great ones should your less invade,
    Or that your weak, though bad, be made
A prey unto the stronger.°

And therefore means to settle   10
    Astraea in her seat again,
    And let down in his golden chain°
The age of better mettle.°

Which deed he doth the rather,
    That even envy may behold   15
    Time not enjoyed his head of gold
Alone beneath his father;°

But that his care conserveth,
    As time, so all time's honours too,
    Regarding still what heaven should do,   20
And not what earth deserveth.

A tumult and clashing of arms heard within.

But hark, what tumult from yond' cave is heard!
    What noise, what strife, what earthquake and alarms!
As° troubled Nature for her maker feared,   25
    And all the Iron Age were up in arms!
Hide me, soft cloud, from their profaner eyes,

Till insolent rebellion take the field,
And as their spirits with their counsels rise,
   I frustrate all, with showing but my shield.°   30

Iron Age presents itself, calling forth the Evils.

[IRON AGE]   Come forth, come forth, do we not hear
              What purpose, and how worth our fear,
                The king of gods hath on us?
              He is not of the iron breed   35
              That would, though Fate did help the deed,
                Let shame in so upon us.
              Rise, rise then up, thou grandame vice
              Of all my issue, Avarice,
                Bring with thee Fraud and Slander,   40
              Corruption with the golden hands,
              Or any subtler ill that stands°
                To be a more commander.°
              Thy boys, Ambition, Pride, and Scorn,
              Force, Rapine, and thy babe last born,   45
                Smooth Treachery, call hither;
              Arm Folly forth, and Ignorance,
               And teach them all our pyrrhic dance;°
                We may triùmph together
              Upon this enemy so great;   50
              Whom if our forces can defeat,
                And but this once bring under,
              We are the masters of the skies,
               Where all the wealth, height, power, lies,
                The sceptre and the thunder.   55
              Which of you would not in a war
              Attempt the price of any scar
                To keep your own states even?
              But here, which of you is that he
              Would not himself the weapon be   60
                To ruin Jove and heaven?
              About it then, and let him feel
              The Iron Age is turned to steel
                Since he begins to threat her.
              And though the bodies here are less   65
              Than were the giants, he'll confess°
                Our malice is far greater.

The antimasque and their dance, two drums, trumpets and a confusion of martial music; at the end of which, Pallas, showing her shield.

[PALLAS] So change and perish, scarcely knowing how, 70
    That 'gainst the gods do take so vain a vow,
    And think to equal with your mortal dates
    Their lives that are obnoxious to no fates.
    'Twas time t'appear, and let their follies see
    'Gainst whom they fought, and with what destiny. 75
    Die all that can remain of you but stone,
    And that be seen awhile, and then be none.

They metamorphosed,° and the scene changed, she calls Astraea and the Golden Age.

PALLAS Now, now, descend, you both beloved of Jove, 80
    And of the good on earth no less the love;
    Descend, you long, long wished and wanted pair,
    And as your softer times divide the air,
    So shake all clouds off with your golden hair,
    For spite is spent: the Iron Age is fled, 85
    And, with her power on earth, her name is dead.

Astraea, [Golden] Age, descending.

ASTRAEA and And are we then
GOLDEN AGE To live again
     With men? 90
ASTRAEA Will Jove such pledges to the earth restore
    As justice?
GOLDEN AGE   Or the purer ore?
PALLAS   Once more.
GOLDEN AGE But do they know
    How much they owe 95
    Below?
ASTRAEA And will of grace receive it, not as due?°
PALLAS If not, they harm themselves, not you.
ASTRAEA True.
GOLDEN AGE   True. 100
CHOIR Let narrow natures, how they will, mistake,
    The great should still be good for their own sake.

They are descended.

PALLAS   Welcome to earth and reign.

ASTRAEA and	But how without a train	105
GOLDEN AGE	Shall we our state sustain?	
PALLAS	Leave that to Jove; therein you are	
	No little part of his Minerva's care.	
	Expect awhile.	

She calls the Poets: 110

You far-famed spirits of this happy isle,
That for your sacred songs have gained the style
Of Phoebus' sons, whose notes the air aspire
Of th'old Egyptian, or the Thracian lyre,°
That Chaucer, Gower, Lydgate, Spenser hight;°   115
Put on your better flames and larger light,
To wait upon the age that shall your names new nourish,
Since virtue pressed shall grow, and buried arts shall flourish.°

Poets descend.

TWO POETS	We come.	
TWO POETS	We come.	
ALL FOUR	Our best of fire	120
	Is that which Pallas doth inspire.	
PALLAS	Then see you yonder souls, set far within the shade,	
	And in Elysian bowers the blessed seats do keep,°	
	That for their living good now semigods are made,	
	And went away from earth, as if but tamed with sleep:	125
	These we must join to wake, for these are of the strain	
	That justice dare defend, and will the age sustain.	
THE CHOIR	Awake, awake, for whom these times were kept,	
	O wake, wake, wake, as you had never slept;	
	Make haste and put on air to be their guard,°	130
	Whom once but to defend is still reward.	
PALLAS	Thus Pallas throws a lightning from her shield.	
CHOIR	To which let all that doubtful darkness yield.	

The Scene of light discovered.

ASTRAEA	Now peace,	
GOLDEN AGE	And love,	
ASTRAEA	Faith	
GOLDEN AGE	Joys,	

BOTH		All, all increase; 135
TWO POETS	And strife,	
TWO POETS	And hate,	
TWO POETS	And fear,	
TWO POETS	And pain,	
ALL FOUR		All cease.

A pause.

PALLAS   No tumour of an iron vein.°
                 The causes shall not come again.

CHOIR   But, as of old, all now be gold.   140
                 Move, move then to these sounds;
                 And do not only walk your solemn rounds,
                 But give those light and airy bounds
                 That fit the *genii* of these gladder grounds.°

The first dance; after which Pallas: 145

[PALLAS]   Already? Do not all things smile?

ASTRAEA   But when they have enjoyed awhile
                 The age's quickening power,°

GOLDEN AGE That every thought a seed doth bring,
                 And every look a plant doth spring,   150
                 And every breath a flower,

PALLAS   Then earth unploughed shall yield her crop,°
                 Pure honey from the oak shall drop,
                 The fountain shall run milk;
                 The thistle shall the lily bear,   155
                 And every bramble roses wear,
                 And every worm make silk.

CHOIR   The very shrub shall balsam sweat,
                 And nectar melt the rock with heat,
                 Till earth have drunk her fill;   160
                 That she no harmful weed may know,
                 Nor barren fern, nor mandrake low,°
                 Nor mineral to kill.

The main dance, after which:

PALLAS   But here's not all, you must do more,   165
                 Or else you do but half restore
                 The age's liberty.

POETS   The male and female used to join,°

And into all delight did coin
   That pure simplicity. 170
Then feature did to form advance,°
And youth called beauty forth to dance,
   And every grace was by.
It was a time of no distrust,
So much of love had nought of lust, 175
   None feared a jealous eye.
The language melted in the ear,
Yet all without a blush might hear;
   They lived with open vow.

CHOIR   Each touch and kiss was so well placed 180
They were as sweet as they were chaste,
   And such must yours be now.

Dance with ladies.

ASTRAEA   What change is here! I had not more
Desire to leave the earth before, 185
   Than I have now to stay;
My silver feet, like roots, are wreathed
Into the ground, my wings are sheathed,
   And I cannot away.

Of all there seems a second birth, 190
It is become a heaven on earth,
   And Jove is present here,
I feel the godhead; nor will doubt
But he can fill the place throughout
   Whose power is everywhere. 195

This, this, and only such as this,
The bright Astraea's region is,
   Where she would pray to live,
And in the midst of so much gold,
Unbought with grace or fear unsold,° 200
   The law to mortals give.°

Galliards and corantos.
Pallas ascending calls them:

PALLAS   'Tis now enough; behold you here,
What Jove hath built to be your sphere; 205
   You hither must retire.°

And as his bounty gives you cause,
Be ready still without your pause
    To show the world your fire.

Like lights about Astraea's throne   210
You here must shine, and all be one,
    In fervour and in flame;
That by your union she may grow,
And, you sustaining her, may know
    The age still by her name;   215

Who vows against or heat or cold
To spin you garments of her gold,
    That want may touch you never;
And making garlands every hour,
To write your names in some new flower,   220
    That you may live for ever.

CHOIR   To Jove, to Jove, be all the honour given,
That thankful hearts can raise from earth to heaven.

THE END

BEN JONSON
Christmas His Masque

Christmas his Masque,
as it was presented at court, 1616

*Enter Christmas with two or three of the guard. He is attired in round
hose, long stockings, a close doublet, a high-crowned hat with a brooch,°
a long thin beard, a truncheon, little ruffs, white shoes, his scarfs and
garters tied cross, and his drum beaten before him.*

CHRISTMAS Why, gentlemen, do you know what you do? Ha! would 5
you ha' kept me out? Christmas, old Christmas? Christmas of
London, and Captain Christmas? Pray you let me be brought
before my Lord Chamberlain,° I'll not be answered else. 'Tis
merry in hall when beards wag all. I ha' seen the time you ha'
wished for me, for a merry Christmas; and now you ha' me, they 10
would not let me in; I must come another time! A good jest, as if
I could come more than once a year. Why, I am no dangerous
person, and so I told my friends o' the guard. I am old Gregory
Christmas° still, and, though I come out of Pope's Head Alley,° as
good a Protestant° as any i' my parish. The truth is, I ha' brought 15
a masque here out o' the City, o' my own making, and do present
it by a set of my sons, that come out of the lanes of London,
good dancing boys all. It was intended, I confess, for Curriers'
Hall,° but because the weather has been open,° and the livery
were not at leisure to see it till a frost come that they cannot work, 20
I thought it convenient, with some little alterations, and the
Groom of the Revels' hand to't, to fit it for a higher place—which
I have done; and though I say it, another manner of device than
your New Year's night. [*He sees the King*] Bones o' bread, the
King! Son Rowland, son Clem, be ready there in a trice; quick, 25
boys.

*Enter his sons and daughters, being ten in number, led in in a string by
Cupid, who is attired in a flat cap° and a prentice's coat, with wings at
his shoulders.*

The names of his children, with their attires:

MISRULE:° *in a velvet cap with a sprig, a short cloak, great yellow*   30
ruff like a reveller, his torch-bearer bearing a rope, a cheese, and a
basket.

CAROL: *a long tawny coat, with a red cap, and a flute at his girdle, his*
torch-bearer carrying a song-book open.

MINCED PIE: *like a fine cook's wife, dressed neat, her man carrying a*   35
pie, dish, and spoons.

GAMBOL: *like a tumbler, with a hoop and bells, his torch-bearer armed*
with a cowlstaff and a blinding cloth.°

POST AND PAIR:° *with a pair-royal of aces in his hat, his garment all*
done over with pairs and purs,° his squire carrying a box, cards, and   40
counters.

NEW-YEAR'S GIFT:° *in a blue coat, serving-man like, with an orange*
and a sprig of rosemary gilt° on his head, his hat full of brooches, with
a collar of gingerbread, his torch-bearer carrying a marchpain, with a
bottle of wine on either arm.
   45

MUMMING: *in a masquing pied suit with a visor, his torch-bearer*
carrying the box,° and ringing it.°

WASSAIL: *like a neat sempster and songster, her page bearing a brown*
bowl dressed with ribbons and rosemary before.

OFFERING: *in a short gown, with a porter's staff in his hand, a withe*   50
borne before him and a basin by his torch-bearer.

BABY CAKE: *dressed like a boy, in a fine long coat, biggin, bib,*
muckender, and a little dagger, his usher bearing a great cake with a
bean and a peas.°

They enter singing.   55

> Now God preserve, as you well do deserve,
>   Your majesties all two there;
> Your highness small, with my good lords all,°
>   And ladies, how do you do there?
> Gi' me leave to ask, for I bring you a masque,   60
>   From little, little, little, little London;
> Which say the king likes, I ha' passed the pikes,
>   If not, old Christmas is undone.

[*Noise outside*]°

CHRISTMAS 'A' peace, what's the matter there?°   65
GAMBOL Here's one o' Friday Street° would come in.
CHRISTMAS By no means, nor out of neither of the Fish Streets°

admit not a man; they are not Christmas creatures. Fish and
fasting days,° foh! Sons, said I well? Look to't.

GAMBOL Nobody out o' Friday Street, nor the two Fish Streets   70
there, do you hear?

CAROL Shall John Butter o' Milk Street° come in? Ask him.

GAMBOL Yes, he may slip in for a torch-bearer, so he melt not too
fast, that he will last till the masque be done.

CHRISTMAS Right son.   75

[*They*] *sing again*

> Our dances' freight, is a matter of eight,
>   And two, the which are wenches;
> In all they be ten, four cocks to a hen,
>   And will swim to the tune like tenches.   80
>
> Each hath his knight for to carry his light,
>   Which some would say are torches,
> To bring them here, and to lead them there,
>   And home again to their own porches.
> Now their intent—   85

Enter Venus, a deaf tirewoman.

VENUS Now all the lords bless me, where am I, trow? Where is
Cupid? Serve the king? They may serve the cobbler well enough,
some of 'em, for any courtesy they have, iwis; they ha' need o'
mending. Unrude people they are, your courtiers; here was thrust   90
upon thrust indeed! Was it ever so hard to get in before, trow?

CHRISTMAS How now? What's the matter?

VENUS A place, forsooth, I do want a place; I would have a good
place to see my child act in before the king and the queen's
majesties (God bless 'em) tonight.   95

CHRISTMAS Why, here is no place for you.

VENUS I was to come in, and I would have come in, or my child
should not have acted here tonight else.

CHRISTMAS What are you, I beseech you?°

VENUS Right forsooth, I am Cupid's mother, Cupid's own mother,   100
forsooth, yes forsooth. I dwell in Pudding Lane;° ay, forsooth, he
is prentice in Love Lane° with a bugle-maker that makes of your
bobs and bird-bolts° for ladies.

CHRISTMAS Good Lady Venus of Pudding Lane, you must go out
for all this.   105

VENUS Yes, forsooth, I can sit anywhere, so I may see my Cupid act.
He is a pretty child, though I say it that perhaps should not, you

will say. I had him by my first husband; he was a smith°
forsooth—we dwelt in Do-little Lane° then—he came a month
before his time, and that may make him somewhat imperfect. But   110
I was a fishmonger's daughter.°

CHRISTMAS No matter for your pedigree, your house;° good Venus,
will you depart?

VENUS Aye, forsooth, he'll say his part, I warrant him, as well as e'er
a play boy of 'em all. I could ha' had money enough for him an I   115
would ha' been tempted, and ha' let him out by the week to the
king's players; Master Burbage has been about and about with me;
and so has old Master Hemminges° too, they ha' need of him.
Where is he, trow 'a? I would fain see him; pray God they have
given him some drink since he came.   120

CHRISTMAS Are you ready, boys? Strike up; nothing will drown this
noise but a drum. 'A' peace yet; I ha' not done. Sing, 'Now their
intent is about to present—'

CAROL Why, here be half of the properties forgotten, father.

OFFERING Post and Pair wants his pur-chops and his pur-dogs.°   125

CAROL Ha' you ne'er a son at the groom-porter's° to beg or borrow
a pair of cards quickly?

GAMBOL It shall not need—here's your son Cheater without; has
cards in his pocket.

OFFERING Odds so; speak to the guard to let him in under the name   130
of a property.

GAMBOL And here's New Year's Gift has an orange and rosemary,
but not a clove to stick in't.

NEW YEAR Why, let one go to the spicery.

CHRISTMAS Fie, fie, fie; it's naught, it's naught, boys.   135

VENUS Why, I have cloves, if it be cloves you want; I have cloves in
my purse, I never go without one in my mouth.

CAROL And Mumming has not his vizard neither.

CHRISTMAS No matter, his own face shall serve for a punishment,
and 'tis bad enough. Has Wassail her bowl and Mince Pie her   140
spoons?

OFFERING Aye, aye; but Misrule doth not like his suit; he says
the players have lent him one too little, on purpose to disgrace
him.

CHRISTMAS Let him hold his peace, and his disgrace will be the less. 145
What? shall we proclaim where we were furnished? Mum! Mum!
'A' peace, be ready, good boys.

Sings again

Now their intent is about to present
   With all the appurtenances,   150
A right Christmas, as of old it was,
   To be gathered out of the dances;

Which they do bring, and afore the king,
   The queen and prince, as it were now
Drawn here by Love, who, over and above,   155
   Doth draw himself i' the gear too.

*Here the drum and fife sounds, and they march about once. At the second
coming up he proceeds in his song.*

Hum drum, sauce for a cony,°
   No more of your martial music,   160
Even for the sake o' the next new stake,°
   For there I do mean to use it.

And now to ye, who in place are to see,
   With roll and farthingale hoopèd;°
I pray you know, though he want his bow,   165
   By the wings, that this is Cupid.

He might go back, for to cry 'what you lack',°
   But that were not so witty;
His cap and coat are enough to note
   That he is the Love o' the city.   170

And he leads on, though he now be gone,
   For that was only his rule;
But now comes in Tom of Bosoms Inn°
   And he presenteth Misrule.

Which you may know, by the very show,   175
   Albeit you never ask it;
For there you may see what his ensigns be,
   The rope, the cheese, and the basket.

This Carol plays, and has been in his days
   A chirping boy, and a kill-pot;   180
Kit Cobbler it is, I'm a father of his,
   And he dwells in the lane called Philpot.°

But who is this? O, my daughter Sis,
  Mince Pie; with her do not dally
On pain o' your life; she's an honest cook's wife,   185
  And comes out of Scalding Alley.°

Next in the trace comes Gambol in place,
  And to make my tale the shorter,
My son Hercules, ta'en out of Distaff Lane,°
  But an active man, and a porter.   190

Now Post and Pair, old Christmas's heir,
  Doth make and a jingling sally;
And wot you who, 'tis one of my two
  Sons, cardmakers in Pur-alley.°

Next in a trice, with his box and his dice,°   195
  Mac-pippin my son, but younger,°
Brings Mumming in, and the knave will win,
  For a' is a costermonger.°

But New Year's Gift of himself makes shift
  To tell you what his name is;   200
With orange on head, and his gingerbread,
  Clem Wasp of Honey Lane 'tis.°

This I you tell, is our jolly Wassail,
  And for Twelfth-night most meet too;°
She works by the ell, and her name is Nell,   205
  And she dwells in Threadneedle Street too.

Then Offering he, with his dish and his tree,°
  That in every great house keepeth,
Is by my son young Littleworth done,
  And in Penny-rich Street he sleepeth.°   210

Last Baby Cake, that an end doth make
  Of Christmas' merry, merry vein-a
Is child Rowlan, and a straight young man,°
  Though he come out of Crooked Lane-a.

There should have been and a dozen, I ween,   215
  But I could find but one more
Child of Christmas, and a Log it was,°
  When I them all had gone o'er.

I prayèd him in a time so trim
  That he would make one to prance it;   220
And I myself would have been the twelfth,
  O, but Log was too heavy to dance it.

Now Cupid, come you on.

CUPID   You worthy wights, king, lords, and knights,
      O queen, and ladies bright,   225
    Cupid invites you to the sights
    He shall present tonight.

VENUS 'Tis a good child; speak out, hold up your head, Love.

CUPID And which Cupid—and which Cupid, etc.°

VENUS Do not shake so, Robin; if thou beest a-cold, I ha' some warm   230
waters for thee here.

CHRISTMAS Come, you put Robin Cupid out with your waters and
your fisling; will you be gone?

VENUS Aye, forsooth; he's a child, you must conceive, and must be
used tenderly. He was never in such an assembly before, forsooth,   235
but once at the warmol 'quest,° forsooth, where he said grace as
prettily as any of the sheriff's hench-boys,° forsooth.

CHRISTMAS Will you peace, forsooth?

CUPID And which Cupid—and which Cupid, etc.

VENUS Aye, that's a good boy, speak plain, Robin. How does his   240
majesty like him, I pray? Will he give him eight pence a day,° think
you? Speak out, Robin.

CHRISTMAS Nay, he is out enough,° you may take him away and
begin your dance. This it is to have speeches.

VENUS You wrong the child, you do wrong the infant; I 'peal to his   245
majesty.

Here they dance

CHRISTMAS Well done, boys, my fine boys, my bully boys.

Sings again

THE EPILOGUE

Nor do you think their legs is all   250
  The commendation of my sons;
For at the artillery-garden they shall°
  As well (forsooth) use their guns.

And march as fine as the muses nine
  Along the streets of London;   255
And i' their brave 'tires, to gi' their false fires,°
  Especially Tom my son.

Now if the lanes and the alleys afford
  Such an ac-ativity as this,
At Christmas next, if they keep their word,   260
  Can the children of Cheapside miss?

Though, put the case, when they come in place,
  They should not dance, but hop,
Their very gold lace with their silk would 'em grace,
  Having so many knights o' the shop!   265

But were I so wise I might seem to advise
  So great a potentate as yourself,
They should, sir, I tell ye, spare't out o' their belly,
  And this way spend some of their pelf;

Aye, and come to the court, for to make you some sport,   270
  At the least once every year;
As Christmas hath done, with his seventh or eighth son,
  And his couple of daughters dear.

THE END

116

BEN JONSON

Pleasure Reconciled to Virtue

Pleasure Reconciled to Virtue
A Masque
As it was presented at Court before
King James, 1618.

The scene was the mountain Atlas,° who had his top ending in the figure of an old man, his head and beard all hoary and frost, as if his shoulders were covered with snow; the rest wood and rock. A grove of ivy at his feet, out of which, to a wild music of cymbals, flutes, and tabors, is brought forth Comus,° the god of cheer or the belly, riding in triumph, his head crowned with roses and other flowers, his hair curled; they that wait upon him crowned with ivy, their javelins done about with it; one of them going with Hercules his bowl° bare before him, while the rest presented him with this 5

HYMN

Room, room, make room for the bouncing belly,° 10
First father of sauce, and deviser of jelly;
Prime master of arts, and the giver of wit,
That found out the excellent engine, the spit,
The plough and the flail, the mill and the hopper,
The hutch and the bolter, the furnace and copper, 15
The oven, the bavin, the mawkin, the peel,
The hearth and the range, the dog and the wheel.°
He, he first invented both hogshead and tun,
The gimlet and vice too, and taught 'em to run.°
And since, with the funnel, an Hippocras bag° 20
He's made of himself, that now he cries swag.°
Which shows, though the pleasure be but of four inches,
Yet he is a weezle, the gullet that pinches,°
Of any delight; and not spares from his back
Whatever to make of the belly a sack. 25
Hail, hail plump paunch, O the founder of taste

For fresh meats, or powdered, or pickle, or paste;
Devourer of broiled, baked, roasted, or sod,
And emptier of cups, be they even or odd;°
All which have now made thee so wide i' the waist   30
As scarce with no pudding thou art to be laced;°
But eating and drinking until thou dost nod,
Thou break'st all thy girdles, and break'st forth a god.

To this, the Bowl-bearer.

[BOWL-BEARER] Do you hear, my friends? To whom do you sing all   35
this now? Pardon me only that I ask you, for I do not look for an
answer; I'll answer myself. I know it is now such a time as the
saturnals° for all the world, that every man stands under the eaves
of his own hat,° and sings what please him; that's the right and the
liberty of it. Now you sing of god Comus here, the belly-god; I   40
say it is well, and I say it is not well. It is well as it is a ballad, and
the belly worthy of it, I must needs say, an 'twere forty yards of
ballad more, as much ballad as tripe.° But when the belly is not
edified by it, it is not well; for where did you ever read or hear
that the belly had any ears? Come, never pump for an answer, for   45
you are defeated. Our fellow Hunger there, that was as ancient a
retainer to the belly as any of us, was turned away for being
unseasonable—not unreasonable, but unseasonable—and now is he
(poor thin-gut) fain to get his living with teaching of starlings,
magpies, parrots, and jackdaws,° those things he would have   50
taught the belly. Beware of dealing with the belly; the belly will
not be talked to, especially when he is full. Then there is no
venturing upon Venter,° he will blow you all up, he will thunder
indeed, la. Some in derision call him the father of farts. But I say
he was the first inventor of great ordnance, and taught us to   55
discharge them on festival days; would we had a fit feast for him
i' faith, to show his activity. I would have something now fetched
in to please his five senses, the throat, or the two senses, the eyes.
Pardon me for my two senses, for I that carry Hercules' bowl i'
the service may see double by my place, for I have drunk like a   60
frog today. I would have a tun now brought in to dance, and so
many bottles about him. Ha! You look as if you would make a
problem of this. Do you see? Do you see? A problem: why bottles?
and why a tun? and why a tun? and why bottles to dance? I say
that men that drink hard, and serve the belly in any place of quality 65
(as The Jovial Tinkers, or The Lusty Kindred°) are living measures
of drink, and can transform themselves, and do every day, to bottles

or tuns when they please; and when they ha' done all they can,
they are, as I say again (for I think I said somewhat like it afore)
but moving measures of drink; and there is a piece i' the cellar can   70
hold more than all they. This will I make good, if it please our new
god but to give a nod, for the belly does all by signs, and I am all
for the belly, the truest clock i' the world to go by.

Here the first antimasque, after which Hercules.°

[HERCULES] What rites are these? Breeds earth more monsters yet?   75
    Antaeus scarce is cold: what can beget°
    This store? and stay! such contraries upon her?°
    Is earth so fruitful of her own dishonour?
    Or 'cause his vice was inhumanity,°
    Hopes she by vicious hospitality   80
    To work an expiation first? And then°
    (Help Virtue!) these are sponges, and not men.
    Bottles? Mere vessels? Half a tun of paunch?
    How? And the other half thrust forth in haunch?
    Whose feast? The belly's? Comus'? And my cup   85
    Brought in to fill the drunken orgies up?
    And here abused? that was the crowned reward
    Of thirsty heroes after labour hard?
    Burdens and shames of nature, perish, die,
    For yet you never lived, but in the sty   90
    Of vice have wallowed, and in that swine's strife
    Been buried under the offence of life.
    Go, reel and fall under the load you make,
    Till your swoll'n bowels burst with what you take.
    Can this be pleasure, to extinguish man?   95
    Or so quite change him in his figure? Can
    The belly love his pain, and be content
    With no delight but what's a punishment?
    These monsters plague themselves, and fitly too,
    For they do suffer what and all they do.   100
    But here must be no shelter, nor no shroud
    For such: sink grove, or vanish into cloud!

*At this, the whole grove vanished, and the whole music was discovered,
sitting at the foot of the mountain, with Pleasure and Virtue seated above
them. The choir invited Hercules to rest with this song.*   105

        Great friend and servant of the good,
        Let cool a while thy heated blood,

And from thy mighty labour cease.
 Lie down, lie down,
And give thy troubled spirits peace,   110
 Whilst Virtue, for whose sake
Thou dost this godlike travail take,
May of the choicest herbage make,
 Here on this mountain bred,
  A crown, a crown   115
 For thy immortal head.

Here Hercules being laid down at their feet, the second antimasque, which
was of pygmies,° appeared.

1st PYGMY Antaeus dead! and Hercules yet live!
 Where is this Hercules? What would I give   120
 To meet him now? Meet him? Nay, three such other
 If they had hand in murder of our brother!°
 With three? With four? With ten? Nay, with as many
 As the name yields. Pray anger there be any°
 Whereon to feed my just revenge, and soon.   125
 How shall I kill him? Hurl him 'gainst the moon,
 And break him in small portions? Give to Greece
 His brain, and every tract of earth a piece?
2nd PYGMY He is yonder.
1st PYGMY   Where?
3rd PYGMY   At the hill foot; asleep.
1st PYGMY Let one go steal his club.
2nd PYGMY   My charge; I'll creep.   130
4th PYGMY He is ours.
1st PYGMY   Yes; peace.
3rd PYGMY   Triumph; we have him, boy.
4th PYGMY Sure, sure; he is sure.
1st PYGMY   Come, let us dance for joy.

At the end of their dance they thought to surprise him, when suddenly,
being awaked by the music, he roused himself, they all run into holes.

SONG

Wake, Hercules, awake; but heave up thy black eye,   135
'Tis only asked from thee to look, and these will die,
 Or fly.
 Already they are fled
Whom scorn had else left dead.

At which Mercury descended from the hill, with a garland of poplar° to   140
crown him.

MERCURY Rest still, thou active friend of Virtue; these
  Should not disturb the peace of Hercules.
  Earth's worms and honour's dwarfs, at too great odds,
  Prove, or provoke the issue of the gods.   145
  See here a crown the agèd hill hath sent thee,
  My grandsire Atlas, he that did present thee°
  With the best sheep that in his fold were found,
  Or golden fruit in the Hesperian ground,
  For rescuing his fair daughters, then the prey   150
  Of a rude pirate, as thou cam'st this way;°
  And taught thee all the learning of the sphere,°
  And how, like him, thou mightst the heavens up-bear,°
  As that thy labour's virtuous recompense.
  He, though a mountain now, hath yet the sense   155
  Of thanking thee for more, thou being still
  Constant to goodness, guardian of the hill;
  Antaeus by thee suffocated here,
  And the voluptuous Comus, god of cheer,
  Beat from his grove, and that defaced. But now   160
  The time's arrived that Atlas told thee of: how
  By unaltered law, and working of the stars,
  There should be a cessation of all jars
  'Twixt Virtue and her noted opposite,
  Pleasure; that both should meet here, in the sight   165
  Of Hesperus, the glory of the west,°
  The brightest star, that from his burning crest
  Lights all on this side the Atlantic seas,
  As far as to thy pillars, Hercules.°
  See where he shines: Justice and Wisdom placed   170
  About his throne, and those with Honour graced,
  Beauty and Love. It is not with his brother
  Bearing the world, but ruling such another°
  Is his renown. Pleasure, for his delight,
  Is reconciled to Virtue; and this night°   175
  Virtue brings forth twelve princes have been bred°
  In this rough mountain and near Atlas' head,
  The hill of knowledge; one, and chief of whom°
  Of the bright race of Hesperus is come,

Who shall in time the same that he is be,   180
And now is only a less light than he.
These now she trusts with Pleasure, and to these
She gives an entrance to the Hesperides,
Fair Beauty's garden; neither can she fear°
They should grow soft, or wax effeminate here,°   185
Since in her sight and by her charge all's done,
Pleasure the servant, Virtue looking on.

*Here the whole choir of music called the twelve masquers° forth from the
lap of the mountain, which then opened, with this song.*

    Ope, agèd Atlas, open then thy lap,   190
    And from thy beamy bosom strike a light,
    That men may read in thy mysterious map
        All lines
        And signs
    Of royal education, and the right.   195
      See how they come and show,
      That are but born to know.
        Descend,
        Descend;
    Though Pleasure lead,   200
      Fear not to follow;
    They who are bred
      Within the hill
      Of skill
    May safely tread   205
      What path they will,
    No ground of good is hollow.

*In their descent from the hill, Daedalus° came down before them, of whom
Hercules questioned Mercury.*

HERCULES But Hermes, stay a little, let me pause.   210
  Who's this that leads?
MERCURY   A guide that gives them laws
  To all their motions, Daedalus the wise.
HERCULES And doth in sacred harmony comprise
  His precepts?
MERCURY   Yes.
HERCULES   They may securely prove
  Then any labyrinth, though it be of love.   215

Here, while they put themselves in form,° Daedalus had his first

SONG

DAEDALUS Come on, come on; and where you go,
So interweave the curious knot,°
As ev'n th'observer scarce may know
Which lines are Pleasure's, and which not.   220
First, figure out the doubtful way°
At which a while all youth should stay,
Where she and Virtue did contend
Which should have Hercules to friend.
Then, as all actions of mankind   225
Are but a labyrinth or maze,
So let your dances be entwined,
Yet not perplex men unto gaze;
But measured, and so numerous too,°
As men may read each act you do;°   230
And when they see the graces meet,
Admire the wisdom of your feet:
For dancing is an exercise
Not only shows the mover's wit,
But maketh the beholder wise,   235
As he hath power to rise to it.°

The first dance. After which Daedalus again:

SONG 2

DAEDALUS O, more, and more; this was so well
As praise wants half his voice to tell;
Again yourselves compose,   240
And now put all the aptness on
Of figure, that proportion
Or colour can disclose.
That if those silent arts were lost,
Design and picture, they might boast   245
From you a newer ground,°
Instructed by the heightening sense
Of dignity and reverence
In your true motions found.
Begin, begin; for look, the fair   250
Do longing listen to what air
You form your second touch,

That they may vent their murmuring hymns
Just to the tune you move your limbs,
  And wish their own were such.   255
   Make haste, make haste, for this
   The labyrinth of beauty is.

The second dance. That ended, Daedalus.

SONG 3

DAEDALUS It follows now you are to prove
    The subtlest maze of all, that's Love, 260
     And if you stay too long,
     The fair will think you do 'em wrong.
    Go, choose among, but with a mind
    As gentle as the stroking wind
     Runs o'er the gentler flowers; 265
    And so let all your actions smile,
    As if they meant not to beguile
     The ladies, but the hours.
    Grace, laughter, and discourse may meet,
     And yet the beauty not go less; 270
    For what is noble should be sweet,
     But not dissolved in wantonness.
     Will you that I give the law
      To all your sport, and sum it?
     It should be such should envy draw, 275
      But ever overcome it.

*Here they danced with the ladies, and the whole revels followed; which
ended, Mercury called to him° in this following speech; which was after
repeated in song by two trebles, two tenors, a bass, and the whole chorus.*

SONG 4

An eye of looking back were well, 280
Or any murmur that would tell
  Your thoughts, how you were sent,
   And went
  To walk with Pleasure, not to dwell.
These, these are hours by Virtue spared 285
Herself, she being her own reward.
  But she will have you know
   That though

Her sports be soft, her life is hard.
You must return unto the hill,   290
  And there advance
With labour, and inhabit still
  That height and crown,
From whence you ever may look down
  Upon triumphèd Chance.   295
She, she it is in darkness shines.
'Tis she that still herself refines
By her own light, to every eye
More seen, more known when Vice
    stands by;
And though a stranger here on earth,   300
In heaven she hath her right of birth.
  There, there is Virtue's seat.
  Strive to keep her your own;
    'Tis only she can make you great,
  Though place here make you known.   305

After which, they danced their last dance, and returned into the scene,
which closed, and was a mountain again, as before.

THE END

ANON.

The Coleorton Masque

A masque presented on Candlemas° night at Coleorton,° by the
Earl of Essex, the Lord Willoughby, Sir Tho. Beaumont, Sir
Walter Devereux, Mr Christopher Denham, Mr Walter T . . .,
Mrs Ann R . . ., Mrs Ann Burneby, Mrs Susan Burneby,
Mrs Elizabeth Beaumont, Mrs Katherine Beaumont, Mrs Susan
Pilkington, to Sir William Seymour and the Lady Frances
Seymour.°

The Antimasque

Enter Bob, the buttery spirit,° singing.

> The buttery key is lost,
> The buttery key is lost,
> And Tom he has got it,°
> He swears they shall pot it,   5
> And every horn be tossed,
> And every horn be tossed,
> And every horn be tossed.
> He will ha' no flinching;
> A pox of all pinching,°   10
> He knows what a hogshead cost.

Enter Puck, the country spirit, stealing in softly.

PUCK O ho ho!° My mad musical boys are ready—is the coast clear
    now? O ho ho!
BOB [*aside*] How now, art thee° there indeed, boy? Old Robin,° alive   15
    and alive's like. Now for a trick upon him. (*He fires his flax*° *and
    claps down behind him, and Puck falls over.*) Buzz ha ha ha, quoth
    the blue fly; hum quoth the bee, etc.° Puck, honest Puck, a fire on
    you, you'll not know your old friends.
PUCK Whoa! Bob o' the buttery! Welcome to Leicestershire again.   20
    As thou lovest me, spirit, tell me—what news abroad? Where the
    vengeance has thou been thus long?

BOB Why, goblin, I'll tell thee boy; all over England, where hospitality (*He sings*)

> Down, down, down it falls.   25
> Down and arise, down and arise it never shall.°

PUCK O ho ho! I knew the downfall of the plough and dairy° would make a hand with the buttery too.

BOB True, Puck, housekeeping is a rag of Rome°—'tis abolished. All good fellowship, called feasting, is turned to a dish of 30 Bibles. The country mirth and pastime, that's Pauncius Pilate, dead and buried;° entertainment, that's now a fooling pleasure for every swabber. In a whole country ye shall have some three great houses smoking, and one of them o' th'old way,° Puck. This new sect, in sincerity 'tis a dry one, and a plaguy soaker of 35 the buttery. Truly, if e'er they drink, drunk 'tis with ale and in private. With ale! Ale, that turdy, dirty, nasty, pissy, farty, lantitantical° liquor, a drink devised by Puritans and pettifoggers to settle the spittle of their palates that their tongues may yet run more at liberty. That villainous drench has been the bane of the 40 buttery.

PUCK O ho, boy, that's not all, Bob, for now every hind is grown a gentleman; gentlemen knights, barons and baronets,° boy. And then my madam, dropped out o' th'dung-cart, or whose father's sheep ha' farted her into a ladyship, must ha' four horses, one more 45 than Phoebus.°

BOB Right, Puck, and then her scurvy hair must be curled and powdered, the chamber stink of bawds and midwives. This wood falls to make her a forepart in a farthingale. Th'hard arable land shall be converted into loose gowns, and the meadows fly up in 50 petticoats.° This robs both buttery and kitchen, boy. Now, roast for his Worship's supper—five cock sparrows and a dittymouse,° with two bears and a dog in rotten pastry-work kept for monuments since his last being sheriff and soaked in piss to preserve the gilding.° His wine the same bottle was sent him a week ago for 55 committing wilful justice.° His Worship's servants board at the alehouse for the most part, and the remnant eat musty bread and onions. Toh! No more of those fellows! And now tell me how thou art used amongst the fairies, those little ringleaders, those white and blue fairies.   60

PUCK O ho, ho, gone° boy, northward ho. They could not live no longer here lad, they must be bountiful. The lass that sweeps clean

and sets water in the chimney would look for somewhat in her
shoe, and where's the money, Bob? Gone boy; there's not nine
shillings left in Little Britain.°   65

BOB Not of white money,° Puck, white fairy money that was all mill
money; but there's store of gold left yet, boy, and a few good
fellows in this corner of the country: here's honest Harry of
Ashby,° Bonny Bob of Lichfield,° besides a brace of my bully
Beaumonts.° This house must ever be my quarter, I'll ne'er be to   70
seek again.

PUCK O, ho ho, boy; hold thee there and I'll bring thee acquainted
with my new company.

BOB Who are they, Puck?

PUCK Why, the black fairies, boy, the dancing spirits of the pits, such   75
as look to Tom's Egyptians° here, and help them hole and drive
sharp their picks and their mandrils, keep away the damp and keep
in their candles,° drain the sough° and hold them out of the
hollows.

BOB And are they good fellows, sirrah? Do they love mirth and   80
drinking, boy? Pray thee, let's see them dance tonight i' th'bottom
o' th'cellar.

PUCK Oh, ho ho, boy, that's my business, Bob. Thou shalt see one
crash presently. I'll but list an my twinkling boys be ready. O ho
ho there, boys!   85

*Here the music sounds a short strain, to which both the spirits move a little
with their bodies.*

BOB Aha, but, Puck, canst thou call them presently?

PUCK By their names, my bonny Bobkin. Now mark, I fetch them.
O ho ho who! Ho ho who! Come away, Turnstake, Gudger,   90
Jagging-tree, Toptree, Jugman, Floats, and Aberience.°

Spirits enter and dance a strain.

BOB Aha, this is brave, Puck.

PUCK Oh, ho! mum, boy,° and mark the motions.

[Spirits] dance it out, then Iris° appears above.   95

IRIS What, spirits abroad, ha?

Here they all gaze up and run out distractly.°

So now the coast is clear.

The clouds close again.° Then the Masque.

The Masque

Favonius° in a green robe descends, with wings and blistered with puffs; 100
buskins white, and gilded; on his head a sun setting. There stood an altar
by with incense fuming, inscribed: Jovi Hospitali Sacrum.°

FAVONIUS Jupiter, whose altar here
  Fumes with incense all the year,
  Where sound hearts and glad desires, 105
  Tables large and living fires
  Crown him, and approve withal
  His best of titles, Hospital,
  He, because it is his will
  More to grace this beauteous hill,° 110
  From the west hath fanned me forth,
  Spite of winter, thus far North;
  Me, whom men do call the kind,
  Favonius, the gentle wind,
  That as soft as lady's breath 115
  When in sighs they would bequeath
  Love to stubborn standers by
  That do scorn the legacy;
  First I come to bless this tower,
  Every bed and every bower; 120
  Sprightly mirth and sparkling wine
  Every brain and cheek refine;
  Safe content and golden slumber,
  Peace and joys sans end or number,
  All the blessings can befall, 125
  Thus I breath upon you all.
  Yet a pair above the rest,
  Of a differing sex, are blessed,
  For whose happy wished repair
  Here these altars loaden are 130
  With new gums, and fresh does rise
  Th'hospitable sacrifice.
  Next the ruler of the sky,
  Honouring this solemnity
  Most for thy sake, child of light,° 135
  Beauteous woman heavenly bright,
  (And what's true, though wondrous rare,
  Th'art as good as thou art fair),°
  Sends me here to usher in

Six brave virtues masculine,   140
Which will prove by moving here
This glad presence virtue's sphere.
Silence, and their names you'll hear:
First and fairest, bravest, best,
And which does include the rest,   145
Nobleness; his race and birth
From heaven, seldom seen in earth,
Whose everywhere deservèd fame
Dwells: Sir Vere Dux, his name.°
Next is Valour, true and tried,   150
Not a boy, that roaring wide
Cries 'God damn me' thrice (all such
Prove but glow-worms in the touch),°
Whose squib-manhood, ere one thinks,
Blazes, cracks, goes out, and stinks.   155
This more is than seeming bold,
Such the Heroës of old;°
His name Sir Arthur, and in field°
A crownèd lion on his shield.
Wisdom and Justice then, which call   160
Sir Sapient and Artegall,°
Virtue's twins, whose upright hands
Atlas-like uphold all lands,
Keep the world it does not run
To the old confusïon.°   165
Next Sir Guyon doth advance,°
The golden virtue, Temperance.
Last in rank, but not the least,
One that joinèd to the rest
Does relish them and make them right,°   170
Calidore, the courteous knight.°
Music, strain a note divine:
Appear you virtues masculine.

Here the scene opens and discovers six women masquers; at which
Favonius, wondering, says: 175

FAVONIUS Ha! How now! Phuh! What have we here? A metamorphosis! Men transformed to women! This age gives example to the
contrary.° Nay, are you there, Mistress Rainbow?° Then Juno° has
some trick upon us.

IRIS (*laughing*) Ladies all, for Juno's sake 180
  Laugh until your hearts do ache;
  Let us laugh both night and day,
  Till we blow this wind away.
  Jove could no way vex his queen
  But to send yon gaudy green 185
  Young Sir Puffin, with a tale°
  For to prove all virtues male.
  He, forsooth, must usher in
  Six brave virtues masculine.
FAVONIUS Well, Iris, Jove shall know this. 190
IRIS But now mark me, fairest fair,
  Juno, regent of the air,
  Heard Jove give this boy his task,
  Slipped away and bound his masque
  In a cloud, and in their room 195
  Charged that these should hither come.
  These are virtue's beauteous race
  That the female sex do grace.
  This is Meekness, fit to be°
  Kin to this, Simplicity, 200
  This Truth-in-Love, that Modesty,
  Silence, and spotless Chastity.°
  These shall prove, whate'er men say,
  We have more of good than they.
  Jove himself, as here you find, 205
  Cast their virtues to the wind;
  But lest this should turn to faction,
  They shall prove my words in action.
FAVONIUS Pretty, i' faith! (*Chafes and puffs*) But, will you dare to do
  this? Well, minion, if I do not make Jove knap thee in forty pieces, 210
  that there shall not be so much of thee left as to make a water-gall,
  or else hang thee on the knob of some thick cloud in thy bowstring,
  let me never reach the middle region° again. You scurvy, pied
  vanity; a fit trumpet for women's commendations—it needs colour
  painting, and thou art nothing else. 215
IRIS Alas, poor wretch, I see thou art e'en at the last gasp—and so is
  all the virtues of thy masque° till we please to revive it. Hear me,
  Favonius, and believe me. 'Tis agreed in heaven that Juno's will
  should be obeyed thus far to have she-masquers first on foot, to
  show the precedency of female virtue. And then I have power to 220

release thy charge from their cloudy prison, to prove that men's
virtue would never appear, did not women contribute lustre
thereunto and help to set it off. Will this content you?

FAVONIUS It must, it seems, of force; women will have their will. I
marvel Juno put not in Wilfulness for a prime virtue.   225

IRIS Well, leave your prating—

*The Sound. Here the first masquers, women six, descend, and while they
pass to the dancing place was sung this.*

SONG°

    Rejoice, all woman kind,
    Juno has her will of Jove.   230
    Each of you that list to prove°
    Shall easy conquest find.
    Be not, O be not blind,
But know your strength, and your own virtues see,
    Which in every several grace   235
    Of the mind or of the face
Gives women right to have priority.

    Brave Amazonian dames
    Made no count of mankind but
    For a fit to be at the rut;   240
    Free fire gives the brightest flames,
    Men's overawing tames
And pedant-like our active spirits smother.
    Learn, virgins, to live free.
    Alas, would it might be   245
Women could live and lie with one another.

Here the women dance the first dance, which done:

IRIS So now, Favonius, I'll unpin your Trojan horse, and let out your
    brave men at arms.
    Shadow, shadow, get thee hence,   250
    Juno's mercy does expense
    This free favour unto those
    Whom she bade thee late enclose.
    She commands them, too, to mix°
    Themselves in pace with yonder six,°   255

(*Here the men were discovered*)

FIG. I A daughter of Niger

FIG. 2 A Knight of Apollo

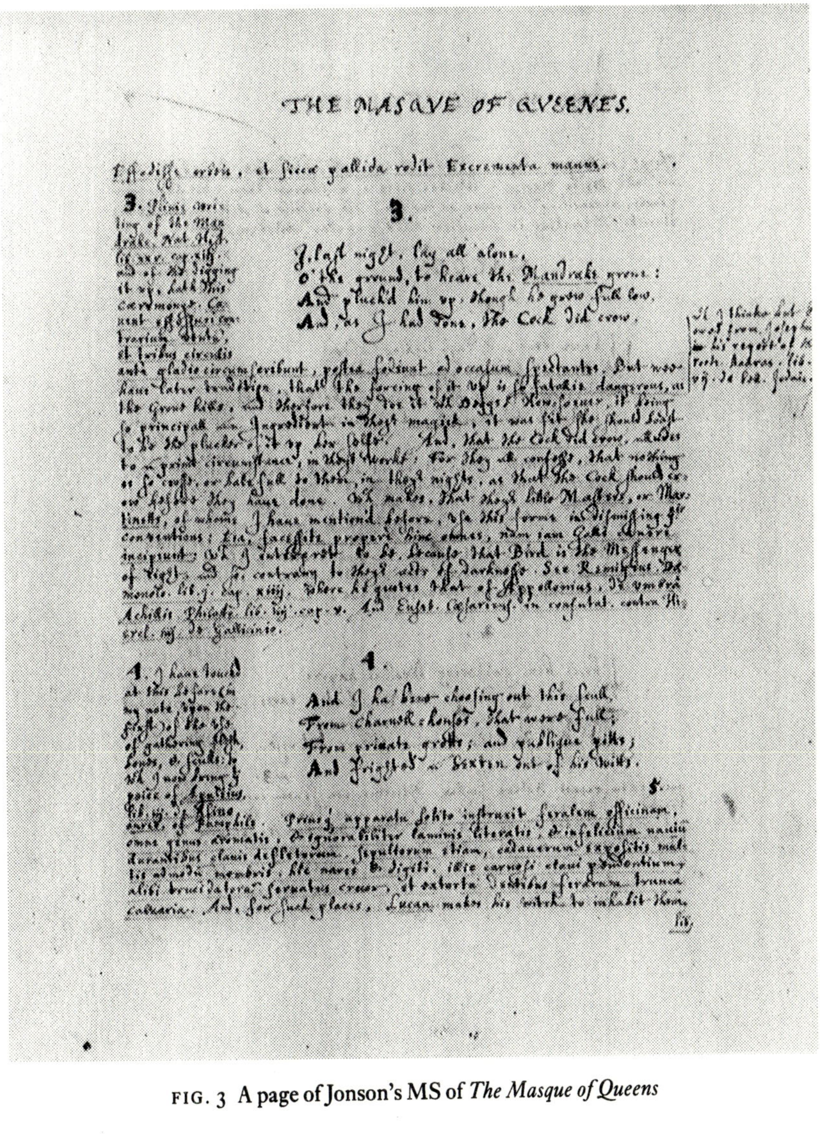

THE MASQVE OF QVEENES.

Effodisse orbis, et sicca pallida rodit Excrementa manus.

3.

3.

    I last night, lay all alone,
    O' the ground, to heare the Mandrake grone:
    And pluckd him up, though he grow full low,
    And, as I had done, the Cock did crow.

FIG. 3 A page of Jonson's MS of *The Masque of Queens*

FIG. 4 Thomyris

FIG. 5 The House of Fame

FIG. 6 Torch-bearer: An Indian

FIG. 7A Turkey

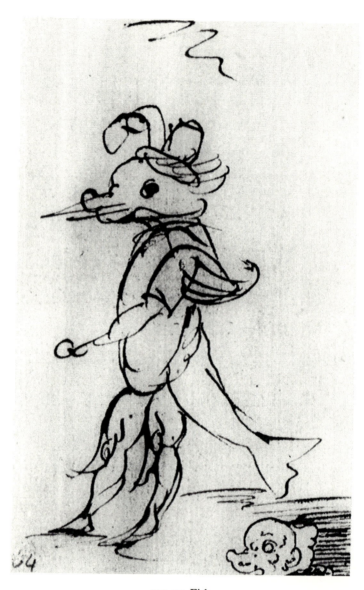

FIG. 7B Fish

FIG. 8 A Dwarf-post from Hell

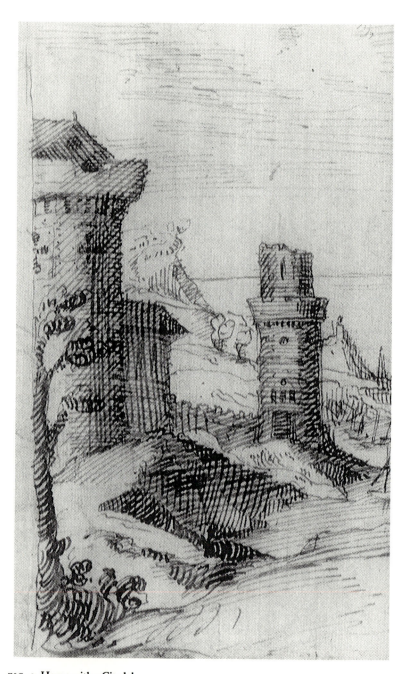

FIG. 9 Haven with a Citadel

FIG. 10 A City in Ruin

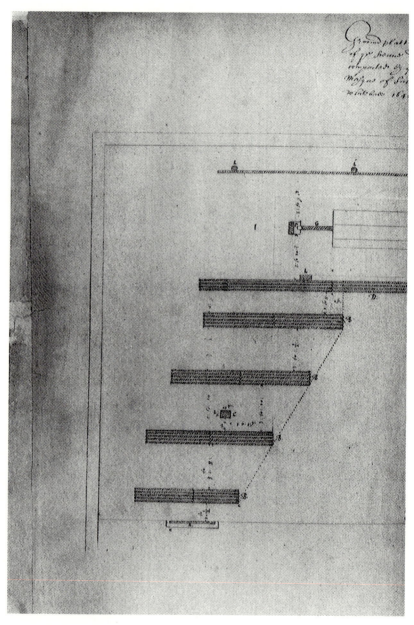

FIG. 11 Ground-plan of Stage and Scenery

And there in lively motion show
Who the other shall outgo.
FAVONIUS Now they appear.
    Sound, music, note divine;   260
    Descend, you virtues masculine.

At the coming in of the men was sung this song. But first Iris says:

IRIS Farewell, Favonius, I leave the convey of them all to you.

[SONG]°

    Now the virtuous male, descend.
    You, that lately so did flout 'em,   265
    Wail your error and amend,
    For what can you do without 'em?

    Like imperfect minerals
    Women are as crude as cold;
    Men, the sun which often falls   270
    On them, turns them into gold.

    Women ciphers are, and want
    Mixture of well-figured men;
    Themselves unsignificant,
    Joined they have a meaning then.   275

    Mix then, and together go,
    This be hers, and that be thine,
    All jars end by coupling so—
    'Tis not long to Valentine.°

Here the men and women dance together, and at the last masquing dance,   280
as they went to their places, was sung this third song.

    This was a sight indeed!
    Who would not break his sleep to see
    The male and the female graces
    Tread in such equal paces   285
    As cannot be decreed
    To which inclines the victory.
    Learn, women, to forsake
    Your coyness, scorn, and proud disdain.
    Men match, though not exceed you,   290
    'Tis Jove hath thus agreed you.

133

And let men warning take,
All strife with women is in vain.

FINIS

At the Going Away

Enter one with a flagon and a glass. In singing he pours out the sack.

Mad Bob o' th'buttery has a loss of late:° 295
'Twas a lucky thing
When they stole his skin
That they missed his plate.°

By me he sends you here liquor of delight.
'Tis a sack right good, 300
Both to clear the blood
And to cheer the spright.

Room, lads and lasses then, make a fair ring.
Come, my bonny boy,
Lady, be not coy, 305
'Tis a scurvy thing.

Run, holy liquor, run, 'tis a precious sight.
Go and cool your thirst
While I taste this first
To the Lady bright. 310

He kneels down and crosses the glass, saying this charm over it:

May this prove to every foe
Shame on earth and worse below;
But to all that wish you wealth,
Grace and honour, 'tis a health. 315

(To my Lady) And now farewell, child of light,
Beauteous woman, heavenly bright,
And (what's true, though wondrous rare)
Th'art as good as thou art fair.
At thy birth, to bless thy fate 320
All the stars in council sat,
All the good ones that dispense
Any bounteous influence.
Every one resolved to give,

Not a voice was negative;   325
By whose doom the graces are
Whole in thee, which others share,
And the virtues used to go°
Single, in thee mixedly flow.
(*To my Lord*) To thee, brave Earl, to urge thy stay   330
What would not our founder say?
But 'tis vain to use that part,
For thou knowest thou hast his heart.
Thou whose tempered soul is white,
Pure and free, as morning light;   335
That does make it all thy ends,
To be honest to thy friends;
Thou whose greatness does not swell thee°
To forget thou art a man,
Nor the things that e'er befell thee°   340
Either vex or alter can.
What thou art, continue still
Consigning those that wish it ill.°
Malice never is withstood
Better, than by being good.   345
Live with heaven, to make thy peace,
By thy virtues friends increase,
No faint hopes nor fears at all:
If the world crack, let it fall.
(*To them all*) Now remains to bid farewell,   350
But or here for ever dwell
Or (your presence having power
To make heaven of every bower)
We not envying others' bliss,
Yet make oft repair to this,   355
Where you find a pair of hearts
Bare of compliment or arts;
But more sound or more devout
Are not in the world throughout.
Deign, then, oft to bless this coast,   360
God dwells where he's honoured most.°

FINIS

BEN JONSON

Neptune's Triumph
for the Return of Albion

Neptune's Triumph for
the Return of Albion.
Celebrated in a Masque at the Court
on the Twelfth Night, 1624

Omnis et ad reducem iam litat ara Deum°
(Martial lib. viii. Epig. xv)

His Majesty being set, and the loud music ceasing, all that is discovered of a scene are two erected pillars dedicated to Neptune, with this inscription upon the one, NEP. RED.;° on the other, SEC. IOV.° The Poet, entering on the stage to disperse the argument,° is called to by the Master-Cook. 5

COOK Do you hear, you, creature of diligence and business! What is the affair that you pluck for° so under your cloak?

POET Nothing but what I colour for, I assure you, and may encounter with, I hope, if Luck favour me, the gamesters' goddess.

COOK You are a votary of hers, it seems by your language. What 10 went you upon? May a man ask you?

POET Certainties indeed, sir, and very good ones; the presentation of a masque. You'll see't anon.

COOK Sir, this is my room and region too, the Banqueting House! And in matter of feast and solemnity nothing is to be presented 15 here but with my acquaintance and allowance to it.

POET You are not his Majesty's confectioner, are you?

COOK No, but one that has as good title to the room, his Master-Cook. What are you, sir?

POET The most unprofitable of his servants I, sir, the Poet. A kind 20 of a Christmas engine, one that is used at least once a year for a trifling instrument of wit, or so.

COOK Were you ever a cook?

136

POET A cook? No, surely.

COOK Then you can be no good poet, for a good poet differs nothing   25
at all from a master-cook. Either's art is the wisdom of the mind.

POET As how, sir?

COOK Expect. I am by my place to know how to please the palates
of the guests; so, you are to know the palate of the times, study
the several tastes, what every nation, the Spaniard, the Dutch, the   30
French, the Walloon, the Neapolitan, the Briton, the Sicilian, can
expect from you.

POET That were a heavy and hard task, to satisfy Expectation, who
is so severe an exactress of duties; ever a tyrannous mistress, and
most times a pressing enemy.   35

COOK She is a powerful great lady, sir, at all times, and must be
satisfied. So must her sister, Madam Curiosity, who hath as dainty
a palate as she, and these will expect.

POET But what if they expect more than they understand?

COOK That's all one, Master Poet, you are bound to satisfy them.   40
For there is a palate of the understanding, as well as of the senses.
The taste is taken with good relishes, the sight with fair objects,
the hearing with delicate sounds, the smelling with pure scents, the
feeling with soft and plump bodies, but the understanding with all
these; for all which you must begin at the kitchen. There the art   45
of poetry was learned and found out, or nowhere, and the same
day with the art of cookery.

POET I should have given it rather to the cellar, if my suffrage had
been asked.

COOK O, you are for the oracle of the bottle,° I see; Hogshead   50
Trismegistus,° he is your Pegasus. Thence flows the spring of your
muses, from that hoof.°
Seducèd poet, I do say to thee,
A boiler, range, and dresser were the fountains
Of all the knowledge in the universe,   55
And that's the kitchen. Where, a master-cook—
Thou dost not know the man, nor canst thou know him
Till thou hast served some years in that deep school
That's both the nurse and mother of the arts,
And hear'st him read, interpret, and demonstrate!   60
A master-cook! Why he is the man of men
For a professor! He designs, he draws,
He paints, he carves, he builds, he fortifies,
Makes citadels of curious fowl and fish;

Some he dry-ditches, some moats round with broths,   65
Mounts marrow-bones, cuts fifty-angled custards,
Rears bulwark pies, and, for his outer works,
He raiseth ramparts of immortal crust,
And teacheth all the tactics at one dinner;
What ranks, what files to put his dishes in—   70
The whole art military! Then he knows
The influence of the stars upon his meats,
And all their seasons, tempers, qualities,
And so, to fit his relishes and sauces!
He 'as Nature in a pot, 'bove all the chemists   75
Or bare-breeched brethren of the Rosy Cross!°
He is an architect, an engineer,
A soldier, a physician, a philosopher,
A general mathematician!
POET   It is granted.
COOK And, that you may not doubt him for a poet—   80
POET This fury shows, if there were nothing else;
  And 'tis divine!
COOK   Then, brother poet—
POET   Brother!°
COOK I have a suit.
POET   What is it?
COOK   Your device.°
POET As you came in upon me I was then
  Offering the argument and this it is.   85
COOK Silence!
POET The mighty Neptune, mighty in his styles,
  And large command of waters and of isles,
  Not as the lord and sovereign of the seas,
  But chief in the art of riding, late did please°   90
  To send his Albion forth, the most his own,°
  Upon discovery, to themselves best known,
  Through Celtiberia; and to assist his course
  Gave him his powerful Manager of Horse,
  With divine Proteus, father of disguise,   95
  To wait upon them with his counsels wise
  In all extremes. His great commands being done,
  And he desirous to review his son,
  He doth despatch a floating isle from hence
  Unto the Hesperian shores, to waft him thence.   100

Where, what the arts were used to make him stay,
And how the sirens wooed him by the way,
What monsters he encountered on the coast,
How near our general joy was to be lost,°
Is not our subject now (though all these make   105
The present gladness greater, for their sake)
But what the triumphs are, the feast, the sport,
And proud solemnities of Neptune's court,
Now he is safe, and Fame's not heard in vain,
But we behold our happy pledge again;   110
That with him loyal Hippius is returned,
Who for it, under so much envy, burned
With his own brightness, till her starved snakes saw°
What Neptune did impose to him was law.

COOK But why not this, till now?

POET   It was not time°   115
To mix this music with the vulgar's chime.
Stay, till th'abortive and extemporal din
Of balladry were understood a sin,
Minerva cried; that what tumultuous verse°
Or prose could make, or steal, they might rehearse,°   120
And every songster had sung out his fit;
That all the country and the city wit
Of bells and bonfires and good cheer was spent,
And Neptune's guard had drunk all that they meant;
That all the tales and stories now were old   125
Of the sea-monster Archy, or grown cold;°
The muses then might venture undeterred,
For they love then to sing, when they are heard.

COOK I like it well, 'tis handsome. And I have
Something would fit this. How do you present 'em?   130
In a fine island, say you?

POET   Yes, a Delos,
Such as when fair Latona fell in travail
Great Neptune made emergent.

COOK   I conceive you.°
I would have had your isle brought floating in, now,
In a brave broth, and of a sprightly green,   135
Just to the colour of the sea; and then
Some twenty sirens singing in the kettle,°
With an Arion mounted on the back°

Of a grown conger, but in such a posture
As all the world should take him for a dolphin.   140
O, 'twould ha' made such music! Ha' you nothing
But a bare island?
POET   Yes, we have a tree too,°
Which we do call the Tree of Harmony,
And is the same with what we read the sun
Brought forth in the Indian Musicana first,   145
And thus it grows: the goodly bole, being got
To certain cubits height, from every side
The boughs decline, which, taking root afresh,
Spring up new boles, and those spring new, and newer,
Till the whole tree become a *porticus*,   150
Or archèd arbour, able to receive
A numerous troop, such as our Albion
And the companions of his journey are;
And this they sit in.
COOK   Your prime masquers?
POET   Yes.
COOK But where's your antimasque now, all this while?   155
I hearken after them.
POET   Faith, we have none.
COOK   None?
POET None, I assure you, neither do I think them
A worthy part of presentation,
Being things so heterogene, to all device
Mere by-works, and at best outlandish nothings.°   160
COOK O, you are all the heaven awry, sir!
For blood of poetry, running in your veins,
Make not yourself so ignorantly simple.
Because, sir, you shall see I am a poet,
No less than cook, and that I find you want   165
A special service here, an antimasque,
I'll fit you with a dish out of the kitchen,
Such as I think will take the present palates,
A metaphorical dish! And do but mark
How a good wit may jump with you. [*Calls*] Are you ready, child? 170
(Had there been masque or no masque, I had made it.)
Child of the boiling house!
[*Enter Child*]
CHILD   Here Father.

COOK Bring forth the pot. It is an *olla podrida*,
    But I have persons to present the meats.°
POET Persons!   175
COOK Such as do relish nothing but *di stato*,°
    But in another fashion than you dream of,
    Know all things the wrong way, talk of the affairs,
    The clouds, the curtains, and the mysteries°
    That are afoot, and, from what hands they have 'em   180
    (The master of the elephant or the camels)°
    What correspondences are held, the posts
    That go and come, and know, almost, their minutes,
    All but their business: therein they are fishes.
    But ha' their garlic, as the proverb says;°   185
    They are our quest of enquiry after news.
POET Together with their learnèd authors?
CHILD   Yes, sir,
    And of the epicene gender, hes and shes;
    Amphibian Archy is the chief.
COOK   Good boy!°
    The child is learnèd too. Note but the kitchen!   190
    Have you put him into the pot for garlic?
CHILD One in his coat shall stink as strong as he, sir,
    And his friend Giblets with him.
COOK   They are two
    That give a part of the seasoning.
POET   I conceive
    The way of your gallimaufry.
COOK   You will like it,°   195
    When they come pouring out of the pot together.
CHILD O, if the pot had been big enough!
COOK   What then, Child?
CHILD I had put in the elephant, and one camel
    At least, for beef.
COOK   But whom ha' you for partridge?
CHILD A brace of dwarfs, and delicate plump birds!   200
COOK And whom for mutton and kid?
CHILD   A fine laced mutton°
    Or two, and either has her frisking husband,
    That reads her the corantos every week.
    Grave Master Ambler, news-master of Paul's°
    Supplies your capon, and grown Captain Buzz   205

(His emissary) underwrites for turkey;
A gentleman of the forest presents pheasant,
And a plump poulterer's wife in Grace's Street°
Plays hen with eggs i' the belly, or a cony,
Choose which you will.

COOK   But where's the bacon, Tom?   210

CHILD Hogrel the butcher and the sow his wife
Are both there.

COOK   It is well; go, dish 'em out.
Are they well boiled?

CHILD   *Podrida!*

POET   What's that? Rotten?

COOK O, that they must be. There's one main ingredient
We have forgot, the artichoke.

CHILD   No, sir.   215
I have a fruiterer with a cold red nose,
Like a blue fig, performs it.

COOK   The fruit looks so.
Good child, go pour 'em out, show their concoction.
They must be rotten boiled, the broth's the best on't,
And that's the dance. The stage here is the charger.   220
And, brother Poet, though the serious part
Be yours, yet envy not the Cook his art.

POET Not I. *Nam lusus ipse triumphus amat.*°

The antimasque is danced by the persons described, coming out of the pot.

POET Well, now, expect the scene itself; it opens!   225

The island is discovered, the masquers sitting in their several sieges. The heavens opening, and Apollo, with Mercury, some Muses, and the Goddess Harmony, make the music, the while the island moves forward, Proteus sitting below; and Apollo sings.

SONG

APOLLO   Look forth, the shepherd of the seas,°   230
             And of the ports that keep'st the keys,°
               And to your Neptune tell,
             His Albion, prince of all his isles,
             For whom the sea and land so smiles,
               Is home returnèd well.   235

CHORUS   And be it thought no common cause,
             That to it so much wonder draws,

And all the heavens' consent
With Harmony to tune their notes,
In answer to the public votes   240
    That for it up were sent.

It was no envious stepdame's rage,
Or tyrant's malice of the age
    That did employ him forth;
But such a wisdom that would prove,   245
By sending him, their hearts and love,
    That else might fear his worth.°

By this time the island hath joined itself with the shore, and Proteus,
Portunus, and Saron° come forth, and go up singing to the state, while the
masquers take time to land.   250

SONG

PROTEUS	Aye! now the pomp of Neptune's triumph shines,
	And all the glories of his great designs
	Are read, reflected in his son's return!
PORTUNUS	How all the eyes, the looks, the hearts here burn
	At his arrival!
SARON	These are the true fires, 255
	Are made of joys!
PROTEUS	Of longings!
PORTUNUS	Of desires!
SARON	Of hopes!
PROTEUS	Of fears!
PORTUNUS	No intermitted blocks,°
SARON	But pure affections, and from odorous stocks!
CHORUS	'Tis incense all that flames!
	And these materials scarce have names! 260
PROTEUS	My king looks higher, as he scorned the wars°
	Of winds, and with his trident touched the stars.
	There is no wrinkle in his brow, or frown,
	But as his cares he would in nectar drown,
	And all the silver-footed nymphs were dressed° 265
	To wait upon him to the ocean's feast;
PORTUNUS	Or here in rows upon the banks were set,
	And had their several hairs made into net
	To catch the youths in, as they come on shore.
SARON	How! Galatea sighing! O, no more.° 270

	Banish your fears;	
PORTUNUS	And Doris, dry your tears.°	
	Albion is come,	
PROTEUS	And Haliclyon too,°	
	That kept his side, as he was charged to do,	
	With wonder.	
SARON	And the sirens have him not,	
PORTUNUS	Though they no practice nor no arts forgot	275
	That might have won him, or by charm or song,	
PROTEUS	Or laying forth their tresses all along	
	Upon the glassy waves;	
PORTUNUS	Then diving;	
PROTEUS	Then,	
	Up with their heads, as they were mad of men;°	
SARON	And there the highest-going billows crown,	280
	Until some lusty sea-god pulled them down.	
CHORUS	See! He is here!	
PROTEUS	Great master of the main,	
	Receive thy dear and precious pawn again.	
CHORUS	Saron, Portunus, Proteus, bring him thus,	
	Safe, as thy subjects' wishes gave him us;	285
	And of thy glorious triumph let it be	
	No less a part, that thou their loves dost see,	
	Than that his sacred head's returned to thee.	

*This sung, the island goes back, whilst the upper chorus takes it from them,
and the masquers prepare for their figure.°*   290

CHORUS	Spring all the graces of the age,	
	And all the loves of time;	
	Bring all the pleasures of the stage,	
	And relishes of rhyme;	
	Add all the softnesses of courts,	295
	The looks, the laughters, and the sports,	
	And mingle all their sweets and salts,°	
	That none may say, the triumph halts.	

*Here the masquers dance their entry. Which done, the first prospective of
a maritime palace, or the house of Oceanus,° is discovered, with loud* 300
music. And the other above is no more seen.

POET Behold the palace of Oceanus!

Hail, reverend structure! Boast no more to us
Thy being able all the gods to feast;
We have seen enough: our Albion was thy guest.   305

Then follows the main dance. After which the second prospect of the sea
is shown, to the former music.

POET Now turn and view the wonders of the deep
    Where Proteus' herds, and Neptune's orcs do keep;
    Where all is ploughed, yet still the pasture's green,   310
    The ways are found, and yet no path is seen.

There Proteus, Portunus, Saron, go up to the ladies with this song.

PROTEUS	Come, noble nymphs, and do not hide
	The joys for which you so provide.
SARON	If not to mingle with the men, 315
	What do you here? Go home again.
PORTUNUS	Your dressings do confess,
	By what we see, so curious parts
	Of Pallas' and Arachne's arts,°
	That you could mean no less. 320
PROTEUS	Why do you wear the silkworms' toils,
	Or glory in the shellfish spoils,
	Or strive to show the grains of ore
	That you have gathered on the shore,
	Whereof to make a stock 325
	To graft the greener emerald on,
	Or any better-watered stone?
SARON	Or ruby of the rock?
PROTEUS	Why do you smell of ambergris,
	Of which was formèd Neptune's niece, 330
	The queen of love, unless you can,
	Like sea-born Venus, love a man?
SARON	Try, put yourselves unto't.
CHORUS	Your looks, your smiles, and thoughts that meet,
	Ambrosian hands and silver feet, 335
	Do promise you will do't.

The revels follow. Which ended, the fleet is discovered, while the three
cornetts play.

POET 'Tis time your eyes should be refreshed at length
    With something new, a part of Neptune's strength.   340

See, yond' his fleet, ready to go or come,
Or fetch the riches of the ocean home,
So to secure him both in peace and wars
Till not one ship alone, but all be stars.

A shout within follows, after which the cook enters.   345

COOK I have another service for you, brother Poet, a dish of pickled
  sailors, fine salt sea-boys, shall relish like anchovies or caviar, to
  draw down a cup of nectar in the skirts of a night.
SAILORS Come away, boys, the town is ours. Hey for Neptune, and
  our young master!   350
POET He knows the compass and the card,
  While Castor sits on the main yard,
  And Pollux too, to help your hales,°
  And bright Leucothe fills your sails;°
  Arion sings, the dolphins swim,   355
  And all the way to gaze on him.

*The antimasque of sailors. Then the last song to the whole music: five
lutes, three cornetts, and ten voices.*

SONG

PROTEUS   Although we wish the triumph still might last
             For such a prince, and his discovery past,   360
             Yet now, great lord of waters and of isles,
             Give Proteus leave to turn unto his wiles;
PORTUNUS   And whilst young Albion doth thy labours ease,
             Dispatch Portunus to thy ports,
SARON   And Saron to thy seas,
             To meet old Nereus, with his fifty girls,°   365
             From agèd Indus laden home with pearls,
             And orient gums to burn unto thy name.
CHORUS   And may thy subjects' hearts be all on flame,
             Whilst thou dost keep the earth in firm estate,
             And 'mongst the winds dost suffer no debate.   370
             But both at sea and land our powers increase,
             With health, and all the golden gifts of peace.°

The last dance.

THE END

146

BEN JONSON
Chloridia

Rites to Chloris and Her Nymphs,
Personated in a Masque at Court
By the Queen's Majesty and her Ladies
At Shrove-Tide, 1631

Unius tellus ante coloris erat.°

The King and Queen's majesty having given their command for the
invention of a new argument, with the whole change of the scene,
wherein her Majesty, with the like number° of her ladies, purposed a
presentation to the King, it was agreed it should be the celebration of
some rites done to the goddess Chloris,° who in a general council   5
of the gods was proclaimed goddess of the flowers, according to that
of Ovid in the *Fasti: Arbitrium tu, Dea, floris habe.*° And was to be
stellified on earth by an absolute decree from Jupiter, who would have
the earth to be adorned with stars, as well as the heaven.

Upon this hinge, the whole invention moved.   10

*The ornament which went about the scene was composed of foliage, or
leaves, heightened with gold, and interwoven with all sorts of flowers, and
naked children playing and climbing among the branches; and in the midst
a great garland of flowers in which was written, CHLORIDIA.*

The curtain being drawn up, the scene is discovered, consisting of   15
*pleasant hills planted with young trees and all the lower banks adorned
with flowers. And from some hollow parts of those hills fountains come
gliding down, which, in the far-off landscape, seemed all to be converted
to a river.*

Over all, a serene sky with transparent clouds, giving a great lustre to   20
the whole work, which did imitate the pleasant spring.

*When the spectators had enough fed their eyes with the delights of the
scene, in a part of the air a bright cloud begins to break forth; and in it
is sitting a plump boy in a changeable garment, richly adorned,
representing the mild Zephyrus.° On the other side of the scene in a*   25

purplish cloud appeareth the Spring, a beautiful maid, her upper
garment green, under it a white robe wrought with flowers, a garland on
her head.

    Here Zephyrus begins his dialogue, calling her forth and making
narration of the gods' decree at large; which she obeys, pretending it is   30
come to earth already, and there begun to be executed by the King's
favour, who assists with all bounties that may be either urged as causes or
reasons of the spring.

THE FIRST SONG

ZEPHYRUS	Come forth, come forth, the gentle Spring,
	And carry the glad news I bring, 35
	To earth, our common mother:
	It is decreed by all the gods
	The heaven of earth shall have no odds,°
	But one shall love another;

        Their glories they shall mutual make;   40
        Earth look on heaven, for heaven's sake;
           Their honours shall be even;
        All emulation cease, and jars;
        Jove will have earth to have her stars
           And lights, no less than heaven.   45

SPRING   It is already done, in flowers
        As fresh and new as are the hours,
           By warmth of yonder sun;
        But will be multiplied on us,
        If from the breath of Zephyrus   50
           Like favour we have won.

ZEPHYRUS   Give all to him: his is the dew,
        The heat, the humour—
SPRING   All the true-°
        Belovèd of the Spring!
ZEPHYRUS   The sun, the wind, the verdure—
SPRING   All   55
        That wisest nature cause can call
           Of quickening any thing.

At which Zephyrus passeth away through the air, and the Spring
descendeth to the earth, and is received by the Naiades, or Napaeae,° who
are the nymphs, fountains, and servants of the season.   60

THE SECOND SONG

FOUNTAINS	Fair maid, but are you come to dwell
	And tarry with us here?
SPRING	Fresh fountains, I am come to tell
	A tale in yond' soft ear,
	Whereof the murmur will do well, 65
	If you your parts will bear.
FOUNTAINS	Our purlings wait upon the Spring
SPRING	Go up with me then; help to sing
	The story to the King.

Here the Spring goes up, singing the argument° to the King; and the   70
fountains follow with the close.

SPRING	Cupid hath ta'en offence of late
	At all the gods, that of the state
	And in their council he was so deserted,
	Not to be called into their guild, 75
	But slightly passed by as a child.
FOUNTAINS	Wherein he thinks his honour was perverted.
SPRING	And though his mother seek to season°
	And rectify his rage with reason,
	By showing he lives yet under her command, 80
	Rebellious, he doth disobey,
	And she hath forced his arms away—°
FOUNTAINS	To make him feel the justice of her hand.
SPRING	Whereat the boy, in fury fell,
	With all his speed is gone to hell, 85
	There to excite and stir up Jealousy
	To make a party 'gainst the gods,
	And set heaven, earth, and hell at odds—
FOUNTAINS	And raise a chaos of calamity.

The song ended, the nymphs fall into a dance to their voices and   90
instruments, and so return into the scene.

The Antimasque

First Entry

A part of the underground opening, out of it enters a dwarf-post from
hell, riding on a curtal, with cloven feet and two lackeys.

These dance, and make the first entry of the antimasque. He alights and speaks.   95

POSTILION Hold my stirrup, my one lackey, and look to my curtal
the other. Walk him well, sirrah, while I expatiate° myself here in
the report of my office. Oh, the furies! How I am joyed with the
title of it! Postilion of hell! Yet no Mercury, but a mere cacodemon
sent hither with a packet of news.° News! Never was hell so   100
furnished of the commodity of news! Love hath been lately there,
and so entertained by Pluto and Proserpine° and all the grandees
of the place as it is there perpetual holiday, and a cessation of
torment granted and proclaimed for ever! Half-famished Tantalus°
is fallen to his fruit, with that appetite as it threatens to undo the   105
whole company of costard-mongers, and has a river afore him
running excellent wine. Ixion° is loosed from his wheel and turned
dancer—does nothing but cut caprioles, fetch friskals, and leads
lavoltas° with the Lamiae! Sisyphus° has left rolling the stone,
and is grown a master bowler—challenges all the prime gamesters,   110
parsons in hell, and gives them odds—upon Tityus° his breast
that, for six of the nine acres, is counted the subtlest bowling
ground in all Tartary. All the furies are at a game called ninepins
or kayles, made of old usurers' bones, and their souls looking on
with delight, and betting on the game. Never was there such   115
freedom of sport! Danaus' daughters° have broke their bottomless
tubs and made bonfires of them. All is turned triumph there. Had
hell-gates been kept with half that strictness as the entry here has
been tonight,° Pluto would have had but a cold court, and
Proserpine a thin presence, though both have a vast territory. We   120
had such a stir to get in, I and my curtal and my two lackeys all
ventured through the eye of a Spanish needle, we had never come
in else, and that was by the favour of one of the guard who was a
woman's tailor, and held ope the passage.° Cupid by commission
hath carried Jealousy from hell, Disdain, Fear, and Dissimulation,   125
with other goblins, to trouble the gods. And I am sent after, post,
to raise Tempest, Winds, Lightnings, Thunder, Rain, and Snow
for some new exploit they have against the earth and the goddess
Chloris, queen of the flowers and mistress of the spring. For joy
of which I will return to myself, mount my bidet in a dance, and   130
curvet upon my curtal.

*The speech ended, the Postilion mounts his curtal, and with his lackeys,
danceth forth as he came in.*

Second Entry

Cupid, Jealousy, Disdain, Fear, and Dissimulation dance together.

Third Entry

The Queen's dwarf,° richly apparelled as a prince of hell, attended by six   135
*infernal spirits; he first danceth alone, and then the spirits, all expressing
their joy for Cupid's coming among them.*

Fourth Entry

*Here the scene changeth into a horrid storm, out of which enters the nymph
Tempest, with four Winds; they dance.*

Fifth Entry

Lightnings, three in number, their habits glistering, expressing that effect   140
in their motion.

Sixth Entry

Thunder alone, dancing the tunes to a noise, mixed, and imitating thunder.

Seventh Entry

*Rain, presented by five persons all swollen and clouded over, their hair
flagging, as if they were wet, and in their hands balls full of sweet water
which, as they dance, sprinkle all the room.*   145

Eighth and last Entry

*Seven with rugged white heads and beards, to express snow, with flakes on
their garments mixed with hail. These having danced return into the
stormy scene whence they came.*

*Here, by the providence of Juno,° the tempest on an instant ceaseth, and
the scene is changed into a delicious place, figuring the bower of Chloris,*   150
*wherein an arbour feigned of goldsmiths' work, the ornament of which was
borne up with terms of satyrs, beautified with festoons, garlands, and all
sorts of fragrant flowers. Beyond all this, in the sky afar off, appeared a
rainbow. In the most eminent place of the bower sat the goddess Chloris
accompanied with fourteen nymphs, their apparel white, embroidered with*   155
silver, trimmed at the shoulders with great leaves of green embroidered with

*gold, falling one under the other. And of the same work were their bases,
their head-tires of flowers mixed with silver and gold, with some sprigs of
egrets° among, and from the top of their dressing, a thin veil hanging down.*

    All which beheld, the nymphs, rivers, and fountains with the Spring   160
sung this rejoicing song.

SONG 3

RIVERS, SPRING, Run out, all the floods, in joy with your silver
FOUNTAINS   feet,
           And haste to meet
           The enamoured Spring,
           For whom the warbling fountains sing   165
           The story of the flowers,
           Preservèd by the Hours°
           At Juno's soft command, and Iris' showers,°
           Sent to quench Jealousy, and all those powers
           Of Love's rebellious war;   170
           Whilst Chloris sits a shining star
           To crown and grace our jolly song,
           Made long
           To the notes that we bring
           To glad the Spring.   175

*Which ended, the goddess and her nymphs descend the degrees into the
room, and dance the entry of the grand masque.*

    After this, another song by the same persons as before.

SONG 4

RIVERS, FOUNTAINS   Tell a truth, gay Spring, let us know
                    What feet they were, that so   180
                    Impressed the earth, and made such various
                        flowers to grow!
SPRING   She that led a queen was at least,
                    Or a goddess 'bove the rest,
                    And all their graces in herself expressed!
RIVERS, FOUNTAINS   O, 'twere a fame to know her name!   185
                    Whether she were the root,°
                    Or they did take th'impression from her
                      foot.

*The masquers here dance their second dance. Which done, the farther
prospect of the scene changeth into air, with a low landscape in part*

covered with clouds. And in that instant, the heaven opening, Juno and   190
Iris are seen, and above them many airy spirits sitting in the clouds.

SONG 5

JUNO	Now Juno and the air shall know
	The truth of what is done below
	From our discoloured bow.
	Iris, what news? 195
IRIS	The air is clear, your bow can tell,
	Chloris renowned, Spite fled to hell;
	The business all is well.
	And Cupid sues—
JUNO	For pardon, does he?
IRIS	He sheds tears 200
	More than your birds have eyes.°
JUNO	The gods have ears.
	Offences made against the deities
	Are soon forgot—
IRIS	If who offends be wise.

Here, out of the earth ariseth a hill, and on the top of it a globe, on which   205
Fame is seen standing with her trumpet in her hand; and on the hill are
seated four persons presenting Poesy, History, Architecture, and Sculpture°
who, together with the nymphs, floods, and fountains, make a full choir;
at which, Fame begins to mount, and moving her wings flieth, singing, up
to heaven.   210

FAME	Rise, golden Fame, and give thy name a birth,
CHORUS	From great and generous actions done on earth.
FAME	The life of Fame is action.
CHORUS	Understood
	That action must be virtuous, great, and good!
FAME	Virtue itself by Fame is oft protected, 215
	And dies despisèd—
CHORUS	Where the Fame's neglected.
FAME	Who hath not heard of Chloris and her bower?
	Fair Iris' act, employed by Juno's power
	To guard the Spring, and prosper every flower
	Whom Jealousy and hell thought to devour? 220
CHORUS	Great actions, oft obscured by time may lie,
	Or envy—
FAME	But they last to memory.

POESY	We that sustain thee, learnèd Poesy,	
HISTORY	And I, her sister, severe History,	
ARCHITECTURE	With Architecture, who will raise thee high,	225
SCULPTURE	And Sculpture, that can keep thee from to die,	
CHORUS	All help to lift thee to eternity.	
JUNO	And Juno through the air doth make thy way,	
IRIS	By her serenest messenger of day.	
FAME	Thus Fame ascends by all degrees to heaven,	230
	And leaves a light here brighter than the seven.°	
CHORUS	Let all applaud the sight:	

    Air first, that gave the bright
    Reflections, day or night!
    With these supports of Fame   235
    That keep alive her name!
    The beauties of the spring,
    Founts, rivers, everything:
    From the height of all,
    To the waters' fall   240
    Resound and sing
The honours of his Chloris to the king.
    Chloris, the queen of flowers,
    The sweetness of all showers,
    The ornament of bowers,   245
    The top of paramours!

Fame being hidden in the clouds, the hill sinks and the heaven closeth. The masquers dance with the lords.

THE END

The names of the masquers as they sat in the bower
The Queen

Countess of Carlisle	Countess of Oxford
Lady Strange	Countess of Berkshire
Lady Anne Cavendish	Countess of Carnarvon
Countess of Newport	Lady Penelope Egerton
Mrs Porter	Mrs Dorothy Savage
Lady Howard	Mrs Elizabeth Savage
Mrs Anne Weston	Mrs Sophia Cary

AURELIAN TOWNSHEND

Tempe Restored

A Masque, presented by the Queen
and fourteen ladies,
to the King's Majesty at Whitehall
on Shrove Tuesday, 1632

The Argument

Circe° by her allurements enamoured a young gentleman on her
person, who awhile lived with her in all sensual delights until, upon
some jealousy conceived, she gave him to drink of an enchanted cup,
and touching him with her golden wand, transformed him into a lion.
After some time she, remembering her former love, retransformed him   5
into his former shape. Which he reassuming took the first occasion by
flight to quit the place, and coming into the presence of his majesty,
whose sight frees him from all fear, he relates the story of his fortune.

When Circe had notice of her lover's escape, it put her into a
furious anger, and then into a lamentation or love passion. But being   10
consolated by her nymphs, she commands that all such delights be
prepared as may sweeten her sorrow; and presently all the
voluntary° beasts under her subjection are introduced to make her
sport. After which, the way being first prepared by Harmony and the
Influences,° Divine Beauty, accompanied with fourteen stars of a   15
happy constellation, descends to the music of the spheres and joineth
with Heroic Virtue, where, in presence of Jove and Cupid, Circe,
knowing the design of the Destinies on this glorious interview,°
voluntarily delivers her golden rod to Minerva. So all the
enchantments being dissolved, Tempe,° which for a time had been   20
possessed by the voluntary beasts of Circe's court, is restored to the
true followers of the muses.

The Description of the Scene

*In the upper part of the border, serving for ornament to the scene, was
painted a fair compartment of scrolls and quadratures, in which was*

written TEMPE RESTAURATUM. *On each side of this lay a figure*   25
bigger than the life; the one a woman with wings on her head like
Mercury, and a pen in her hand, the other a man looking down in a book
lying open before him, a torch lighted in his hand. That figured Invention,
this Knowledge.° Near to these were children holding ugly masks before
their faces, in action as if they would affright them, others riding on tame   30
beasts, and some blowing such wreathen trumps° as make confused noise;
in the corners sat other children hardening of darts in lamps. But Invention
and Knowledge seem not to be diverted from their study by these childish
bugbears. In the midst of the two sides of this border, in short niches, sat
two ugly figures, the one a woman with a forked tongue and snaky locks,   35
and the under part of a satyr. This hag held in her hand a smiling vizard
crowned with roses, and was figured for Envy, under the mask of
Friendship. On the other side was sitting as horrid a man-satyr, with a
wreath of poppy on his head and a frog sitting on the forepart thereof, and
above a bat flying; this represented Curious Ignorance.° The rest of the   40
border was filled up with several fancies, which lest I should be too long
in the description of the frame, I will go to the picture itself; and indeed
these shows are nothing else but pictures with light and motion.°

A curtain being drawn up, the lightsome scene appeared, showing a
delicious place by nature and art, where, in a valley environed with hills   45
afar off, was seated a prospect of curious arbours of various forms. The
first order, of marble pilasters, between which were niches of rock work and
statues, some spurting water received into vases beneath them, and others
standing on pedestals. On the returns of these pilasters run slender
cornicements, from which was raised a second order of gracious terms with   50
women's faces, which bear up the ornaments. Under this to a leaning
height was a balustrata enriched. All this second story seemed of silver
work mixed with fresh verdures, which on the tops of these arbours covered
some of the returns, in the form of types,° with tender branches dangling
down; others were covered flat, and had flowerpots of gold for finishing.   55
Behind these appeared the tops of slender trees, whose leaves seemed to
move with a gentle breath coming from the far-off hills.

Out of this pleasant place comes in haste a young gentleman,° looking
often back, as if he feared a pursuit; and being come into the midst of the
room, looking still distractedly about him, he wipes his face with a   60
handkerchief, and then advanceth towards the state, and speaks.°

THE FUGITIVE FAVOURITE Was I a lion, that am now afraid?
   I fear no danger; nor I fear no death
   But to be retransformed into a beast;
   Which while I was, although I must confess   65

I was the bravest (what could she do less
That saw me subject to no base desire?)
Yet was there in me a Promethean fire°
That made me covet to be man again,
Governed by reason, and not ruled by sense.　　　　　70
　　Therefore I shun this place of residence,
And fly to virtue; in whose awful sight
She dares not come but in a mask, and crouch
As low as I did for my liberty.
　　Her bower is pleasant and her palace rich,　　　　75
Her fare delicious, and her language fine;
But shall the soul, the minion of the gods,
Stoop to her vassals? or stand by and starve
While they sit swelling in her chair of state?
'Tis not her rod, her philtres nor her herbs　　　　80
(Though strong in magic) that can bound men's minds,
And make them prisoners where there is no wall:
It is consent that makes a perfect slave,
And sloth that binds us to lust's easy trades,
Wherein we serve out our youth's 'prenticeship,　　　85
Thinking at last Love should enfranchise us,
Whom we have never either served or known:
'He finds no help, that uses not his own.'°

The speech ended, the Gentleman lies down at the feet of the lords'
seats.°　　　　　　　　　　　　　　　　　　　　　　90
　　Then the further part of the scene opening, there appears seated on the
side of a fruitful hill a sumptuous palace, with an open terrace before it,
and a great stair of return descending into the lower grounds; the upper
part environed with walls of marble, alongst which were planted cypress
trees. From the foot of the hill Circe, attended by the naiades and dryads,°　　95
comes forth in fury for the escape of the young gentleman her lover, and
having traversed the stage with an angry look, sings to her lute.

THE SONG OF CIRCE
(represented by Madam Coniack)°

CIRCE　　　Dissembling traitor, now I see the cause
　　　　　　Of all thy fawning was but to be free.　　　　100
　　　　　　'Twas not for nothing thou hadst teeth
　　　　　　　　and claws,
　　　　　　For thou hast made a cruel prey of me.

157

HER FOUR	Ingratitude is apt to slink away,	
NYMPHS	And shun that bounty which it cannot pay.	
CIRCE	And he is gone (ay me) is stol'n from hence,	105
	And this poor casket of my breast hath left	
	Without a heart, that should for recompense	
	Have locked in two. O most inhuman theft!	
NYMPHS	Send not your sighs after a fickle mind,	
	That sails the faster for such gales of wind.	110
CIRCE	Then take my keys, and show me all my wealth!	
	Lead me abroad! Let me my subjects view!	
	Bring me some physic, though that bring no health,	
	And feign me pleasures, since I find none true.	
CHORUS	Ye willing servants! and ye souls confined	115
	To several shapes by powerful herbs and art,	
	Appear, transformed each in your several kind,	
	And strive to temper the distempered heart	
	Of sullen Circe, stung with Cupid's dart.	

Her song ended, she sits, and before her are presented all the antimasques, 120
consisting of Indians and Barbarians (who naturally are bestial) and
others which are voluntaries, and but half transformed into beasts.
  Here come forth all the antimasques.°

First	*7 Indians adoring their 1 Pagoda*	
Second	*1 Hare, 2 Hounds*	125
Third	*4 Lions*	
Fourth	*3 Apes, an ass like a pedant, teaching them prick-song*	
Fifth	*6 Barbarians*	
Sixth	*5 Hogs*	

The Last antimasque consisting of 130

> *2 Indians*
> *2 Hounds*
> *2 Apes*
> *1 Ass*
> *2 Lions* 135
> *2 Barbarians*
> *2 Hogs*

  The antimasques being past, Circe and her nymphs retire towards
the palace from whence she came, and the scene returns into the vale of
Tempe. 140

Harmony comes forth attended by a chorus of music, and under her conduct fourteen Influences of the stars, which are to come. She with the chorus goes up to the state and sings.

HARMONY (presented by Mrs Shepherd)

    Not as myself, but as the brightest star   145
    That shines in heaven, come to reign this
        day;
    And these the beams and influences
        are
    Of constellations, whose planetic sway,
    Though some foresee, all must alike
        obey.

CHORUS   Such a conjunction of auspicious lights,   150
                  Meet but in honour of some regal rites.°

HARMONY AND Ladies, lend us your ears!
HER CHOIR   And let no lover's sigh be heard!
                  Or suit (though just) be now preferred.
                    A consort of the spheres   155
                  Admits no whisper, nor no sound,
                  But what is descant to their ground.°
                    Nor can we hold ye long
                    For there are stars to rise,
                    That far above our song   160
                    Are music to all eyes.

They retire

A SARABAND

If any beauty here
In her own glass appear
Or lover's eye most clear,   165
Looking but up, she may with small ado
Perceive that flatters, and her servant too.

Her song ended, they retire with a saraband, and the fourteen Influences fall into their dance. Which being past, they are placed on the degrees by the lords and ladies, where they sit to see the masque.   170
   Then the scene is changed into an oriental sky, such as appears at the sun rising, and afar off is seen a landscape and a calm sea, which did terminate the horizon. In the hither part was a haven with a citadel, and opposite to that were broken grounds and craggy rocks.

In the midst of the air the eight spheres in rich habits were seated on a 175
cloud, which in a circular form was on each side continued unto the highest
part of the heaven, and seemed to have let them down as in a chain.°

To the music of these spheres there appeared two other clouds descending,
and in them were discovered eight stars. These being come to the middle
region of the sky, another greater cloud came down above them, which by 180
little and little descending, discovered other glistering stars to the number
of six. And above all, in a chariot of goldsmith's work richly adorned with
precious gems, sat Divine Beauty, over whose head appeared a brightness
full of small stars that environed the top of the chariot, striking a light
round about it. 185

The eight stars that first descended, being by this time past the spheres,
came forth, and the clouds on which they sat with a swift motion returning
up again, and the other still descending, showed a pleasing contention
between them as they passed. When Divine Beauty and her attendants
were lighted, that great cloud that bare them flies up again, leaving the 190
chariot standing on the earth.

This sight altogether was, for the difficulty of the engining and the
number of the persons, the greatest that hath been seen here in our time.
For the apparitions of such as came down in the air, and the choruses
standing beneath, arrived to the number of fifty persons, all richly attired, 195
showing the magnificence of the court of England. The description of the
several habits of the main masque, antimasques, with all the persons
employed, would make a book alone as big as this, and ask more time in
setting down than can be now spared. Only thus much: the Queen's
majesty was in a garment of watchet satin with stars of silver embroidered 200
and embossed from the ground, and on her head a crown of stars mixed
with some small falls of white feathers, and the ladies were in the same
manner. The stuff was rich and the form noble, and all suiting to the
munificence of so great a Queen.

THE HIGHEST SPHERE (represented by Mr Lanier) 205
      When Divine Beauty will vouchsafe to stoop
      And move to earth, 'tis fit the heavenly spheres
      Should be her music, and the starry troop
      Shine round about her, like the crown she wears.
CHORUS   No mortal breast 210
      Can entertain
      So great a guest,
      And such a train.
HIGHEST I cannot blame ye if ye gaze,

SPHERE	And give small ear to what I say;	215
	For such a presence will amaze,	
	And send the senses all one way.	
CHORUS	The music that ye hear is dull,	
	But that ye see is sweet indeed,°	
	In every part exact and full,	220
	From whence there doth an air proceed,	
	On which th'Intelligences feed,	
	Where fair and good, inseparably	
	conjoined,	
	Create a Cupid, that is never blind.	

The Queen and the ladies dance their entry, after which Harmony and the   225
highest sphere sing, assisted by all the choruses together.

THE SONG

HARMONY	How rich is earth, and poor the skies,	
	Deprived of heavenly Beauty's eyes,	
	Whose image men adore.	
THE EIGHTH	Heroic Virtue is that kind	230
SPHERE	Of beauty that attracts the mind,	
	And men should most implore.	
THE REST OF	Janus was happy, that could see°	
THE SPHERES	Two ways at once; and happier he	
	That round about him kept	235
	Watches that never slept.°	
CHORUSES	But we most happy that behold	
	Two that have turned this age to gold,	
	Making old Saturn's reign°	
	In theirs come back again.	240
	And since more th'object than the sight	
	Makes each spectator blest,	
	How are we ravished with delight,	
	That see the best.	

The masquers dance their main dance, which done, and the Queen seated   245
under the state by his majesty, the scene is again changed into a shady
wood, and a new heaven appears, differing in shape and colour from the
other. In the midst of which, Jove, sitting on an eagle, is seen hovering in
the air with a glory beyond him. And at that instant Cupid from another
part of the heaven comes flying forth, and having passed the scene, turns   250

161

soaring about like a bird; and at the same time Pallas, Circe, and her four
nymphs appear on the stage, the great chorus consisting of five and thirty
musicians standing below to assist them.

CUPID	It is but justice to torment a heart	
	That tortured thousands, and my gentle reign	255
	So wronged with acting of a tyrant's part.	
	I must restrain	
	My power abused, and right my injured train.	
JUPITER	Thou claim'st her subjects, and I claim the soil	
	As sovereign lord. The hecatombs she brings,°	260
	Though great oblations, yet deduced from spoil,°	
	Are sordid things,	
	And scent of earth: virtue pure incense brings.	
CIRCE	The gods more freedom did allow,	
	When Jove turned Io to a cow.	265
PALLAS	Are mortal creatures grown so proud	
	To tax the sky for every cloud?°	
CIRCE	Man-maid, begone!°	
PALLAS	Though I could turn thee to a stone,°	
	I'll beg thy peace—	
JUPITER	Dear daughter, cease!	270
CIRCE	Cease, dreadful Jove! Finding thy drift,	
	My bounty shall prevent thy gift:	
	This matchless pair	
	I make my heir;	
	All I possess I here resign;	275
	Thou hast thy will, and I have mine.	
JUPITER	She gives but what she cannot keep.	
CUPID	Then was the wound I gave her deep.	
BOTH	'Twas I, whose power none can withstand,	
	That opened both her heart and hand.	280

THE VALEDICTION

How would they mourn to lose ye quite,
That are so loth to say goodnight.
Yet we may plead in our excuse,
Should you these loans of love forsake,
The gods themselves such sums would take,   285
   And pay us use.

When this was past, the eagle with Jove flew up, and Cupid took his flight
through the air, after which the heavens close. Pallas and Circe return into
the scene with the nymphs and chorus; and so concluded the last
intermedium.° After which the Queen and her ladies began the revels with   290
the King and his lords, which continued all the night.

The Allegory°

In the young gentleman who Circe had first enamoured on her
person, and after, through jealousy conceived, transformed into a lion,
and again remembering her former love retransformed into his former
shape, is figured an incontinent man, that striving with his affections   295
is at last, by the power of reason, persuaded to fly from those sensual
desires which had formerly corrupted his judgement.

Circe here signifies desire in general, the which hath power on all
living creatures, and being mixed of the divine and sensible, hath
diverse effects, leading some to virtue and others to vice. She is   300
described as a queen, having in her service and subjection the
nymphs, which participate of divinity, figuring the virtues, and the
brute beasts, denoting the vices. The description of her person, of
extraordinary beauty, and sweetness of her voice, shows that desire is
moved either by sight or hearing to love virtue or the contrary; and   305
the beautiful aspect of her enchanted palace, glistering with gold and
precious ornaments, that desire cannot be moved without appearance
of beauty,° either true or false.

The dryads and naiades, nymphs of the woods and waters, that is
to say, the good spirits diffused through all the universe, are servants   310
to this queen, and live with her in all liberty and pleasure, whose
employment is to gather the most exquisite herbs and flowers of the
earth for the service of the mistress, figuring the virtues and sciences,
by which the desire of man's spirits are prepared and disposed to
good. The beasts in part transformed, who contrary to their natures   315
make her sport, represents unto us that sensual desire makes men lose
their virtue and valour, turning parasites and slaves to their brutish
affections. That these intemperate beasts of Circe's court should for
a time possess Tempe, the happy retreat of the muses and their
followers, is meant the enchantments of vicious impostures, that by   320
false means seek to extirpate the true lovers of science and virtue, to
whom of right only that place belongs.

That Divine Beauty, accompanied with a troop of stars of a happy constellation, joining with Heroic Virtue, should dissolve the enchantments, and Circe voluntarily deliver her golden rod to Minerva, is   325
meant that a divine beam coming from above, with a good inclination and a perfect habit of virtue made by the harmony of the irascible and concupiscible parts obedient to the rational and highest part of the soul, making man only a mind using the body and affections as instruments, which being his true perfection, brings him to all the   330
happiness which can be enjoyed here below.

In Heroic Virtue is figured the King's majesty, who therein transcends as far common men as they are above beasts, he truly being the prototype to all the kingdoms under his monarchy of religion, justice, and all the virtues joined together.   335

So that corporeal beauty, consisting in symmetry, colour, and certain unexpressible graces, shining in the Queen's majesty, may draw us to the contemplation of the Beauty of the soul, unto which it hath analogy.

All the verses were written by Mr Aurelian Townshend. The   340
subject and allegory of the masque, with the descriptions, and apparatus of the scenes, were invented by Inigo Jones, Surveyor of his Majesty's Work.

FINIS

The Names of the Influences

represented by

Lord Herbert	Lady Mary Villiers
Lord Ellesmere	Lady Elizabeth Cecil
Lord Rich of Holland	Lady Alice Egerton
Mr Henry Howard of Berkshire	Lady Elizabeth Feilding
Lord Grey of Stamford	Lady Frances Howard of Berkshire
Mr Philip Herbert	Lady Elizabeth Grey of Stamford
Mr Charles Cavendish	Lady Diana Cecil

The Names of the Masquers

The Queen's Majesty

Countess Oxford
Countess Carnarvon
Lady Anne Russell
Lady Anne Cavendish
Lady Mary Russell
Mrs Victory Cary
Mrs Weston

Countess Carlisle
Countess Newport
Lady Katherine Egerton
Lady Anne Feilding
Lady Howard
Mrs Paget
Mrs Sophia Cary

THOMAS CAREW
Coelum Britannicum

A Masque at
Whitehall in the Banqueting House
on Shrove Tuesday Night
the 18 of February, 1634

Non habeo ingenium; Caesar sed iussit: habebo.
Cur me posse negem, posse quod ille putat?°

The Description of the Scene

*The first thing that presented itself to the sight was a rich ornament° that
enclosed the scene, in the upper part of which were great branches of foliage
growing out of leaves and husks, with a cornice at the top; and in the
midst was placed a large compartment composed of grotesque work, wherein
were harpies° with wings and lions' claws, and their hinder parts converted* 5
*into leaves and branches. Over all was a broken frontispiece, wrought with
scrolls and mask-heads of children, and within this a table adorned with a
lesser compartment with this inscription:* COELUM BRITANNICUM.°
*The two sides of this ornament were thus ordered: first, from the ground
arose a square basement, and on the plinth stood a great vase of gold, richly* 10
*enchased and beautified with sculptures of great relief, with fruitages
hanging from the upper part. At the foot of this sat two youths naked, in their
natural colours. Each of these with one arm supported the vase, on the cover
of which stood two young women in draperies, arm in arm, the one figuring
the Glory of Princes and the other Mansuetude,° their other arms° bore up* 15
an oval, in which to the King's majesty was this impresa: *a lion with an
imperial crown on his head; the word,* Animum sub pectore forti.° *On the
other side was the like composition, but the design of the figures varied, and
in the oval on the top, being borne up by Nobility and Fecundity, was this
impresa to the Queen's majesty: a lily° growing with branches and leaves,* 20
and three lesser lilies springing out of the stem; the word, Semper inclita
virtus.° *All this ornament was heightened with gold, and for the invention
and various composition was the newest and most gracious that hath been done
in this place.*

The curtain was watchet and a pale yellow in panes, which flying up   25
on the sudden, discovered the scene,° representing old arches, old palaces,
decayed walls, parts of temples, theatres, basilicas, and thermae, *with*
confused heaps of broken columns, bases, cornices, and statues, lying as
underground, and altogether resembling the ruins of some great city of the
ancient Romans or civilized Britons. This strange prospect detained the   30
eyes of the spectators some time, when to a loud music Mercury descends.
On the upper part of his chariot stands a cock in action of crowing; his
habit was a coat of flame-colour girt to him, and a white mantle trimmed
with gold and silver; upon his head a wreath with small falls of white
feathers, a caduceus in his hand, and wings at his heels. Being come to the   35
ground he dismounts and goes up to the state.

MERCURY From the high senate of the gods, to you
   Bright glorious twins of love and majesty,
   Before whose throne three warlike nations bend
   Their willing knees, on whose imperial brows   40
   The regal circle prints no awful frowns
   To fright your subjects, but whose calmer eyes
   Shed joy and safety on their melting hearts
   That flow with cheerful loyal reverence,
   Come I, Cyllenius, Jove's ambassador:°   45
   Not, as of old, to whisper amorous tales
   Of wanton love into the glowing ear
   Of some choice beauty in this numerous train;
   Those days are fled, the rebel flame is quenched
   In heavenly breasts, the gods have sworn by Styx°   50
   Never to tempt yielding mortality
   To loose embraces. Your exemplar life°
   Hath not alone transfused a zealous heat
   Of imitation through your virtuous court,
   By whose bright blaze your palace is become   55
   The envied pattern of this underworld,
   But the aspiring flame hath kindled heaven;
   Th'immortal bosoms burn with emulous fires,
   Jove rivals your great virtues, royal sir,
   And Juno, madam, your attractive graces;   60
   He his wild lusts, her raging jealousies
   She lays aside, and through th'Olympic hall,
   As yours doth here, their great example spreads.
   And though of old, when youthful blood conspired

With his new empire, prone to heats of lust,   65
He acted incests, rapes, adulteries
On earthly beauties, which his raging queen,
Swol'n with revengeful fury, turned to beasts,
And in despite he retransformed to stars,
Till he had filled the crowded firmament   70
With his loose strumpets and their spurious race,
Where the eternal records of his shame
Shine to the world in flaming characters;
When in the crystal mirror of your reign
He viewed himself, he found his loathsome stains.°   75
And now, to expiate the infectious guilt
Of those detested luxuries, he'll chase
Th'infamous lights from their usurpèd sphere,
And drown in the Lethean flood their cursed°
Both names and memories. In whose vacant rooms   80
First you succeed, and of the wheeling orb
In the most eminent and conspicuous point,
With dazzling beams and spreading magnitude,
Shine, the bright pole star of this hemisphere.
Next, by your side in a triumphant chair,   85
And crowned with Ariadne's diadem,°
Sits the fair consort of your heart and throne.
Diffused about you, with that share of light
As they of virtue have derived from you,
He'll fix this noble train of either sex.   90
So to the British stars this lower globe
Shall owe its light, and they alone dispense
To th'world a pure refinèd influence.°

Enter Momus,° attired in a long, darkish robe all wrought over with
poniards, serpents' tongues, eyes, and ears; his beard and hair 95
parti-coloured,° and upon his head a wreath stuck with feathers, and a
porcupine in the forepart.

MOMUS By your leave, mortals. Good den, cousin Hermes; your
pardon, good my lord ambassador; I found the tables of your arms
and titles in every inn betwixt this and Olympus, where your 100
present expedition is registered, your nine thousandth, nine hundred ninety-ninth legation. I cannot reach the policy why your
master breeds so few statesmen; it suits not with his dignity that
in the whole empyreum there should not be a god fit to send on

these honourable errands but your self, who are not yet so careful   105
of his honour or your own as might become your quality, when
you are itinerant. The hosts upon the highway cry out with open
mouth upon you for supporting pilfery in your train, which,
though as you are the god of petty larceny° you might protect, yet
you know it is directly against the new orders, and opposes the   110
reformation in diameter.

MERCURY   Peace, railer, bridle your licentious tongue,
And let this presence teach you modesty.

MOMUS   Let it if it can. In the meantime I will acquaint it with my
condition. Know, gay people, that though your poets who enjoy   115
by patent a particular privilege to draw down any of the deities
from Twelfth Night till Shrove Tuesday, at what time there is
annually a most familiar intercourse between the two courts,° have
as yet never invited me to these solemnities, yet it shall appear by
my intrusion this night that I am a very considerable person upon   120
these occasions, and may most properly assist at such entertainments. My name is Momus-ap-Somnus-ap-Erebus-ap-Chaos-ap-
Demagorgon-ap-Eternity.° My offices and titles are: The Supreme
Theomastix,° Hypercritic of Manners, Protonotary° of Abuses,
Arch-Informer,° Dilator General, Universal Calumniator, Eternal   125
Plaintiff, and Perpetual Foreman of the Grand Inquest. My
privileges are an ubiquitary, circumambulatory, speculatory, inter-
rogatory, redargutory immunity over all the privy lodgings, behind
hangings, doors, curtains, through keyholes, chinks, windows,
about all venereal lobbies, sconces, or redoubts, though it be to the   130
surprise of a perdu° page or chambermaid, in and at all courts of
civil and criminal judicature, all councils, consultations, and
parliamentary assemblies, where, though I am but a woolsack god,°
and have no vote in the sanction of new laws, I have yet a
prerogative of wresting the old to any whatsoever interpretation,   135
whether it be to the behoof or prejudice of Jupiter his crown and
dignity, for or against the rights of either house of patrician or
plebeian gods. My natural qualities are to make Jove frown, Juno
pout, Mars chafe, Venus blush, Vulcan glow, Saturn quake,
Cynthia pale, Phoebus hide his face, and Mercury here take his   140
heels. My recreations are witty mischiefs, as when Saturn gelt his
father,° the Smith° caught his wife and her bravo in a net of
cobweb-iron, and Hebe° through the lubricity of the pavement
tumbling over the halfpace, presented the emblem of the forked
tree, and discovered to the tanned Ethiops the snowy cliffs of   145

Calabria with the grotto of Puteolum.° But that you may arrive at
the perfect knowledge of me by the familiar illustration of a bird
of mine own feather, old Peter Aretine,° who reduced all the
sceptres and mitres of that age tributary to his wit, was my parallel;
and Frank Rabelais° sucked much of my milk too. But your   150
modern French hospital of oratory° is mere counterfeit, an arrant
mountebank, for though fearing no other tortures than his sciatica,
he discourses of kings and queens with as little reverence as of
grooms and chambermaids, yet he wants their fang-teeth and
scorpion's tail; I mean that fellow who to add to his stature thinks   155
it a greater grace to dance on his tiptoes like a dog in a doublet°
than to walk like other men on the soles of his feet.

MERCURY No more, impertinent trifler, you disturb
The great affair with your rude, scurrilous chat.
What doth the knowledge of your abject state   160
Concern Jove's solemn message?

MOMUS Sir, by your favour, though you have a more especial
commission of employment from Jupiter, and a larger entertainment from his exchequer, yet as a freeborn god I have the liberty
to travel at mine own charges, without your pass or countenance   165
legatine.° And, that it may appear a sedulous acute observer may
know as much as a dull phlegmatic ambassador, and wears a treble
key° to unlock the mysterious ciphers of your dark secrecies, I will
discourse the politic state of heaven to this trim audience——

At this the scene changeth, and in the heaven is discovered a sphere, with   170
stars placed in their several images, borne up by a huge naked figure (only
a piece of drapery hanging over his thigh) kneeling and bowing forwards,
as if the great weight lying on his shoulders oppressed him; upon his head
a crown; by all which he might easily be known to be Atlas.

——You shall understand that Jupiter, upon the inspection of I   175
know not what virtuous precedents extant (as they say) here in this
court, but as I more probably guess, out of the consideration of the
decay of his natural abilities,° hath before a frequent convocation
of the superlunary peers in a solemn oration recanted, disclaimed,
and utterly renounced all the lascivious extravagancies and riotous   180
enormities of his forepast licentious life, and taken his oath on
Juno's breviary, religiously kissing the two-leaved book,° never
to stretch his limbs more betwixt adulterous sheets, and hath
with pathetical remonstrances exhorted, and under strict penalties

enjoined, a respective conformity in the several subordinate deities. 185
And because the libertines of antiquity, the ribald poets, to
perpetuate the memory and example of their triumphs over
chastity to all future imitation, have in their immortal songs
celebrated the martyrdom of those strumpets under the persecu-
tion of the wives, and devolved to posterity the pedigrees of their 190
whores, bawds, and bastards, it is therefore by the authority
aforesaid enacted, that this whole army of constellations be immediately disbanded and cashiered, so to remove all imputation of
impiety from the celestial spirits, and all lustful influences upon
terrestrial bodies; and consequently, that there be an inquisition 195
erected° to expunge in the ancient, and suppress in the modern
and succeeding poems and pamphlets all past, present, and future
mention of those abjured heresies, and to take particular notice of
all ensuing incontinences, and punish them in their high commission court. Am not I in election to be a tall statesman, think 200
you, that can repeat a passage at a council table thus punctually?
MERCURY I shun in vain the importunity
With which this snarler vexeth all the gods;
Jove cannot scape him. Well, what else from heaven?
MOMUS Heaven! Heaven is no more the place it was; a cloister of 205
Carthusians, a monastery of converted gods. Jove is grown old and
fearful, apprehends a subversion of his empire, and doubts lest
Fate should introduce a legal succession in the legitimate heir by
repossessing the Titanian line,° and hence springs all this innovation. We have had new orders° read in the presence chamber by 210
the vice-president of Parnassus, too strict to be observed long.
Monopolies are called in, sophistication of wares° punished, and
rates imposed on commodities. Injunctions are gone out to the
nectar brewers for the purging of the heavenly beverage of a
narcotic weed which hath rendered the Ideas confused in the 215
divine intellects, and reducing it to the composition used in
Saturn's reign. Edicts are made for the restoring of decayed
housekeeping, prohibiting the repair of families to the metropolis;
but this did endanger an Amazonian mutiny, till the females put
on a more masculine resolution of soliciting businesses in their own 220
persons, and leaving their husbands at home for stallions of
hospitality.° Bacchus hath commanded all taverns to be shut, and
no liquor drawn after ten at night. Cupid must go no more so
scandalously naked, but is enjoined to make him breeches, though
of his mother's petticoats. Ganymede° is forbidden the bedcham- 225

ber, and must only minister in public. The gods must keep no
pages nor grooms of their chamber under the age of twenty-five,
and those provided of a competent stock of beard. Pan may not
pipe, nor Proteus juggle, but by especial permission. Vulcan was
brought to an *ore tenus*° and fined, for driving in a plate of iron   230
into one of the sun's chariot wheels and frost-nailing his horses
upon the fifth of November° last, for breach of a penal statute
prohibiting work upon holidays, that being the annual celebrations
of the Gigantomachy.° In brief, the whole state of the hierarchy
suffers a total reformation, especially in the point of reciprocation   235
of conjugal affection. Venus hath confessed all her adulteries, and
is received to grace by her husband, who, conscious of the great
disparity betwixt her perfections and his deformities,° allows those
levities as an equal counterpoise; but it is the prettiest spectacle to
see her stroking with her ivory hand his collied cheeks, and with   240
her snowy fingers combing his sooty beard. Jupiter too begins to
learn to lead his own wife—I left him practising in the milky
way°—and there is no doubt of an universal obedience, where the
Lawgiver himself in his own person observes his decrees so
punctually; who, besides, to eternize the memory of that great   245
example of matrimonial union which he derives from hence, hath
on his bedchamber door and ceiling, fretted with stars, in capital
letters engraven the inscription of CARLOMARIA. This is as
much, I am sure, as either your knowledge or instructions can
direct you to, which I, having in a blunt round tale, without   250
state-formality, politic inferences, or suspected rhetorical elegan-
cies already delivered, you may now dexterously proceed to the
second part of your charge, which is the raking of yon heavenly
sparks up in the embers, or reducing the ethereal lights to their
primitive opacity and gross dark subsistence. They are all   255
unriveted from the sphere, and hang loose in their sockets, where
they but attend the waving of your caduce, and immediately they
reinvest their pristine shapes, and appear before you in their own
natural deformities.

MERCURY Momus, thou shalt prevail. For since thy bold   260
Intrusion hath inverted my resolves,
I must obey necessity, and thus turn
My face to breathe the Thunderer's just decree
'Gainst this adulterate sphere, which first I purge
Of loathsome monsters and misshapen forms.   265
Down from her azure concave thus I charm

The Lernean Hydra, the rough unlicked Bear,°
The watchful Dragon, the storm-boding Whale,
The Centaur, the horned goatfish Capricorn,°
The snake-haired Gorgon, and fierce Sagittar: 270
Divested of your gorgeous starry robes,
Fall from the circling orb, and ere you suck
Fresh venom in, measure this happy earth;
Then to the fens, caves, forests, deserts, seas,
Fly, and resume your native qualities.   275

*They dance in those monstrous shapes the first antimasque, of natural
deformity.*

MOMUS Are not these fine companions, trim playfellows for the
  deities? Yet these and their fellows have made up all our conversation for some thousands of years. Do not you fair ladies   280
  acknowledge yourselves deeply engaged now to those poets your
  servants, that in the height of commendation have raised your
  beauties to a parallel with such exact proportions, or at least ranked
  you in their spruce society? Hath not the consideration of these
  inhabitants rather frighted your thoughts utterly from the contem- 285
  plation of the place? But now that those heavenly mansions are to
  be void, you that shall hereafter be found unlodged will become
  inexcusable, especially since virtue alone shall be sufficient title,
  fine, and rent. Yet if there be a lady not competently stocked that
  way, she shall not on the instant utterly despair, if she carry a   290
  sufficient pawn of handsomeness; for however the letter of the law
  runs, Jupiter, notwithstanding his age and present austerity, will
  never refuse to stamp beauty, and make it current with his own
  impression.° But to such as are destitute of both, I can afford but
  small encouragement. Proceed, cousin Mercury; what follows?   295
MERCURY Look up, and mark where the bright zodiac
  Hangs like a belt about the breast of heaven;
  On the right shoulder, like a flaming jewel,
  His shell with nine rich topazes adorned,
  Lord of this Tropic, sits the scalding Crab.   300
  He, when the sun gallops in full career
  His annual race, his ghastly claws upreared,
  Frights at the confines of the torrid zone
  The fiery team, and proudly stops their course,
  Making a solstice, till the fierce steeds learn   305
  His backward paces, and so retrograde

Post downhill to th'opposèd Capricorn.°
Thus I depose him from his lofty throne:°
Drop from the sky, into the briny flood,
There teach thy motion to the ebbing sea;   310
But let those fires that beautified thy shell
Take human shapes, and the disorder show
Of thy regressive paces here below.

The second antimasque is danced in retrograde paces, expressing obliquity
in motion.   315

MOMUS This crab, I confess, did ill become the heavens; but there
   is another° that more infests the earth, and makes such a solstice
   in the politer arts and sciences as they have not been observed for
   many ages to have made any sensible advance. Could you but lead
   the learned squadrons with a masculine resolution past this point 320
   of retrogradation, it were a benefit to mankind worthy the power
   of a god, and to be paid with altars; but that not being the work
   of this night, you may pursue your purposes. What now succeeds?
MERCURY Vice, that unbodied in the appetite
   Erects his throne, hath yet, in bestial shapes,   325
   Branded by nature with the character
   And distinct stamp of some peculiar ill,
   Mounted the sky, and fixed his trophies there:
   As fawning flattery in the little Dog,
   I' th'bigger, churlish murmur; cowardice   330
   I' th'timorous Hare, ambition in the Eagle,
   Rapine and avarice in th'adventurous Ship
   That sailed to Colchis for the Golden Fleece;
   Drunken distemper in the Goblet flows,
   I' th'Dart and Scorpion biting calumny,   335
   In Hercules and the Lion furious rage,
   Vain ostentation in Cassiope.
   All these I to eternal exile doom,
   But to this place their emblemed vices summon,
   Clad in those proper figures by which best   340
   Their incorporeal nature is expressed.

The third antimasque is danced of these several vices, expressing the
deviation from virtue.

MOMUS From henceforth it shall be no more said in the proverb,
   when you would express a riotous assembly, that hell, but heaven 345
   is broke loose. This was an arrant gaol-delivery; all the prisons of

your great cities could not have vomited more corrupt matter. But, cousin Cyllenius, in my judgement it is not safe that these infectious persons should wander here to the hazard of this island; they threatened less danger when they were nailed to the firmament. I should conceive it a very discreet course, since they are provided of a tall vessel of their own ready rigged, to embark them all together in that good ship called the Argo, and send them to the plantation in New England,° which hath purged more virulent humours from the politic body than guaiacum and all the West Indian drugs have from the natural bodies of this kingdom. Can you devise how to dispose them better?

MERCURY They cannot breathe this pure and temperate air
Where virtue lives, but will with hasty flight
'Mongst fogs and vapours seek unsound abodes.
Fly after them from your usurpèd seats,
You foul remainders of that viperous brood.
Let not a star of the luxurious race
With his loose blaze stain the sky's crystal face.

All the stars are quenched, and the sphere darkened.
Before the entry of every antimasque the stars in those figures in the sphere which they were to represent were extinct, so as, by the end of the antimasques, in the sphere no more stars were seen.

MOMUS Here is a total eclipse of the eighth sphere,° which neither Booker, Allestree,° nor any of you prognosticators, no, nor their great master Tycho° were aware of. But yet in my opinion there were some innocent and some generous constellations, that might have been reserved for noble uses: as the Scales and Swords to adorn the statue of Justice, since she resides here on earth only in picture and effigy. The Eagle had been a fit present for the Germans, in regard their bird hath mewed most of her feathers lately.° The Dolphin° too had been most welcome to the French, and then had you but clapped Perseus on his Pegasus, brandishing his sword, the Dragon yawning on his back under the horse's feet, with Python's dart through his throat, there had been a divine St George for this nation.° But since you have improvidently shuffled them altogether, it now rests only that we provide an immediate succession, and to that purpose I will instantly proclaim a free election.

Oyez, Oyez, Oyez!° By the father of the gods, and the king of men: Whereas we, having observed a very commendable practice

350

355

360

365

370

375

380

385

175

taken into frequent use by the princes of these latter ages, of perpetuating the memory of their famous enterprises, sieges, battles, victories, in picture, sculpture, tapestry, embroideries, and other manufactures, wherewith they have embellished their public 390 palaces, and taken into our more distinct and serious consideration the particular Christmas hangings° of the guard chamber of this court, wherein the naval victory of '88° is to the eternal glory of this nation exactly delineated; and whereas we likewise, out of a prophetical imitation of this so laudable custom, did for many 395 thousand years before adorn and beautify the eighth room of our celestial mansion, commonly called the Star Chamber,° with the military adventures, stratagems, achievements, feats, and defeats performed in our own person, whilst yet our standard was erected and we a combatant in the amorous warfare: it hath notwithstand- 400 ing, after mature deliberation and long debate, held first in our own inscrutable bosom° and afterwards communicated with our Privy Council, seemed meet to our omnipotency, for causes to ourself best known, to unfurnish and disarray our foresaid Star Chamber of all those ancient constellations which have for so many 405 ages been sufficiently notorious, and to admit into their vacant places such persons only as shall be qualified with exemplar virtue and eminent desert, there to shine in indelible characters of glory to all posterity. It is therefore our divine will and pleasure, voluntarily and out of our own free and proper motion, mere grace, 410 and special favour, by these presents to specify and declare to all our loving people, that it shall be lawful for any person whatsoever that conceiveth him or her self to be really endued with any heroical virtue or transcendent merit worthy so high a calling and dignity, to bring their several pleas and pretences before our right 415 trusty and well-beloved cousin and counsellor, Don Mercury, and god Momus, etc., our peculiar delegates for that affair, upon whom we have transferred an absolute power to conclude, and determine without appeal or revocation, accordingly as to their wisdoms it shall in such cases appear behoveful and expedient. Given at our 420 palace in Olympus the first day of the first month in the first year of the Reformation.

Plutus enters; an old man full of wrinkles, a bald head, a thin white beard, spectacles on his nose, with a bunched back and attired in a robe of cloth of gold. 425
   Plutus appears.

MERCURY Who's this appears?

MOMUS This is a subterranean fiend, Plutus, in this dialect termed
    Riches or the god of gold; a poison, hid by Providence in the
    bottom of seas and navel of the earth from man's discovery, where,   430
    if the seeds begun to sprout above ground, the excrescence was
    carefully guarded by dragons, yet at last by human curiosity
    brought to light, to their own destruction; this being the true
    Pandora's box whence issued all those mischiefs that now fill the
    universe.   435

PLUTUS That I prevent the message of the gods
    Thus with my haste, and not attend their summons,
    Which ought in justice call me to the place
    I now require of right, is not alone
    To show the just precedence that I hold   440
    Before all earthly, next the immortal powers,
    But to exclude the hope of partial grace
    In all pretenders, who, since I descend
    To equal trial, must by my example,
    Waiving your favour, claim by sole desert.°   445
      If Virtue must inherit, she's my slave.
    I lead her captive in a golden chain
    About the world; she takes her form and being
    From my creation; and those barren seeds
    That drop from heaven, if I not cherish them   450
    With my distilling dews and fotive heat,
    They know no vegetation, but, exposed
    To blasting winds of freezing poverty,
    Or not shoot forth at all, or budding, wither.
    Should I proclaim the daily sacrifice   455
    Brought to my temples by the toiling rout,
    Not of the fat and gore of abject beasts,
    But human sweat and blood poured on my altars,
    I might provoke the envy of the gods.
    Turn but your eyes and mark the busy world   460
    Climbing steep mountains for the sparkling stone,
    Piercing the centre for the shining ore,
    And the ocean's bosom to rake pearly sands,
    Crossing the torrid and the frozen zones
    'Midst rocks and swallowing gulfs for gainful trade,   465
    And through opposing swords, fire, murdering cannon,
    Scaling the wallèd town for precious spoils.

Plant in the passage to your heavenly seats
These horrid dangers, and then see who dares
Advance his desperate foot. Yet am I sought,   470
And oft in vain, through these and greater hazards.
I could discover how your deities
Are for my sake slighted, despised, abused;
Your temples, shrines, altars, and images
Uncovered, rifled, robbed, and disarrayed   475
By sacrilegious hands. Yet is this treasure
To th'golden mountain where I sit adored
With superstitious solemn rites conveyed,
And becomes sacred there, the sordid wretch
Not daring touch the consecrated ore,   480
Or with profane hands lessen the bright heap.
But this might draw your anger down on mortals
For rendering me the homage due to you.
Yet what is said may well express my power
Too great for earth, and only fit for heaven.   485
    Now, for your pastime, view the naked root
Which in the dirty earth and base mould drowned
Sends forth this precious plant and golden fruit.
You lusty swains, that to your grazing flocks
Pipe amorous roundelays, you toiling hinds   490
That barb the fields and to your merry teams
Whistle your passions, and you mining moles
That in the bowels of your mother earth
Dwell the eternal burden of her womb,
Cease from your labours when Wealth bids you play;   495
Sing, dance, and keep a cheerful holiday.

*They dance the fourth antimasque, consisting of country people, music, and
measures.*

MERCURY Plutus, the gods know and confess your power,
    Which feeble virtue seldom can resist,   500
Stronger than towers of brass, or chastity.
Jove knew you when he courted Danaë,°
And Cupid wears you on that arrow's head
That still prevails. But the gods keep their thrones
To install Virtue, not her enemies.   505
They dread thy force, which even themselves have felt—
Witness Mount Ida, where the martial maid
And frowning Juno did to mortal eyes

178

Naked, for gold, their sacred bodies show.°
Therefore for ever be from heaven banished.   510
But since with toil from undiscovered worlds
Thou art brought hither, where thou first didst breathe
The thirst of empire into regal breasts,
And frightedst quiet Peace from her meek throne,
Filling the world with tumult, blood, and war,   515
Follow the camps of the contentious earth,
And be the conqueror's slave; but he that can
Or conquer thee, or give thee Virtue's stamp,
Shall shine in heaven a pure immortal lamp.

MOMUS Nay, stay, and take my benediction along with you. I could,   520
being here a co-judge, like others in my place, now that you are
condemned, either rail at you or break jests upon you; but I rather
choose to loose a word of good counsel, and entreat you to be more
careful in your choice of company, for you are always found either
with misers, that not use you at all, or with fools, that know not   525
how to use you well. Be not hereafter so reserved and coy to men
of worth and parts, and so you shall gain such credit as at the next
sessions you may be heard with better success. But till you are thus
reformed, I pronounce this positive sentence: that wheresoever you
shall choose to abide, your society shall add no credit or reputation   530
to the party, nor your discontinuance or total absence be matter of
disparagement to any man; and whosoever shall hold a contrary
estimation of you shall be condemned to wear perpetual motley,
unless he recant his opinion. Now you may void the court.

Poenia° enters, a woman of a pale colour, large brims of a hat upon her   535
head, through which her hair started up like a fury; her robe was of a dark
colour full of patches; about one of her hands was tied a chain of iron, to
which was fastened a weighty stone, which she bore up under her arms.
Poenia enters.   540

MERCURY What creature's this?

MOMUS The antipodes to the other—they move like two buckets, or
as two nails drive out one another;° if Riches depart, Poverty will
enter.

POVERTY I nothing doubt, great and immortal powers,   545
But that the place your wisdom hath denied
My foe, your justice will confer on me,
Since that which renders him incapable
Proves a strong plea for me. I could pretend,
Even in these rags, a larger sovereignty   550

Than gaudy Wealth in all his pomp can boast.
For mark how few they are that share the world.
The numerous armies, and the swarming ants
That fight and toil for them, are all my subjects;
They take my wages, wear my livery.   555
Invention, too, and Wit are both my creatures,
And the whole race of Virtue is my offspring.
As many mischiefs issue from my womb,
And those as mighty, as proceed from gold.
Oft o'er his throne I wave my awful sceptre,   560
And in the bowels of his state command,
When 'midst his heaps of coin and hills of gold
I pine and starve the avaricious fool.
But I decline those titles, and lay claim
To heaven, by right of divine Contemplation.   565
She is my darling; I in my soft lap,
Free from disturbing cares, bargains, accounts,
Leases, rents, stewards, and the fear of thieves,
That vex the rich, nurse her in calm repose,
And with her all the virtues speculative,   570
Which, but with me, find no secure retreat.
   For entertainment of this hour, I'll call
A race of people to this place that live
At nature's charge, and not importune heaven
To chain the winds up or keep back the storms,   575
To stay the thunder, or forbid the hail
To thresh the unreaped ear; but to all weathers,
Both chilling frost and scalding sun, expose
Their equal face. Come forth, my swarthy train,
In this fair circle dance, and as you move,   580
Mark and foretell happy events of love.

They dance the fifth antimasque of gypsies.

MOMUS I cannot but wonder that your perpetual conversation with
   poets and philosophers hath furnished you with no more logic, or
   that you should think to impose upon us so gross an inference, as   585
   because Plutus and you are contrary, therefore whatsoever is
   denied of the one must be true of the other; as if it should follow
   of necessity, because he is not Jupiter, you are. No, I give you to
   know, I am better versed in cavils with the gods than to swallow
   such a fallacy; for though you two cannot be together in one place, 590

yet there are many places that may be without you both, and such
is heaven, where neither of you are likely to arrive. Therefore let
me advise you to marry your self to Content, and beget sage
apophthegms and goodly moral sentences in dispraise of Riches,
and contempt of the world.   595
MERCURY Thou dost presume too much, poor needy wretch,
  To claim a station in the firmament
  Because thy humble cottage, or thy tub°
  Nurses some lazy or pedantic virtue
  In the cheap sunshine, or by shady springs   600
  With roots and pot-herbs, where thy rigid hand,
  Tearing those human passions from the mind
  Upon whose stocks fair blooming virtues flourish,
  Degradeth nature, and benumbeth sense,
  And Gorgon-like turns active men to stone.   605
  We not require the dull society
  Of your necessitated temperance,
  Or that unnatural stupidity
  That knows nor joy nor sorrow, nor your forced
  Falsely exalted passive fortitude   610
  Above the active. This low, abject brood
  That fix their seats in mediocrity
  Become your servile minds, but we advance
  Such virtues only as admit excess;
  Brave bounteous acts, regal magnificence,   615
  All-seeing prudence, magnanimity
  That knows no bound, and that heroic virtue
  For which antiquity hath left no name,
  But patterns only, such as Hercules,
  Achilles, Theseus. Back to thy loathed cell,   620
  And when thou seest the new enlightened sphere,
  Study to know but what those worthies were.

*Tiche° enters, her head bald behind, and one great lock before, wings at
her shoulders, and in her hand a wheel; her upper parts naked, and the
skirt of her garment wrought all over with crowns, sceptres, books, and*   625
such other things as express both her greatest and smallest gifts.

MOMUS See where Dame Fortune comes; you may know her by her
  wheel and that veil over her eyes, with which she hopes like a
  seeled pigeon to mount above the clouds and perch in the eighth
  sphere. Listen, she begins.   630

FORTUNE I come not here, you gods, to plead the right
    By which antiquity assigned my deity,
    Though no peculiar station 'mongst the stars,
    Yet general power to rule their influence;
    Or boast the title of omnipotent   635
    Ascribed me then, by which I rivalled Jove,
    Since you have cancelled all those old records;
    But confident in my good cause and merit,
    Claim a succession in the vacant orb.
    For since Astraea fled to heaven, I sit°   640
    Her deputy on earth; I hold her scales,
    And weigh men's fates out, who have made me blind
    Because themselves want eyes to see my causes,
    Call me inconstant 'cause my works surpass
    The shallow fathom of their human reason.   645
    Yet here, like blinded Justice, I dispense
    With my impartial hands their constant lots,
    And if desertless impious men engross
    My best rewards, the fault is yours, you gods,
    That scant your graces to mortality,   650
    And, niggards of your good, scarce spare the world
    One virtuous, for a thousand wicked men.
    It is no error to confer dignity,
    But to bestow it on a vicious man.
    I gave the dignity, but you made the vice;   655
    Make you men good, and I'll make good men happy.
    That Plutus is refused dismays me not;
    He is my drudge, and the external pomp
    In which he decks the world proceeds from me,
    Not him—like harmony, that not resides   660
    In strings or notes, but in the hand and voice.
    The revolutions of empires, states,
    Sceptres, and crowns are but my game and sport,
    Which, as they hang on the events of war,
    So those depend upon my turning wheel.   665
      You warlike squadrons, who in battles joined
    Dispute the right of kings, which I decide,
    Present the model of that martial frame
    By which, when crowns are staked, I rule the game.

They dance the sixth antimasque, being the representation of a battle.   670

MOMUS Madam, I should censure you *pro falso clamore*, for prefer-
ring a scandalous cross-bill° of recrimination against the gods; but
your blindness shall excuse you. Alas! what would it advantage you
if virtue were as universal as vice is? It would only follow that, as
the world now exclaims upon you for exalting the vicious, it would   675
then rail as fast at you for depressing the virtuous. So they would
still keep their tune, though you changed their ditty.

MERCURY The mists in which future events are wrapped,
  That oft succeed beside the purposes
  Of him that works, his dull eyes not discerning   680
  The first great cause, offered thy clouded shape
  To his enquiring search; so in the dark
  The groping world first found thy deity,
  And gave thee rule over contingencies,
  Which, to the piercing eye of Providence,   685
  Being fixed and certain, where past and to come
  Are always present, thou dost disappear,
  Losest thy being, and art not at all.
  Be thou then only a deluding phantom,
  At best a blind guide, leading blinder fools;   690
  Who, would they but survey their mutual wants
  And help each other, there were left no room
  For thy vain aid. Wisdom, whose strong-built plots
  Leave nought to hazard, mocks thy futile power.
  Industrious labour drags thee by the locks,   695
  Bound to his toiling car, and not attending
  Till thou dispense, reaches his own reward.
  Only the lazy sluggard yawning lies
  Before thy threshold, gaping for thy dole,
  And licks the easy hand that feeds his sloth.   700
  The shallow, rash, and unadvisèd man
  Makes thee his stale, disburdens all the follies
  Of his misguided actions on thy shoulders.
  Vanish from hence, and seek those idiots out
  That thy fantastic godhead hath allowed,   705
  And rule that giddy, superstitious crowd.

*Hedone° (Pleasure) a young woman with a smiling face, in a light, lascivious
habit, adorned with silver and gold; her temples crowned with a garland of
roses, and over that a rainbow circling her head down to her shoulders.*
  Hedone enters.   710

MERCURY What wanton's this?

MOMUS This is the sprightly Lady Hedone, a merry gamester; this
    people call her Pleasure.

PLEASURE The reasons, equal judges, here alleged
    By the dismissed pretenders, all concur   715
    To strengthen my just title to the sphere.
    Honour, or Wealth, or the contempt of both,
    Have in themselves no simple real good,
    But as they are the means to purchase Pleasure,
    The paths that lead to my delicious palace.   720
    They for my sake, I for mine own am prized.
    Beyond me nothing is; I am the goal,
    The journey's end, to which the sweating world
    And wearied nature travels. For this, the best
    And wisest sect of all philosophers°   725
    Made me the seat of sùpreme happiness.
    And though some, more austere, upon my ruins
    Did, to the prejudice of nature, raise
    Some petty low-built virtues, 'twas because
    They wanted wings to reach my soaring pitch.   730
    Had they been princes born, themselves had proved
    Of all mankind the most luxurious.
    For those delights, which to their low condition
    Were obvious, they with greedy appetite
    Sucked and devoured; from offices of state,   735
    From cares of family, children, wife, hopes, fears
    Retired, the churlish Cynic in his tub
    Enjoyed those pleasures which his tongue defamed.
    Nor am I ranked 'mongst the superfluous goods.
    My necessary offices preserve   740
    Each single man, and propagate the kind.
    Then am I universal as the light,
    Or common air we breathe. And since I am
    The general desire of all mankind,
    Civil felicity must reside in me.   745
    Tell me what rate my choicest pleasures bear,
    When for the short delight of a poor draught
    Of cheap cold water, great Lysimachus
    Rendered himself slave to the Scythians.°
    Should I the curious structure of my seats,   750
    The art and beauty of my several objects,

Rehearse at large, your bounties would reserve
For every sense a proper constellation.
But I present their persons to your eyes.
   Come forth, my subtle organs of delight,   755
With changing figures please the curious eye,
And charm the ear with moving harmony.

They dance the seventh antimasque of the five senses.

MERCURY Bewitching siren, gilded rottenness,
   Thou hast with cunning artifice displayed   760
   The enamelled outside and the honeyed verge
   Of the fair cup where deadly poison lurks.
   Within, a thousand sorrows dance the round,
   And like a shell, Pain circles thee without;
   Grief is the shadow waiting on thy steps,   765
   Which, as thy joys 'gin towards their west decline,
   Doth to a giant's spreading form extend
   Thy dwarfish stature. Thou thyself art Pain,
   Greedy, intense Desire; and the keen edge
   Of thy fierce appetite oft strangles thee   770
   And cuts thy slender thread. But still the terror
   And apprehension of thy hasty end
   Mingles with gall thy most refinèd sweets.
   Yet thy Circean charms transform the world.°
   Captains, that have resisted war and death,   775
   Nations, that over Fortune have triumphed,
   Are by thy magic made effeminate.
   Empires, that knew no limits but the poles,
   Have in thy wanton lap melted away.
   Thou wert the author of the first excess   780
   That drew this reformation on the gods.
   Canst thou then dream those powers that from heaven have
   Banished th'effect, will there enthrone the cause?
   To thy voluptuous den fly, witch, from hence;
   There dwell, for ever drowned in brutish sense.   785
MOMUS I concur, and am grown so weary of these tedious pleadings
   as I'll pack up too and be gone. Besides, I see a crowd of other
   suitors pressing hither; I'll stop 'em, take their petitions, and prefer
   'em above; and as I came in bluntly without knocking, and nobody
   bid me welcome, so I'll depart as abruptly without taking leave,   790
   and bid nobody farewell.

[*Exit Momus*]°

MERCURY [*To Henrietta Maria*] These, with forced reasons and
    strained arguments,
Urge vain pretences, whilst your actions plead,
And with a silent importunity   795
Awake the drowsy justice of the gods
To crown your deeds with immortality.
The growing titles of your ancestors,
These nations' glorious acts, joined to the stock
Of your own royal virtues, and the clear   800
Reflex they take from the imitation
Of your famed court, make Honour's story full,
And have to that secure fixed state advanced
Both you and them, to which the labouring world,
Wading through streams of blood, sweats to aspire.   805
Those ancient worthies of these famous isles
That long have slept, in fresh and lively shapes
Shall straight appear, where you shall see yourself
Circled with modern heroes, who shall be
In act whatever elder times can boast   810
Noble or great, as they in prophecy
Were all but what you are. Then shall you see
The sacred hand of bright Eternity
Mould you to stars, and fix you in the sphere.
To you, your royal half, to them she'll join   815
Such of this train as with industrious steps
In the fair prints your virtuous feet have made,
Though with unequal paces, follow you.
This is decreed by Jove, which my return
Shall see performed. But first behold the rude   820
And old abiders here, and in them view
The point from which your full perfections grew.
You naked, ancient, wild inhabitants
That breathed this air and pressed this flowery earth,
Come from those shades where dwells eternal night,   825
And see what wonders time hath brought to light.

*Atlas and the sphere vanisheth, and a new scene appears of mountains,
whose eminent height exceed the clouds which passed beneath them; the
lower parts were wild and woody. Out of this place comes forth a more*

grave antimasque of Picts, the natural inhabitants of this isle, ancient   830
Scots and Irish; these dance a Pyrrhica,° or martial dance.

    *When this antimasque was past, there began to arise out of the earth the
top of a hill, which by little and little grew to be a huge mountain° that
covered all the scene. The under-part of this was wild and craggy, and
above somewhat more pleasant and flourishing; about the middle part*   835
*of this mountain were seated the three kingdoms of England, Scotland,
and Ireland, all richly attired in regal habits appropriated to the
several nations, with crowns on their heads, and each of them bearing
the ancient arms of the kingdoms they represented. At a distance above
these sat a young man in a white embroidered robe, upon his fair hair an*   840
*olive garland with wings at his shoulders, and holding in his hand a
cornucopia filled with corn and fruits, representing the Genius of these
kingdoms.*

THE FIRST SONG

GENIUS   Raise from these rocky cliffs your heads,
                             Brave sons, and see where Glory spreads   845
                             Her glittering wings, where Majesty,
                             Crowned with sweet smiles, shoots from
                                 her eye
                             Diffusive joy, where Good and Fair
                             United sit in Honour's chair.
                             Call forth your agèd priests and crystal streams   850
                             To warm their hearts and waves in these bright
                             beams.

KINGDOMS *1.*   From your consecrated woods,
                             Holy Druids
         2.   Silver floods,
                             From your channels fringed with flowers,
         3.   Hither move; forsake your bowers   855
         1.   Strewed with hallowed oaken leaves,
                             Decked with flags and sedgy sheaves,
                             And behold a wonder.
         3.   Say,
                             What do your duller eyes survey?
CHORUS OF   We see at once in dead of night   860
DRUIDS AND   A sun appear, and yet a bright
RIVERS   Noonday, springing from star-light.
GENIUS   Look up, and see the darkened sphere
                             Deprived of light; her eyes shine there;

187

CHORUS		These are more sparkling than those were.	865
KINGDOMS	*1.*	These shed a nobler influence,	
	2.	These by a pure intelligence	
		Of more transcendent virtue move;	
	3.	These first feel, then kindle love.	
	1,2.	From the bosoms they inspire	870
		These receive a mutual fire;	
	1,2,3.	And where their flames impure return,	
		These can quench as well as burn.	

GENIUS   Here the fair victorious eyes
Make Worth only Beauty's prize;   875
Here the hand of Virtue ties
'Bout the heart love's amorous chain;
Captives triumph, vassals reign
And none live here but the slain.

CHORUS   These are th'Hesperian bowers, whose fair
                   trees bear   880
Rich golden fruit, and yet no dragon near.°

GENIUS   Then from your imprisoning womb,
Which is the cradle and the tomb
Of British worthies (fair sons) send
A troop of heroes, that may lend   885
Their hands to ease this loaden grove,
And gather the ripe fruits of love.

KINGDOMS *1,2,3.*   Open thy stony entrails wide,
And break old Atlas, that the pride
Of three famed kingdoms may be spied.   890

CHORUS   Pace forth thou mighty British Hercules,
With thy choice band, for only thou and these
May revel here, in Love's Hesperides.

At this the under-part of the rock opens, and out of a cave are seen to
come the masquers, richly attired like ancient heroes, the colours yellow,   895
embroidered with silver; their antique helms curiously wrought, and great
plumes on the top; before them a troop of young lords and noblemen's sons
bearing torches of virgin wax; these were apparelled after the old British
fashion in white coats embroidered with silver, girt, and full gathered, cut
square-collared, and round caps on their heads, with a white feather   900
wreathen about them. First these dance with their lights in their hands,
after which the masquers descend into the room and dance their entry.

The dance being past, there appears in the further part of the heaven coming down a pleasant cloud, bright and transparent, which, coming softly downwards before the upper part of the mountain, embraceth the 905 *Genius, but so as through it all his body is seen; and then rising again with a gentle motion bears up the Genius of the three kingdoms, and being past the airy region, pierceth the heavens and is no more seen. At that instant the rock with the three kingdoms on it sinks, and it is hidden in the earth. This strange spectacle gave great cause of admiration, but* 910 *especially how so huge a machine, and of that great height, should come from under the stage, which was but six foot high.*

THE SECOND SONG

KINGDOMS *1.*	Here are shapes formed fit for heaven;	
2.	These move gracefully and even;	
3.	Here the air and paces meet	915
	So just, as if the skilful feet	
	Had struck the viols. *1, 2, 3.* So the ear	
	Might the tuneful footing hear.	
CHORUS	And had the music silent been,	
	The eye a moving tune had seen.	920
GENIUS	These must in the unpeopled sky	
	Succeed, and govern Destiny.	
	Jove is temp'ring purer fire,	
	And will with brighter flames attire	
	These glorious lights. I must ascend	925
	And help the work.	
KINGDOMS	*1.* We cannot lend	
	Heaven so much treasure. *2.* Nor that pay,	
	But rendering what it takes away.	
3.	Why should they that here can move	
	So well, be ever fixed above?	930
CHORUS	Or be to one eternal posture tied,	
	That can into such various figures slide?	
GENIUS	Jove shall not, to enrich the sky,	
	Beggar the earth; their fame shall fly	
	From hence alone, and in the sphere	935
	Kindle new stars, whilst they rest here.	
KINGDOMS *1,2,3.*	How can the shaft stay in the quiver,	
	Yet hit the mark?	
GENIUS	Did not the river	
	Eridanus° the grace acquire	

	In heaven and earth to flow;	940
	Above in streams of golden fire,	
	In silver waves below?	
KINGDOMS *1,2,3.*	But shall not we, now thou art gone,	
	Who wert our nature, wither,	
	Or break that triple union	945
	Which thy soul held together?	
GENIUS	In Concord's pure, immortal spring	
	I will my force renew,	
	And a more active virtue bring	
	At my return. Adieu.	950
KINGDOMS	Adieu. CHORUS Adieu.	

The masquers dance their main dance; which done, the scene again is varied into a new and pleasant prospect, clean differing from all the other; the nearest part showing a delicious garden with several walks and parterres set round with low trees, and on the sides against these walks 955 *were fountains and grots, and in the furthest part a palace, from whence went high walks upon arches, and above them open terraces planted with cypress trees, and all this together was composed of such ornaments as might express a princely villa.*

From hence the chorus, descending into the room, goes up to the state. 960

THE THIRD SONG
BY THE CHORUS GOING UP TO THE QUEEN

Whilst thus the darlings of the gods
  From Honour's temple to the shrine
Of Beauty and these sweet abodes
  Of Love we guide, let thy divine
Aspects (bright Deity) with fair   965
And halcyon beams, becalm the air.

We bring Prince Arthur, or the brave
  St George himself (great Queen) to you,
You'll soon discern him; and we have
  A Guy, a Bevis, or some true°   970
Round-Table knight as ever fought
For lady, to each beauty brought.

Plant in their martial hands, war's seat,
  Your peaceful pledges of warm snow,
And, if a speaking touch, repeat   975

In love's known language tales of woe;
Say, in soft whispers of the palm,
As eyes shoot darts, so lips shed balm.

For though you seem like captives, led
    In triumph by the foe away,   980
Yet on the conqu'rors neck you tread,
    And the fierce victor proves your prey.
What heart is then secure from you,
That can, though vanquished, yet subdue?

The song done, they retire, and the masquers dance the revels with the 985
ladies, which continued a great part of the night.
    The revels being past, and the King's majesty seated under the state by
the Queen, for conclusion to this masque there appears, coming forth from
one of the sides as moving by a gentle wind, a great cloud, which arriving
at the middle of the heaven, stayeth. This was of several colours, and so 990
great that it covered the whole scene. Out of the further part of the heaven
begins to break forth two other clouds, differing in colour and shape; and
being fully discovered there appeared sitting in one of them Religion, Truth,
and Wisdom. Religion was apparelled in white, and part of her face was
covered with a light veil, in one hand a book, and in the other a flame of 995
fire. Truth in a watchet robe, a sun upon her forehead and bearing in her
hand a palm; Wisdom in a mantle wrought with eyes and hands, golden
rays about her head, and Apollo's cithera in her hand. In the other cloud
sat Concord, Government, and Reputation. The habit of Concord was
carnation, bearing in her hand a little faggot of sticks bound together, and 1000
on the top of it a heart, and a garland of corn on her head. Government
was figured in a coat of armour, bearing a shield, and on it a Medusa's
head; upon her head a plumed helm, and in her right hand a lance.
Reputation, a young man in a purple robe wrought with gold, and wearing
a laurel wreath on his head. These being come down in an equal distance 1005
to the middle part of the air, the great cloud began to break open, out of
which struck beams of light; in the midst, suspended in the air, sat Eternity
on a globe; his garment was long, of a light blue, wrought all over with
stars of gold, and bearing in his hand a serpent bent into a circle, with his
tail in his mouth. In the firmament about him was a troop of fifteen stars, 1010
expressing the stellifying of our British heroes; but one more great and
eminent than the rest, which was over his head, figured his Majesty. And
in the lower part was seen afar off the prospect of Windsor Castle, the
famous seat of the most honourable Order of the Garter.°

THE FOURTH SONG
Eternity, Eusebia, Alethia, Sophia, Homonoia, Dicaearche, Euphemia° 1015

ETERNITY   Be fixed, you rapid orbs, that bear
            The changing seasons of the year
            On your swift wings, and see the old
            Decrepit sphere grown dark and cold;
            Nor did Jove quench her fires: these bright   1020
            Flames have eclipsed her sullen light;
            This royal pair, for whom Fate will
            Make motion cease and time stand still,
            Since good is here so perfect, as no worth
            Is left for after-ages to bring forth.   1025

EUSEBIA   Mortality cannot with more
            Religious zeal the gods adore.

ALETHIA   My truths, from human eyes concealed,
            Are naked to their sight revealed.

SOPHIA   Nor do their actions from the guide   1030
            Of my exactest precepts slide.

HOMONOIA   And as their own pure souls entwined,
            So are their subjects' hearts combined.

DICAEARCHE So just, so gentle is their sway,
            As it seems empire to obey.   1035

EUPHEMIA   And their fair fame, like incense hurled
            On altars, hath perfumed the world.

SOPHIA   Wisdom,

ALETHIA   Truth,

EUSEBIA   Pure Adoration,

HOMONOIA   Concord,

DICAEARCHE   Rule,

EUPHEMIA   Clear Reputation,

CHORUS   Crown this king, this queen, this nation.   1040
            Wisdom, Truth, etc.

ETERNITY   Brave spirits, whose adventurous feet
              Have to the mountain's top aspired,
            Where fair Desert and Honour meet,
              Here, from the toiling press retired,   1045
            Secure from all disturbing evil,
            For ever in my temple revel.

            With wreaths of stars circlèd about,
              Gild all the spacious firmament,

And smiling on the panting rout   1050
   That labour in the steep ascent,
With your resistless influence guide
Of human change th'incertain tide.

EUS. ALE. SOP. But oh, you royal turtles, shed,
   When you from earth remove,   1055
On the ripe fruits of your chaste bed,
   Those sacred seeds of Love.

CHORUS Which no power can but yours dispense,
Since you the pattern bear from hence.

HOM. DIC. EUP. Then from your fruitful race shall flow   1060
   Endless succession,
Sceptres shall bud, and laurels blow
   'Bout their immortal throne.

CHORUS Propitious stars shall crown each birth,
Whilst you rule them, and they the earth.   1065

*The song ended, the two clouds with the persons sitting on them ascend;
the great cloud closeth again, and so passeth away overthwart the scene,
leaving behind it nothing but a serene sky. After which, the masquers dance
their last dance, and the curtain was let fall.*

The Names of the Masquers

The King's Majesty

Duke of Lennox	Lord Fielding
Earl of Devonshire	Lord Digby
Earl of Holland	Lord Dungarvan
Earl of Newport	Lord Dunluce
Earl of Elgin	Lord Wharton
Viscount Grandison	Lord Paget
Lord Rich	Lord Salton

The names of the young lords and noblemen's sons

Lord Walden	Mr Thomas Howard
Lord Cranborne	Mr Thomas Egerton
Lord Brackley	Mr Charles Cavendish
Lord Chandos	Mr Robert Howard
Mr William Herbert	Mr Henry Spencer

BEN JONSON

Love's Welcome at Bolsover

Love's Welcome.
The King and Queen's Entertainment
At Bolsover, at the Earl of Newcastle's,
The thirtieth of July, 1634.

THE SONG AT THE BANQUET
SUNG BY TWO TENORS AND A BASS

CHORUS	If Love be called a lifting of the sense	
	To knowledge of that pure intelligence	
	Wherein the soul hath rest and residence,°	
1 TENOR	When were the senses in such order placed?°	
2 TENOR	The sight, the hearing, smelling, touching, taste,	5
	All at one banquet?	
BASS	Would it ever last!	
1 TENOR	We wish the same. Who set it forth thus?	
BASS	Love!	
2 TENOR	But to what end, or to what object?	
BASS	Love!	
1 TENOR	Doth Love then feast itself?	
BASS	Love will feast Love!°	
2 TENOR	You make of Love a riddle or a chain,	10
	A circle, a mere knot: untie't again.	
BASS	Love is a circle, both the first and last	
	Of all our actions, and his knot's too fast.	
1 TENOR	A true-love knot will hardly be untied,	
	And if it could, who would this pair divide?	15
BASS	God made them such, and Love;	
1 TENOR	Who is a ring,	
	The likest to the year of any thing,	
2 TENOR	And runs into itself.	
BASS	Then let us sing,	
	And run into one sound.	

CHORUS   Let welcome fill
                Our thoughts, hearts, voices, and that one word trill   20
                Through all our language, 'welcome, welcome' still.

                COMPLEMENT

1 TENOR   Could we put on the beauty of all creatures,
2 TENOR   Sing in the air and notes of nightingales,
1 TENOR   Exhale the sweets of earth, and all her features,
2 TENOR   And tell you, softer than in silk, these tales,   25
BASS   'Welcome' should season all for taste.
CHORUS   And hence,
                At every real banquet to the sense,
                Welcome, true welcome, fill the complements.

*After the banquet the King and Queen, retired,° were entertained with
Coronel Vitruvius° his oration to his dance of mechanics.*   30

VITRUVIUS, Come forth; boldly put forth i' your holiday clothes,
    every mother's son of you. This is the King and Queen's majestical
    holiday. My lord has it granted from them; I had it granted from
    my lord, and do give it unto you *gratis*, that is *bona fide*, with the
    faith of a surveyor, your Coronel Vitruvius. Do you know what a   35
    surveyor is, now? I tell you, a supervisor! A hard word, that; but
    it may be softened and brought in, to signify something. An
    overseer! One that oversee-eth you. A busy man! And yet I must
    seem busier than I am (as the poet° sings, but which of them I will
    not now trouble myself to tell you). O Captain Smith! our   40
    hammer-armed° Vulcan! with your three sledges,° you are our
    music; you come a little too tardy, but we remit that to your
    polt-foot,° we know you are lame. Plant yourselves there, and beat
    your time out at the anvil. Time and measure are the father and
    mother of music you know, and your Coronel Vitruvius knows a   45
    little. O Chesil, our curious carver and Master Maul, our free-
    mason, Squire Sumner our carpenter and Twybil his man,° stand
    you four there i' the second rank, work upon that ground. And
    you, Dresser the plumber, Quarrel the glazier, Fret the plasterer,
    and Beater° the mortar-man, put all you on i' the rear, as finishers   50
    in true footing,° with tune and measure. Measure is the soul of a
    dance, and tune the tickle-foot thereof. Use holiday legs, and have
    'em; spring, leap, caper, and jingle; pumps and ribands shall be
    your reward, till the soles of your feet swell with the surfeit of your
    light and nimble motion. (*They begun to dance.*) Well done, my   55

musical, arithmetical, geometrical gamesters! or rather, my true mathematical boys! It is carried in number, weight, and measure, as if the airs were all harmony and the figures a well-timed proportion!° I cry still: deserve holidays, and have 'em. I'll have a whole quarter of the year cut out for you in holidays, and laced with statute-tunes and dances, fitted to the activity of your trestles, to which you shall trust, lads, in the name of your Iniquo° Vitruvius. Hey for the lily, for and the blended rose.°   60

The dance ended. And the King and Queen having a second banquet set down before them from the clouds by two Loves,° one as the King's, with a bough of palm in his hand cleft a little at the top, the other as the Queen's, differenced by their garlands only: his of white and red roses, the other of lilies interweaved, gold, silver, purple, etc. They were both armed and winged, with bows and quivers, cassocks, breeches, buskins, gloves, and perukes alike. They stood silent awhile, wondering at one another, till at last the lesser of them began to speak.   65   70

EROS Another Cupid?
ANTEROS   Yes, your second self,
  A son of Venus, and as mere an elf
  And wag as you.
EROS   Eros?
ANTEROS   No, Anteros,
  Your brother Cupid, yet not sent to cross   75
  Or spy into your favours here at court.
EROS What then?
ANTEROS   To serve you, brother, and report
  Your graces from the Queen's side to the King's,
  In whose name I salute you.
EROS   Break my wings
  I fear you will.
ANTEROS   O be not jealous, brother!   80
  What bough is this?
EROS   A palm
ANTEROS   Give me't.
EROS   Another
  You may have.
ANTEROS   I will this.

Anteros snatched at the palm, but Eros divided it.

EROS   Divide it.
ANTEROS   So.

This was right brother-like! The world will know   85
By this one act, both natures. You are Love,
I, Love-again. In these two spheres we move,
Eros and Anteros.
EROS   We ha' cleft the bough,
And struck a tally of our loves too, now.°
ANTEROS I call to mind the wisdom of our mother   90
Venus, who would have Cupid have a brother—
EROS To look upon and thrive. Me seems I grew
Three inches higher sin' I met with you.
ANTEROS It was the counsel that the oracle gave
Your nurses, the glad Graces, sent to crave   95
Themis' advice. You do not know (quoth she)°
The nature of this infant. Love may be
Brought forth thus little, live awhile alone,
But ne'er will prosper if he have not one
Sent after him to play with.
EROS   Such another   100
As you are, Anteros, our loving brother.
ANTEROS Who would be always planted in your eye;
For love, by love, increaseth mutually.
EROS We, either looking on each other, thrive;
ANTEROS Shoot up, grow galliard—
EROS   Yes, and more alive!   105
ANTEROS When one's away, it seems we both are less.
EROS I was a dwarf, an urchin, I confess,
Till you were present.
ANTEROS   But a bird of wing
Now, fit to fly before a queen or king.
EROS I ha' not one sick feather sin' you came,   110
But turned a jollier Cupid—
ANTEROS   Than I am.
EROS I love my mother's brain could thus provide
For both in court, and give us each our side
Where we might meet.
ANTEROS   Embrace.
EROS   Circle each other.
ANTEROS Confer, and whisper.
EROS   Brother with a brother.   115
ANTEROS And by this sweet contention for the palm
Unite our appetites, and make them calm.

197

EROS To will and nill one thing.

ANTEROS   And so to move°
Affection in our wills, as in our love.

EROS It is the place sure breeds it, where we are;   120

ANTEROS The King and Queen's court, which is circular°
And perfect;

EROS   The pure school that we live in,
And is of purer love the discipline.

PHILALETHES° No more of your poetry, pretty Cupids, lest presum-
ing on your little wits you profane the intention of your service.   125
The place, I confess, wherein (by the providence of your mother
Venus) you are now planted, is the divine school of love. An
academy or court, where all the true lessons of love are throughly
read and taught; the reasons, the proportions and harmony, drawn
forth in analytic tables, and made demonstrable to the senses.   130
Which if you, brethren, should report and swear to, would hardly
get credit above a fable, here in the edge of Derbyshire (the region
of ale) because you relate it in rhyme.° O, that rhyme is a shrewd
disease, and makes all suspected it would persuade. Leave it, pretty
Cupids, leave it. Rhyme will undo you, and hinder your growth   135
and reputation in court more than any thing beside you have either
mentioned or feared. If you dabble in poetry once, it is done of°
your being believed or understood here. No man will trust you in
this verge, but conclude you for a mere case of canters,° or a pair
of wandering gypsies.   140

Return to yourselves, little deities, and admire the miracles you
serve, this excellent king and his unparalleled queen, who are the
canons, the decretals, and whole school-divinity of love. Contem-
plate and study them. Here shall you read Hymen, having lighted
two torches, either of which inflame mutually but waste not; one   145
Love by the other's aspect increasing, and both in the right lines
of aspiring; the Fates spinning them round and even threads, and
of their whitest wool,° without brack or purl; Fortune and Time
fettered at their feet with adamantine chains, their wings de-
plumed, for starting from them; all amiableness in the richest dress   150
of delight and colours, courting the season to tarry by them, and
make the Idea of their felicity perfect, together with the love,
knowledge, and duty of their subjects perpetual. So wisheth the
glad and grateful client seated here, the overjoyed master of the
house; and prayeth that the whole region about him could speak   155
but his language. Which is, that first the people's love would let

that people know their own happiness, and that knowledge could
confirm their duties to an admiration of your sacred persons,
descended, one from the most peaceful, the other the most
warlike,° both your pious and just progenitors; from whom, as out   160
of peace came strength, and out of the strong came sweetness,° so
in you, joined by holy marriage in the flower and ripeness of years,
live the promise of a numerous succession to your sceptres, and a
strength to secure your own islands, with their own ocean, but
more, your own palm branches, the types of perpetual victory. To   165
which, two words be added, a zealous Amen, and ever rounded
with a crown of welcome. Welcome, welcome!

WILLIAM DAVENANT

Salmacida Spolia

Salmacida Spolia
A Masque
Presented by the King and Queen's Majesties at Whitehall
on Tuesday the 21 day of January 1640

The Subject of the Masque

Discord, a malicious Fury, appears in a storm, and by the invocation
of malignant spirits proper to her evil use, having already put most
of the world into disorder, endeavours to disturb these parts, envying
the blessings and tranquillity we have long enjoyed.

These incantations are expressed by those spirits in an antimasque;   5
who on a sudden are surprised and stopped in their motion by a secret
power whose wisdom they tremble at, and depart as foreknowing that
wisdom will change all their malicious hope of these disorders into a
sudden calm, which after their departure is prepared by a dispersed
harmony° of music.   10

This secret wisdom, in the person of the King attended by his
nobles, and under the name of Philogenes, or 'Lover of his People',
hath his appearance prepared by a chorus, representing the beloved
people, and is instantly discovered environed with those nobles in the
throne of Honour.   15

Then the Queen, personating the chief heroine, with her martial
ladies, is sent down from heaven by Pallas° as a reward of his
prudence for reducing the threatening storm into the following calm.

*In the border that enclosed the scenes and made a frontispiece to all the
work, in a square niche on the right hand, stood two figures of women, one*   20
*of them expressing much majesty in her aspect, apparelled in sky colour,
with a crown of gold on her head and a bridle in her hand, representing
Reason;° the other embracing her was in changeable silk with wings at her
shoulders, figured for Intellectual Appetite, who while she embraceth
Reason, all the actions of men are rightly governed. Above these, in a*   25
second order, were winged children, one riding on a furious lion° which he

seems to tame with reins and a bit, another bearing an antique ensign, the third hovering above with a branch of palm in his hand, expressing the victory over the perturbations. In a niche on the other side stood two figures joining hands; one a grave old man in a robe of purple, with a heart of 30 *gold in a chain about his neck, figured for Counsel,° the other a woman in a garment of cloth of gold, in her hand a sword with a serpent winding about the blade, representing Resolution, both these being necessary to the good means of arriving to a virtuous end.*

Over these and answering to the other side was a round altar raised 35 *high, and on it the bird of Pallas,° figured for Prudence. On either side were children with wings, one in act of adoration, another holding a book, and a third flying over their heads with a lighted torch in his hand, representing the Intellectual Light accompanied with Doctrine and Discipline, and alluding to the figures below, as those on the other side.* 40

Above these ran a large frieze with a cornicement, in the midst whereof was a double compartment rich and full of ornament. On the top of this sat Fame with spreaded wings, in act, sounding a trumpet of gold. Joining to the compartment in various postures lay two figures in their natural colours as big as the life; one holding an anchor representing Safety, the 45 *other expressing Riches° with a cornucopia, and about her stood antique vases of gold. The rest of this frieze was composed of children with significant signs to express their several qualities: Forgetfulness of Injuries, extinguishing a flaming torch on an armour; Commerce, with ears of corn; Felicity, with a basket of lilies; Affection to the Country, holding a* 50 *grasshopper;° Prosperous Success, with the rudder of a ship; Innocence, with a branch of fern; all these expressing the several goods, followers of peace and concord, and forerunners of human felicity; so as the work of this front, consisting of picture qualified with moral philosophy, tempered delight with profit.* 55

In the midst of the aforesaid compartment in an oval table was written:

SALMACIDA SPOLIA.

The ancient adages are these:

Salmacida spolia sine sanguine sine sudore, potius quam
Cadmia victoria, ubi ipsos victores pernicies opprimit.° 60

But before I proceed in the descriptions of the scenes, it is not amiss briefly to set down the histories from whence these proverbs took their original.

For the first: Melas and Arevanias of Argos and Troezen conducted a common colony to Halicarnassus in Asia, and there drave out the 65 barbarous Carie and Lelegi, who fled up to the mountains; from whence they made many incursions, robbing and cruelly spoiling the Grecian inhabitants, which could by no means be prevented.

On the top of the right horn of the hill which surrounds Halicarnassus in form of a theatre is a famous fountain of most clear water and exquisite taste, called Salmacis. It happened that near to this fountain one of the colony, to make gain by the goodness of the water, set up a tavern and furnished it with all necessaries, to which the barbarians resorting (enticed by the delicious taste of this water, at first some few, and after many together in troops) of fierce and cruel natures were reduced of their own accord to the sweetness of the Grecian customs.

The other adage is thus derived: the city of Thebes, anciently called Cadmia, had war with Adrastus, the Argive king, who raised a great army of Arcadians and Messenians and fought a battle with them near Ismenia, where the Thebans were overthrown, turned their backs, and fled into their city. The Peloponnesians, not accustomed to scale walled towns, assaulting furiously but without order, were repulsed from the walls by the defendants, and many of the Argives slain. At that instant the besieged making a great sally, and finding the enemy in disorder and confusion, cut them all in pieces, only Adrastus excepted, who was saved by flight. But this victory was gotten with great damage and slaughter of the Thebans, for few of them returned alive into their city.

The allusion is, that his Majesty, out of his mercy and clemency approving the first proverb, seeks by all means to reduce tempestuous and turbulent natures into a sweet calm of civil concord.

A curtain flying up, a horrid scene appeared of storm and tempest. No glimpse of the sun was seen, as if darkness, confusion, and deformity had possessed the world and driven light to heaven; the trees bending, as forced by a gust of wind, their branches rent from their trunks, and some torn up by the roots. Afar off was a dark wrought sea, with rolling billows breaking against the rocks, with rain, lightning, and thunder. In the midst was a globe of the earth, which at an instant falling on fire, was turned into a Fury,° her hair upright, mixed with snakes, her body lean, wrinkled, and of a swarthy colour, her breasts hung bagging down to her waist, to which with a knot of serpents was girt red bases, and under it tawny skirts down to her feet. In her hand she brandished a sable torch, and looking askance with hollow envious eyes came down into the room.

FURY Blow winds! until you raise the seas so high
    That waves may hang like tears in the sun's eye;

70

75

80

85

90

95

100

105

That we, when in vast cataracts they fall,
May think he weeps at nature's funeral.
Blow winds! and from the troubled womb of earth,
Where you receive your undiscovered birth,°   110
Break out in wild disorders, till you make
Atlas beneath his shaking load to shake.
How am I grieved the world should everywhere
Be vexed into a storm save only here!
Thou over-lucky, too-much-happy isle,   115
Grow more desirous of this flattering style!
For thy long health can never altered be
But by thy surfeits on felicity.
And I, to stir the humours that increase
In thy full body, overgrown with peace,°   120
Will call those Furies hither who incense
The guilty, and disorder innocence.
Ascend! ascend! you horrid sullen brood
Of evil spirits, and displace the good!
The great, make only wiser to suspect   125
Whom they have wronged by falsehood or neglect.
The rich, make full of avarice as pride,
Like graves or swallowing seas unsatisfied,
Busy to help the state, when needy grown,
From poor men's fortunes, never from their own.   130
The poor, ambitious make, apt to obey
The false, in hope to rule whom they betray,
And make religion to become their vice,°
Named to disguise ambitious avarice.

The speech ended, three Furies make their entry, presented by Mr Charles   135
Murray, Mr Seymour, Mr Tartareau.
   *This antimasque being past,° the scene changed into a calm, the sky serene;
afar off Zephyrus appeared, breathing a gentle gale; in the landscape were
cornfields and pleasant trees sustaining vines fraught with grapes, and in
some of the furthest parts villages, with all such things as might express a*   140
*country in peace, rich and fruitful. There came breaking out of the heavens
a silver chariot, in which sat two persons, the one a woman in a watchet
garment, her dressing of silver mixed with bulrushes, representing Concord;
somewhat below her sat the Good Genius of Great Britain, a young man
in a carnation garment embroidered all with flowers, an antique sword*   145
*hung in a scarf,° a garland on his head, and in his hand a branch of platan
mixed with ears of corn. These in their descent° sung together.*

SONG I

Good Genius of Great Britain, Concord

CONCORD   Why should I hasten hither, since the good
                 I bring to men is slowly understood?

GENIUS   I know it is the people's vice   150
                 To lay too mean, too cheap a price
                 On every blessing they possess;
                 Th'enjoying makes them think it less.

CONCORD   If then the need of what is good
                 Doth make it loved or understood,
                 Or 'tis by absence better known,   155
                 I shall be valued when I'm gone.

GENIUS   Yet stay, O stay! if but to please
                 The great and wise Philogenes.

CONCORD   Should dews not fall, the sun forbear   160
                 His course, or I my visits here,
                 Alike from these defects would cease
                 The power and hope of all increase.

GENIUS   Stay then, O stay! if but to ease
                 The cares of wise Philogenes.   165

CONCORD   I will! and much I grieve, that though the best
                 Of kingly science harbours in his breast,
                 Yet 'tis his fate to rule in adverse times,
                 When wisdom must awhile give place to crimes.

Being arrived at the earth and descended from the chariot, they sing this   170
short dialogue; and then departed several ways to incite the beloved people
to honest pleasures and recreations which have ever been peculiar to this
nation.°

BOTH   O who but he could thus endure
                   To live and govern in a sullen age,   175
                 When it is harder far to cure
                   The people's folly than resist their rage?

After which there followed these several Entries of Antimasques:

Entry 1

Wolfgangus Vandergoose, spagyric, operator to the Invisible Lady styled
the Magical Sister of the Rosicross,° *with these receipts following and*   180

many other rare secrets, undertakes in short time to cure the defects of
nature and diseases of the mind:

1. *Confection of hope and fear to entertain lovers.*
2. *Essence of dissimulation, to enforce love.*
3. *Julep of fruition, to recreate the hot fevers of love.*   185
4. *Water of dalliance, to warm an old courage.*
5. *A subtle quintessence drawn from mathematical points and lines,*
   filtered through a melancholy brain, to make eunuchs engender.
6. *Pomado of the bark of comeliness, the sweetness of wormwood,*
   with the fat of gravity, to anoint those that have an ill mind.   190
7. *Spirit of Satyrus' high capers, and Bacchus' whirling vertigos,*
   to make one dance well.
8. *One dram of the first matter,° as much of the rust of Time's*
   scythe, mixed with the juice of Medea's° herbs; this, in an
   electuary, makes all sorts of old people young.   195
9. *An opiate of the spirit of muscadine taken in good quantity to*
   bedward, to make one forget his creditors.
10. *Powder of Menippus'° tree and the rind of hemp,° to consolate*
    those who have lost their money.
11. *Treacle of the gall of serpents and the liver of doves, to initiate*   200
    a neophyte courtier.
12. *An easy vomit of the fawning of a spaniel,* Gallo-belgicus,°
    and the last coranto, hot from the press, with the powder of
    some lean jests, to prepare a disprovu's° welcome to rich men's
    tables.   205
13. *A gargarism of* Florio's First Fruits, Diana de Montemayor,°
    and the scraping of Spanish Romanzas distilled in balneo, *to*
    make a sufficient linguist without travelling or scarce knowing
    himself what he says.
14. *A bath made of a catalogue from the mart and common places,*   210
    taken in a Frankfurt dryfat;° in his diet he must refrain all
    real knowledge and only suck in vulgar opinions, using the
    fricassee of confederacy; will make ignorants in all professions
    to seem and not to be.

Entry 2

Four old men richly attired the	*Mr Boroughs*	215
shapes proper to the persons,	*Mr Skipwith*	
presented by	*Mr Pert*	
	Mr Ashton	

Entry 3

Three young soldiers in several	*Mr Hearne*
fashioned habits, but costly, and	*Mr Slingsby*
presented to the life by	*Mr Chumley*

220

Entry 4

A nurse and three children in long coats, with bibs, biggins, and muckenders.

Entry 5

An ancient Irishman, presented by   Mr Jay

Entry 6

An ancient Scottishman, presented by   Mr Atkins

225

Entry 7

An old-fashioned Englishman and	*Mr Arpe*
his mistress, presented by	*Mr Will. Murray*

These three antimasques were well and naturally set out.

Entry 8

Doctor Tartaglia and two pedants	*Mr Rimes*
of Francolin,° *presented by*	*Mr Warder*
	Mr Villiers

230

Entry 9

Four grotesques or drollities, in the most fantastical shapes that could be devised.

Entry 10

The Invisible Lady, magical sister of the Rosicross.

Entry 11

A shepherd, presented by   Mr Charles Murray

235

Entry 12

A farmer and his wife, presented by Mr Skipwith

Entry 13

A country gentleman,	*Mr Boroughs*
his wife, and his bailiff,	*Mr Ashton*
presented by	*Mr Pert*

Entry 14

An amorous courtier richly	*Mr Seymour*	240
apparelled, presented by		

Entry 15

Two roaring boys,° *their suits answering their profession.*

Entry 16

Four mad lovers and as madly clad.

Entry 17

A jealous Dutchman,	*Mr Arpe*	
his wife, and her Italian	*Mr Rimes*	245
lover, presented by	*Mr Tartareau*	

Entry 18

Three Swisses, one a little Swiss	*Mr Cotterell*
who played the wag with them	*Mr Newton*
as they slept, presented by	*Mr Jeffrey Hudson*°

Entry 19

Four antic° *cavaliers,*	*Mr Arpe*	250
imitating a manage	*Mr Jay*	
and tilting	*Mr Atkins*	
	Mr Tartareau	

Entry 20

A Cavallerizzo and two pages.

All which antimasques were well set out and excellently danced, and the 255
tunes fitted to the persons.

*The antimasques being past, all the scene was changed into craggy rocks
and inaccessible mountains. In the upper parts, where any earth could
fasten, were some trees, but of strange forms, such as only grow in remote
parts of the Alps and in desolate places; the furthest of these was hollow* 260
*in the midst and seemed to be cut through by art, as the Pausilipo near
Naples,*° *and so high as the top pierced the clouds; all which represented
the difficult way which heroes are to pass ere they come to the Throne of
Honour.*

The chorus of the beloved people came forth, led by Concord and the 265
*Good Genius of Great Britain, their habits being various and rich. They
go up to the state and sing.*

SONG II
To the Queen Mother°

When with instructed eyes we look upon
  Our blessings that descend so fast 270
From the fair partner of our monarch's throne,
  We grieve, they are too great to last.

But when those growing comforts we survey°
  By whom our hopes are longer lived,
Then gladly we our vows and praises pay 275
  To her from whom they are derived.

And since, great Queen, she is derived from you,
  We here begin our offerings;
For those who sacrificed to rivers knew
  Their first rites due unto their springs.° 280

The stream from whence our blessings flow, you bred;
  You in whose bosom even the chief and best
Of modern victors laid his weary head°
  When he rewarded victories with rest;
Your beauty kept his valour's flame alive, 285
Your Tuscan wisdom taught it how to thrive.°

Inviting the King's appearance in the Throne of Honour

To be printed, not sung°

Why are our joys detained by this delay?
  Unless, as in a morning overcast, 290
We find it long ere we can find out day;
  So, whilst our hopes increase, our time doth waste.
Or are you slow 'cause th'way to Honour's throne,
  In which you travail now, is so uneven,°
Hilly and craggy, or as much unknown 295
  As that uncertain path which leads to heaven?
O that philosophers (who through those mists
  Low nature casts do upper knowledge spy)
Or those that smile at them (o'er-weening priests)°
  Could with such sure, such an undoubted eye, 300
Reach distant heaven, as you can Honour's throne;
  Then we should shift our flesh t'inhabit there,
Where, we are taught, the heroës are gone,
  Though now content with earth, 'cause you are here.

The song ended, they return up to the stage and divide themselves on each 305
side. Then the further part of the scene disappeared, and the King's
majesty and the rest of the masquers were discovered sitting in the Throne
of Honour, his Majesty highest in a seat of gold, and the rest of the lords
about him. This throne was adorned with palm trees, between which stood
statues of the ancient heroes. In the under parts on each side lay captives 310
bound in several postures,° lying on trophies of armours, shields, and
antique weapons, all his throne being feigned of goldsmith's work. The
habit of his Majesty and the masquers was of watchet, richly embroidered
with silver; long stockings set up of white; their caps silver with scrolls of
gold and plumes of white feathers. 315

SONG III
To the King when he appears with his lords in the Throne of Honour

Those quarrelling winds (that deafened unto death
    The living, and did wake men dead before)
Seem now to pant small gusts, as out of breath,
    And fly, to reconcile themselves on shore. 320

If it be kingly patience to outlast
    Those storms the people's giddy fury raise
Till like fantastic winds themselves they waste,
    The wisdom of that patience is thy praise.

Murmur's a sickness epidemical: 325
    'Tis catching, and infects weak common ears;
For through those crooked, narrow alleys, all
    Invaded are and killed by whisperers.

This you discerned, and by your mercy taught
    Would not (like monarchs that severe have been) 330
Invent imperial arts to question thought,
    Nor punish vulgar sickness as a sin.°

Nor would your valour, when it might subdue,
    Be hindered of the pleasure to forgive.
Th'are worse than overcome, your wisdom knew, 335
    That needed mercy to have leave to live.

Since strength of virtues gained you Honour's throne,
    Accept our wonder and enjoy your praise!
He's fit to govern there and rule alone°
    Whom inward helps, not outward force, doth raise. 340

209

Whilst the chorus sung this song, there came softly from the upper part of the heavens a huge cloud of various colours, but pleasant to the sight; which descending to the midst of the scene opened, and within it was a transparent brightness of thin exhalations, such as the gods are feigned to descend in; in the most eminent place of which her Majesty sat,   345 *representing the chief heroine, environed with her martial ladies; and from over her head were darted lightsome rays that illuminated her seat; and all the ladies about her participated more or less of that light, as they sat near or further off. This brightness with many streaks of thin vapours about it, such as are seen in a fair evening sky, softly descended; and as*   350 *it came near to the earth the seat of Honour by little and little vanished, as if it gave way to these heavenly graces. The Queen's majesty and her ladies were in Amazonian habits of carnation, embroidered with silver, with plumed helms, baldrics with antique swords hanging by their sides, all as rich as might be; but the strangeness of the habits was most*   355 *admired.*

SONG IV
When the Queen and her ladies descended

You that so wisely studious are
To measure and to trace each star,
How swift they travel and how far,   360
  Now number your celestial store,
Planets or lesser lights, and try
If in the face of all the sky
  You count so many as before.

If you would practise how to know   365
The chief for influence or show,
Level your pèrspectives below,
  For in this nether orb they move!
Each here (when lost in's doubtful art)°
May by his eyes advance his heart,   370
  And through his optic learn to love!°

But what is she that rules the night?
That kindles ladies with her light,
And gives to men the power of sight?
  All those who can her virtue doubt   375
Her mind will in her face advise;
For through the casements of her eyes
  Her soul is ever looking out.°

And with its beams she doth survey
Our growth in virtue or decay, 380
Still lighting us in Honour's way!
All that are good she did inspire!
Lovers are chaste, because they know
It is her will they should be so.
The valiant take from her their fire! 385

When this heavenly seat touched the earth, the King's majesty took out
the Queen, and the lords the ladies, and came down into the room and
danced their entry; betwixt which and the second dance was this song.

SONG V
After the first dance

Why stand you still, and at these beauties gaze, 390
As if you were afraid,
Or they were made
Much more for wonder than delight?
Sure those whom first their virtue did amaze
Their feature must at last invite. 395

Time never knew the mischiefs of his haste,
Nor can you force him stay
To keep off day.
Make then fit use of triumphs here.
It were a crime 'gainst pleasant youth, to waste 400
This night in over-civil fear.

Move then like Time, for Love as well as he
Hath got a calendar,
Where must appear
How evenly you these measures tread; 405
And when they end, we far more grieved shall be
Than for his hours when they are fled.

The second dance ended, and their Majesties being seated under the state,
the scene was changed into magnificent buildings composed of several
selected pieces of architecture. In the furthest part was a bridge over a 410
river, where many people, coaches, horses, and such like were seen to pass
to and fro. Beyond this on the shore were buildings in prospective, which,
shooting far from the eye, showed as the suburbs of a great city.
From the highest part of the heavens came forth a cloud far in the scene,
in which were eight persons richly attired, representing the spheres. This, 415

211

joining with two other clouds which appeared at that instant full of music,
covered all the upper part of the scene; and at that instant, beyond all
these, a heaven opened full of deities; which celestial prospect, with the
chorus below, filled all the whole scene with apparitions and harmony.

SONG VI
To the King and Queen by a chorus of all 420

So musical as to all ears
Doth seem the music of the spheres,°
Are you unto each other still,
Tuning your thoughts to either's will.

All that are harsh, all that are rude, 425
Are by your harmony subdued;
Yet so into obedience wrought
As if not forced to it, but taught.

Live still, the pleasure of our sight,
Both our examples and delight; 430

So long, until you find the good success
Of all your virtues in one happiness;

Till we so kind, so wise, and careful be
In the behalf of our posterity,

That we may wish your sceptres ruling here, 435
(Loved even by those who should your justice fear)
When we are gone, when to our last remove
We are dispatched, to sing your praise above.

After this song the spheres passed through the air, and all the deities
ascended; and so concluded this masque, which was generally approved of, 440
especially by all strangers° that were present, to be the noblest and most
ingenious that hath been done here in that kind.

The invention, ornament, scenes, and apparitions, with their des-
criptions, were made by Inigo Jones, Surveyor General of his Majesty's
Works. 445

What was spoken or sung, by William Davenant, her Majesty's servant.
The subject was set down by them both.

The music was composed by Lewis Richard, Master of her Majesty's
Music.

FINIS

The Names of the Masquers

The King's Majesty	The Queen's Majesty
Duke of Lennox	Duchess of Lennox
Earl of Carlisle	Countess of Carnarvon
Earl of Newport	Countess of Newport
Earl of Lanark/Limerick°	Countess of Portland
Lord Russell	Lady Andover
Lord Herbert	Lady Margaret Howard
Lord Paget	Lady Kellymekin
Lord Fielding	Lady Frances Howard
Master Russell	Mistress Cary
Master Thomas Howard	Mistress Nevill

EXPLANATORY NOTES

ABBREVIATIONS

Q = Quarto; F = Folio.

Editions

BoMasques	T. J. B. Spencer and Stanley Wells, A *Book of Masques in Honour of Allardyce Nicoll* (Cambridge: Cambridge University Press, 1967).
Brotanek	Rudolf Brotanek, *Die englischen Maskenspiele* (Vienna and Leipzig, 1902).
Brown	Cedric Brown (ed.), *The Poems and Masques of Aurelian Townshend* (Reading: Reading University Press, 1983).
Davis	Walter R. Davis (ed.), *The Works of Thomas Campion* (London: Faber and Faber, 1969).
Dunlap	Rhodes Dunlap (ed.), *The Poems of Thomas Carew with his Masque Coelum Britannicum* (Oxford: Clarendon Press, 1949).
Dutton	Richard Dutton (ed.), *Jacobean and Caroline Masques*, 2 vols. (Nottingham: Nottingham Drama Texts, 1981, 1989).
Evans	G. Blakemore Evans, 'The Memorable Masque', in Allan Holaday (ed.), *The Plays of George Chapman: The Comedies* (Urbana, Chicago, and London: University of Illinois Press, 1970).
H&S	C. H. Herford, Percy and Evelyn Simpson (eds.), *Ben Jonson*, vols. 7 and 10 (Oxford: Clarendon Press, 1941, 1950).
O	Stephen Orgel (ed.), *Ben Jonson: The Complete Masques* (New Haven, Conn., and London: Yale University Press, 1969).
O&S	Stephen Orgel and Roy Strong (eds.), *Inigo Jones: The Theatre of the Stuart Court*, 2 vols. (London, Berkeley, and Los Angeles: Sotheby Parke Bernet and University of California Press, 1973).
Tilley	Morris Palmer Tilley (ed.), *A Dictionary of the Proverbs in England in the Sixteenth and Seventeenth Centuries* (Ann Arbor: University of Michigan Press, 1950).
Vivian	Percival Vivian (ed.), *Campion's Works* (Oxford: Clarendon Press, 1909).

Masque Titles

Bar	*Barriers at a Marriage*
Bla	*The Masque of Blackness*
Bols	*Love's Welcome at Bolsover*
Cav	*The Caversham Entertainment*

CBrit	*Coelum Britannicum*
Chlo	*Chloridia*
Chr	*Christmas His Masque*
Cole	*The Coleorton Masque*
Gold	*The Golden Age Restored*
Hay	*The Lord Hay's Masque*
LRest	*Love Restored*
MemM	*The Memorable Masque*
Nept	*Neptune's Triumph for the Return of Albion*
PlRec	*Pleasure Reconciled to Virtue*
Qu	*The Masque of Queens*
Salm	*Salmacida Spolia*
TempR	*Tempe Restored*
Teth	*Tethys' Festival*

The Masque of Blackness

This was the work that established Jonson and Inigo Jones as the major providers of masques for the next two and a half decades. In presenting the Queen and her ladies in black-face Jonson was responding to Queen Anne's express wish, and he did so with a display of witty learning, managing both to assert the nobility and beauty of blackness, and yet present the ladies' arrival at court as the result of their desire to be turned white by the power of the King. There was, however, the problem that at the end of the masque there could be no immediate transformation of the ladies back into their 'real' selves; perhaps Jonson intended from the beginning to answer this masque with the *Masque of Beauty*, which was eventually performed in 1608.

The masque was extremely expensive, up to £3,000 being spent upon it. Though well received by foreigners present, the indecorum of the black-faced masquers and their flimsy apparel shocked some native observers, and the performance seems to have been surrounded with problems; John Chamberlain, an indefatigable news-letter writer of the period, records controversy amongst the ambassadors invited, chaos from the press of people, a precipitous demolition of the banquet afterwards, and the arrest of a loose woman caught prosecuting her business on the terrace.

The texts of *Blackness* and *Beauty*, with *The Haddington Masque*, were published together in quarto in 1608, and in the Folio of 1616. One MS, BL Royal MS 17.B.xxxi, survives. Jonson himself annotated the text: the most important of these notes are signalled below by 'J'.

6 *in these*: i.e. these masques.

7 *rage . . . carcasses*: the Tudor custom of permitting the audience to take down scenery and plunder decorations seems to have survived into the early Stuart period.

13 *Leo the African*: his *Description of Africa* was published in 1526; he is here added to the three classical authorities Jonson cites.

14 *Niger*: 'Some take it to be the same with Nilus, which is by Lucan called *Melas*, signifying *Niger* [black]. Howsoever, Pliny . . . hath this: "The river Niger has the same nature as the Nile . . ." ' (J; my trans. of Latin).

16 *certain lake*: Lake Chad.

20 *Landtschap*: landscape (painted on the front curtain). The Dutch form is a signal of novelty of the word, which *OED* first records in 1598.

21 *falling*: the curtain was dropped rather than drawn.

23 *artificial sea . . . break*: a machine turned, raising and lowering a series of painted cloths.

25 *tritons*: sea-gods.

35 *Upon . . . advanced*: J cites Lucian as authority for Nilus 'sitting upon a hippopotamus', and explains 'the ancients induced Oceanus always with a bull's head, on account of the violence of the winds by which he is stirred up and driven, or because he is borne against the shore raging like a bull'. Oceanus was the Atlantic Ocean, the limit of the ancient world.

45 *Oceaniae*: sea-nymphs, daughters of Oceanus and Tethys.

51 *extravagant*: (1) unusual; (2) moving about.

59 *their hair . . . pyramids*: MS; not in Q, F.

67 *scene . . . forth*: the painted backdrop and the wave machine seemed like a single sea.

68 *level . . . state*: the vanishing point of the perspective was at the level of the King's throne ('*the state*')—he alone viewed from the perfect position.

72 *night piece*: the upper part of the scenery, through which the moon later descends.

80 *son . . . Oceanus*: 'All rivers are said to be the sons of the *Ocean*; for as the ancients thought, out of the vapours exhaled by the heat of the sun rivers and fountains were begotten. And both by Orpheus . . . and Homer . . . Oceanus is celebrated as father and source of gods and things, *because nothing is born or decays without moisture*' (J).

85 *full of life*: Queen Anne was six months pregnant at the time of the masque, a fact perhaps also reflected in her symbol at the end of the masque (see below, l. 245).

97 *Mix . . . stream*: Jonson's marginal note suggests that the fiction, though improbable in nature, is authorized by Virgil's words in his tenth Eclogue about Arethusa not mixing her stream with the briny wave.

98 *diademe*: (diadem) spelling preserved for rhyme.

100 *squarèd . . . bodies*: 'Heavenly bodies perfectly transformed into an earthly realm' (O).

108 *hell . . . industry*: Horace, *Odes* I. iii. 36: 'herculean effort overcame hell'.

114 *first . . . earth*: 'It is a conjecture of the old ethnics [pagans], that they which dwell under the south were the first begotten of the earth' (J).

117 *formal cause*: an Aristotelian term: creator of the form or essence of things.

137 *Phaëton*: son of Apollo, who could not control the horses of the sun god, drove the sun too near the earth, and was destroyed before he could set the world alight. This is the poetic fiction which has distressed the Ethiopian ladies.

145 *them*: 'The Poets' (J).

150 *charged . . . revilings*: 'a custom of the Ethiops' (J).

161 *Ethiops never dream*: J cites Pliny for this belief.

170 *greater light*: King James.

174 *Mauritania*: land of the Moors in North Africa.

175 *Lusitania*: Portugal and western Spain.

176 *Aquitania*: south-west France.

177 *designed*: both 'indicated' and 'appointed'.

181 *Albion*: 'Orpheus in his *Argonautica* calls it "white land" ' (J).

182 *Neptune's son*: James. 'Alluding to the rite of styling princes after the name of their princedoms; so is he still Albion, and Neptune's son that governs. As also his being dear to Neptune, in being so embraced by him' (J).

184 *Deucalion*: Greek equivalent of Noah; both survived a great flood.

194 *present passion*: immediate outburst.

197 *Æthiopia*: 'The Ethiopians worshipped the moon by that surname' (J).

208 *Pythagoras . . . glass*: he was supposed to be able to reflect messages written in blood on a mirror on to the moon.

212 *Britannia . . . admires*: the triple realms of heaven, earth, and underworld wonder at the three kingdoms of England, Scotland, and Wales united by James.

213 *her name*: James reintroduced the name 'Britain' in 1604. Despite l. 222 below, it was, in fact, less than popular.

216 *Hesperus . . . spread*: evening to dawn, west to east.

219 *A world . . . world*: referring to the frequently invoked idea of Britain as a distinct and fortunate world of its own.

220 *tried . . . pride*: 'experienced the ideal of it through England's own pride in herself' (O).

226 *blanch an Ethiop*: a proverbial impossibility.

231 *Indent . . . traces*: make an impression on the land with their dancing footsteps.

238 *every couple . . . fans*: the ladies advanced in pairs, displaying fans to the audience, on one of which was the pair of names, on the other a picture which represented their allegorical nature. The names are largely Jonson's coinage; the emblems are drawn from Renaissance sources such as Valeriano's *Hieroglyphica*. The names of the Oceaniae come from Hesiod's *Theogony*.

244 *The Names*: the meanings of the names in order are: abundance, splendour, transparent, flexibility, swiftness, spotless, moisture, coldness, sweetness, delicacy, weight, revolving (circular). *The symbols*, in order, refer to fertility, a twenty-sided figure standing for water, purity, the salamander not harmed by fire, education, the globe of the earth.

316 *year . . . round*: if Jonson already had the *Masque of Beauty* specifically in mind, they had to wait until 1608, since marriage masques occupied the next two years.

322 *Dian*: the moon.

330 *first masque*: of the three printed in the 1608 Quarto.

Barriers at a Marriage

For the wedding of Frances Howard, daughter of Thomas, Earl of Suffolk, and Robert Devereux, third Earl of Essex, Jonson provided a pair of entertainments. The masque of *Hymenaei* was performed on 5 January 1606, in the Banqueting House, and was followed the next night by the *Barriers* here printed. Both entertainments were paid for by friends of the couple, rather than by the King. The bride was about 13 years old, her husband almost 15. The marriage was arranged to heal old factional wounds, and this is reflected in the way the combatants in the *Barriers* are lined up largely according to their affiliation to the Essex or Howard families, so that their reconciliation at the end has a specific political application. The marriage, however, was to founder in annulment in 1613, and in the scandal of the Overbury murder, revealed in 1615. The later history of the couple prompted Jonson to remove all mention of its occasion when he reprinted the work in the 1616 Folio.

The theme of the work, the contest between virginity and marriage, was a standard debating topic—though the Renaissance reversed the centuries-old tendency for the argument to validate virginity. Jonson seems to have drawn some of the details of the argument from Erasmus's *Colloquia*, particularly from *Proci et Puella*, and from the examples of persuasive and dissuasive letters in *De Conscribendis Epistolis*.

'Barriers' were tournaments where a bar was erected the length of the tiltyard or hall to separate combatants. They were highly regulated occasions, whether involving tilting on horseback, or, as here, a foot combat in which the number of pushes with the pikes and strokes with the sword would be prescribed.

The preface to the whole work is reproduced here, since it is one of the most important formulations of the theory of masque.

The masque was published in 1606 in quarto, and again in the Folio of 1616. Since Jonson's later alterations were dictated by political expediency this edition follows the Quarto.

15 *or . . . or*: either . . . or.

26 *Vaticana . . . delectentur*: 'They can drink bad wine if they like.'

28 *Praetereant . . . stomachum*: 'They can carry on, if it does not upset their stomachs.' This and the preceding quotation are adapted from Martial x. xlv. 5–6.

32 *battle*: piece of music representing a battle.

36 *palm*: emblem of truth because it always springs up, no matter how much it is pressed down.

42 *time . . . industry*: 'Truth is feigned to be the daughter of Saturn, who, indeed, with the ancients was no other than Time' (J).

44 *figure . . . fight*: signals that the debate is a mental as well as a physical struggle.

49 *Best . . . related*: Opinion suggests that Truth has described her own birth in the preceding speech.

53 *fit . . . position*: maintain this argument, which is suitable to the celebration of marriage.

59 *Opinion*: 'Hippocrates . . . describeth her: "a woman who does not look evil, but bold and vehement". To which Cesare Ripa in his *Iconology* alludeth in these words: "a face neither beautiful nor unpleasant" ' (J). Ripa's *Iconologia*, first published in 1593 and with many editions thereafter, was a collection of emblematic representations pillaged by Jonson, Jones, and others for its useful depictions and descriptions of abstract qualities.

73 *heaven's . . . birth*: both Christ and his mother Mary, and Cupid and his mother Venus are implied.

89 *approved . . . superficies*: demonstrated that lines and surfaces are not moved.

101 *satiety*: Q; F reads 'society'.

110 *Euripus*: 'A narrow sea, between Aulis, a port of Boeotia, and the Isle of Euboea' (J).

117 *moon . . . declines*: a variation on Plutarch's assertion that a wife should not be like the moon, but should shine most in the company of her husband (*Moralia* i. 304–5).

121 *begged monopolies*: wives are hidden away out of the same sense of shame

that affects those who have gained their commercial monopolies by begging them from courtiers or the king.

143 *one . . . sway*: husband and wife form a mutual pair because she agrees to obey him.

150 *how a flower . . .*: version of Catullus lxii. 39–58.

close . . . grows: grows hidden in an enclosed place.

155 *same . . . desired*: a complex construction. O suggests 'same' is the subject of 'is' and object of 'have desired': H&S follow Gifford in emending to ''tis withered'.

161 *Hymen*: god of marriage.

170 *elm . . . husband*: the Romans trained vines on elms; a standard emblem for marriage.

173 *unmanured*: literally 'uncultivated' (though a rather insensitively chosen word, even in 1606).

189 *They placed*: when they were in position.

209 *Whose names . . . Mr Digby*: omitted in F.

210 *bar*: barrier over which the tournament was conducted.

211 *join*: in fighting.

221 *music*: Q; F 'masque'.

237 *dove . . . serpents*: cf. Matt. 10: 16, 'wise as serpents, harmless as doves'.

241 *curious*: elaborately made.

256 *related*: just described.

259 *disclosed*: uncovered, exposed to view.

265 [*Opinion's . . . removed*]: At some point after l. 261 Opinion must be stripped to reveal her true garment underneath.

291 *Vivite . . . munus*: 'Live in harmony, and learn to perform our duty' (Claudian, *Carmina Minora* xxv. 130).

The Lord Hay's Masque

The masque was performed on 6 January 1607. The bridegroom was a Scottish favourite, who had secured considerable financial advantages from King James, and, indeed, was to be a conspicuous spender throughout his life. His bride was Honora Denny, whose father Sir Edward Denny, a client of Thomas Howard, Earl of Suffolk and kinsman of Thomas Cecil, Earl of Exeter, had to be persuaded into letting his daughter marry the Scotsman. The marriage suited James's policy of encouraging his much-desired project of uniting England and Scotland, and it is possible that the masque was paid for by the Cecil and Howard families as a demonstration of their loyalty to the King's wishes.

Campion's masque takes the union of the realms as its political subject, but offers a balanced view, articulating many of the anxieties felt by the King's English subjects, especially concerning James's generosity to the Scots. In choosing Diana as the mythological figure whose contest with Phoebus animates the masque, Campion seems to allude to Queen Elizabeth, whose acceptance of James as her heir blessed the idea of union, but whose chaste life and (relatively) temperate court contrasted with the practices of her successor. The insistence on temperance at the end of the masque is particularly significant.

The setting and costumes may have been designed by Inigo Jones—though this is but an inference drawn from the similarity between the masquer's costume illustrated as the frontispiece of the printed text (Fig. 2) and other of his designs. Campion himself wrote the music to at least two of the songs, and other music was written by Thomas Lupo and Thomas Giles (who probably choreographed the dances).

The masque was published in 1607 in a quarto text which is the basis of this edition. A manuscript containing six of the songs from the masque is at Hatfield House (144.268).

2 *King of Great Britain*: James adopted this style by Proclamation in 1604, against the wishes of many.

3 *Scythians*: story from Herodotus iv. 70.

10 *stirred it to an equal flood*: mixed all the blood equally (Davis).

20 *he that marries . . . men*: alluding both to James's words to parliament: 'I am the Husband, and all the whole Isle is my lawful Wife', and to his encouragement of intermarriage between Scots and English.

21 *An Epigram*: Merlin's prophecies of the return of Arthur were frequently invoked as foretelling the advent of James.

43 *Ad Invictissimum . . . parens*: 'To the most Invincible, most Serene James, King of Great Britain. I am uncertain, O King, whether you be the father of England and of united Scotland, or the husband, or neither, or both at once. That one man should join to himself a pair of wives at the same time, this, by your own prohibition, we believe unlawful. And further, for a parent to violate daughters in a marital embrace, who does not think this to be a sin? But by divine good fortune both marry you; yet only one is your consort, one also the conjugal love. What a wondrous marriage, in that you are able to marry what is both a pair and one. You alone, James, have such power. Divided lands you easily unite into one and further make them one for ever, in name and in reality. To offspring and brides you have been made father and husband, to the united pair a husband indeed and in your love a parent.'

65 *But if . . . bays*: since he cannot adequately praise the young lord, he will not be able to express the mature man he will become, and thus gain the 'bays', the poet's laurel crown.

73 *Hayes*: Campion's chosen spelling, retained for the rhyme.

79 *habits*: both name and dress are 'estranged' from the masquers' 'real' identities.

88 *Haeredem . . . avos*: 'The newly-wed bride shall, as is the hope, produce an Anglo-Scottish heir; the one whom he hereafter shall beget shall be British. So a new posterity, from two kingdoms sprung, shall ennoble its goodly forebears on both sides.'

97 *great hall*: the hall, which was used since the Banqueting House was being rebuilt, was 40 feet wide, 70 feet long.

100 *screen*: the rear wall of the hall in front of passageway and kitchens. An accurate diagram is given in O&S, 120.

102 *bass . . . lutes*: different sizes of lute, the 'mean' smaller than the bass lute, and therefore higher in pitch.

105 *Chapel voices*: singers who were choristers of the Chapel Royal.

109 *double veil*: two curtains.

121 *window*: the window in the hall.

145 *nine*: three and its multiples are important throughout the design of this work at every level. The three major deities—Phoebus, Diana, and Hesperus (Venus) who unites them—suggest the Orphic triad of Heaven, Earth, and Love.

149 *worthies*: nine famous figures from classical, biblical, and medieval history.

151 *first leaf*: as frontispiece; see Fig. 2.

152 *heat and youth*: the opposition and then combination of male heat and fire with female cold and moisture are part of the standard iconology of marriage celebrations.

155 *Flora*: according to Ovid, Flora was married to Zephyrus.

changeable taffeta: of colour changing in different lights.

158 *Zephyrus*: 'The western wind, of all the most mild and pleasant, who with Venus the Queen of love is said to bring in the spring, when natural heat and appetite reviveth, and the glad earth begins to be beautified with flowers' (Campion).

white: contradicts the 'sky-blue taffeta'; perhaps a misprint for 'wide'?

167 *Hesperus*: 'The Evening star foreshows that the wished marriage night is at hand, and for that cause is supposed to be the friend of bridegrooms and brides' (Campion).

177 *at the sound whereof*: music initiates every movement of the masque, underlining its symbolic importance.

180 *Sylvans*: woodland semi-deities. One must have been played by a boy.

194 *kindlier*: 'befitting' is secondary meaning.

201 *must still be mingled*: an allusion to the uniting of the roses of York and Lancaster by Henry VII, used by James as precedent for his own unification of the kingdoms.

204 *Divers divers flowers affect*: different people adopt different flowers as theirs.

243 *Who . . . wife?*: cf. *Barriers* headnote and *passim*.

256 *levels fair*: both 'aims well' and 'lies down'.

258 *Io, Hymen*: salute to the marriage god; cf. Catullus lxi. 117.

260 *Diana*: 'The moon and queen of virginity, is said to be regent and empress of night, and is therefore by night defended as in her quarrel for the loss of the bride, her virgin' (Campion).

267 *veils*: the curtains which have hidden the bower of Night.

274 *Cynthia*: alternative name for Diana.

283 *throughly blown*: fully in bloom.

297 *thieves*: as the Knights of Apollo stand for the male, Scottish side of the marriage, their representation as 'thieves' might be held to articulate very frequently expressed English fears of the Scots' pillaging the riches of the kingdom—and seizing the marriageable women.

299 *Phoebus*: Apollo, god of the sun, but also a figure for King James (see ll. 310–32).

305 *gilt*: the original spelling 'guilt' perhaps suggests that James has rewarded them richly, but in so doing has laid them open to accusation of excess.

329 *highest gem that hung*: Hesperus presents a talismanic stone associated with the moon. The use of the past tense may link it with Queen Elizabeth, who was often represented in costume adorned with lunar jewels.

335 *leese*: variant form of 'lose', retained for the rhyme.

336 *This is her pleasure*: typographically differentiated in Quarto, perhaps for emphasis.

347 *Next Love*: following immediately after Love in order of precedence.

354 *Thracian harp*: instrument of Orpheus, the legendary musician, born in Thrace.

356 *Amphion*: son of Zeus, who with his lyre charmed rocks to build the walls of Thebes. With Orpheus he was routinely invoked to exemplify the power of music.

358 *Can music these enjoy?*: a textual crux. Q reads 'can music then joye? joy mountains moves'. The emendation offered here derives from Jonathan C. George in *Notes and Queries*, 206 (1971), 454–5. 'These' refers back

to the dancing stones, and the verb has a transitive sense 'to put into a joyous condition'. Joy which moves mountains is a biblical commonplace. The logic, then, is that since music produces a joy which moves stones, while heavenly joy moves mountains, music can certainly make the trees dance for joy.

360 *religious oak*: the oak at Dodona, sacred to Zeus, prophesied in the rustling of its leaves (Homer, *Odyssey* xiv. 327 ff.).

362 *Aeneas*: in Virgil's *Aeneid* iii. 24 ff. a tree from which he tears a branch is the transformed Polydorus, who warns him to leave Thrace.

378 *because*: implies a necessary function of music in any masque—to cover up the noise of stage machinery.

391 *Mete*: traverse, but also 'measure out'. The dancers move from Diana's tree to the throne of James.

402 *sylvan shadows*: the disguise of trees.

407 *began to yield*: 'Either by the simplicity, negligence, or conspiracy of the painter, the passing away of the trees was somewhat hazarded, the patterns of them the same day having been shown with much admiration, and the nine trees being left unset together even to the same night' (Campion).

412 *false habit*: the restoration is not complete until the knights have acknowledged the power of Diana.

431 *Like . . . receive*: speaking to the second three trees, who will be touched and transformed like the first.

432 *best of numbers is contained in three*: three is the number of the Trinity, and of perfection. It is also the number uniting the male one with female two, and therefore appropriate to marriage.

441 *first music*: the Sylvans.

444 *manner of an echo*: not a true Echo song, but the effect of *cori spezzati* (spaced choirs) popular in Renaissance music.

447 *bearing five voices*: singing in five parts made up of the six Chapel voices plus the four Sylvans (also probably members of the Chapel).

449 *distinguished by the place*: the consorts are distinct aurally because of their placement.

451 *forty-two*: the figure is puzzling; the totals given here add up to thirty-eight, unless extra Sylvans, or the hoboys, or Zephyrus (or some combination thereof) are counted in.

459 *rarely became*: excellently suited.

461 *distraction*: separation, from Lat. 'pulling apart'.

523 *rights*: also 'rites' (spelt the same in the period).

551 *before*: in front of the bower.

558 *leaden . . . grows*: becomes heavy-eyed and heavy-spirited.

561 *turtles*: turtle-doves (an emblem of faithful love).

566 *change of music and measure*: a change of pulse, perhaps from 2/4 to 3/4.

588 *buskin . . . bays*: the dignity of tragedy (buskins were the footwear of Roman tragic actors) or of the laureate poet.

603 *by the great*: wholesale.

611 *Quid . . . medici*: 'Why do you involve yourself in verses? Is it that verses, sportively written, do befit a physician, seated in his chair? O Phoebus, you are a musician, a physician, and a celebrated poet too; the charm of poetry helps the sick when art demands it. Believe you me, one who has no taste for the poet's song, the same has not native talents nor the skill of a physician.'

At the end of the masque Campion printed five pieces of music. Two were songs from the masque, the other three were tunes for dances to which Campion added words to make them singable to the lute or viol. They are not reprinted here.

The Masque of Queens

This 1609 masque is especially significant in the history of the genre for its introduction of the full-blown antimasque, set not merely as 'foil' to the main masque, but as representation of the forces of disorder over which the masquers triumph. Though Queen Anne was the patron of the masque, and may well have had a significant part to play in its design, as Jonson's preface indicates, the choice of witches as antimasque figures allowed Jonson to pay a compliment to the King, whose interest in the subject is attested by his work *Demonology*. The masque is also noteworthy for the extravagant fullness of its annotation, undertaken at the request of Prince Henry, and signifying the seriousness with which Jonson wished his high and hearty learnings to be taken. (Only a very few of these notes have been reproduced in this edition; most specify sources, and only those with direct bearing upon understanding have been used.)

Current critical debate centres on the extent to which the work represents a political attitude specific to the Queen. It is noteworthy that the queens personated by the noble ladies are praised for active rather than passive virtue, in significant opposition to James's love of peace. Feminist readings have also found the antimasque of hags problematic. The witches may represent a demonized version of male fear of women, but it is perhaps equally possible that, though Jonson grounds his witch-lore firmly in scholarship, the performance might have emphasized the ridiculous self-delusions of witchcraft as much as its menace.

The work was published in quarto in 1609, and in the 1616 Folio. In addition Jonson prepared a fine holograph manuscript for Prince Henry (BL Royal MS. 18 A), of which one page is reproduced (Fig. 3). This text is based on the Folio, but the dedication to Prince Henry, in MS and Quarto, is of such central interest that it is given below. (Henry died in 1612, before the Folio was printed.)

> To the glory of our own, and grief of other nations:
> My Lord Henry, Prince of Great Britain, etc.

Sir,

When it hath been my happiness (as would it were more frequent) but to see your face, and, as passing by, to consider you, I have with as much joy as I am now far from flattery in professing it, called to mind that doctrine of some great inquisitors in Nature, who hold every royal and heroic form to partake and draw much to it of the heavenly virtue. For whether it be that a divine soul, being to come into a body, first chooseth a palace fit for itself, or, being come, doth make it so, or that Nature be ambitious to have her work equal, I know not. But what is lawful for me to understand and speak, that I dare; which is, that both your virtue and your form did deserve your fortune. The one claimed that you should be born a prince; the other makes that you do become it. And when Necessity (excellent lord) the mother of the Fates, hath so provided that your form should not more insinuate you to the eyes of men than your virtue to their minds, it comes near a wonder to think how sweetly that habit flows in you, and with so hourly testimonies, which to all posterity might hold the dignity of examples. Amongst the rest, your favour to letters and these gentler studies that go under the title of Humanity is not the least honour of your wreath. For if once the worthy professors of these learnings shall come, as heretofore they were, to be the care of princes, the crowns their sovereigns wear will not more adorn their temples, nor their stamps live longer in their medals than in such subject's labours. Poetry, my lord, is not born with every man, nor every day; and in her general right it is now my minute to thank your highness, who not only do honour her with your ear, but are curious to examine her with your eye and enquire into her beauties and strengths. Where, though it hath proved a work of some difficulty to me to retrieve the particular authorities (according to your gracious command, and a desire born out of judgement) to those things which I writ out of fullness and memory of my former readings, yet, now I have overcome it, the reward that meets me is double to one act; which is, that thereby your excellent understanding will not only justify me to your own knowledge, but decline the stiffness of others' original ignorance, already armed to censure. For which singular bounty, if my fate, most excellent prince and only delicacy of mankind, shall reserve me to the age of your actions, whether in the camp or the council chamber, that I may write at nights the deeds of your days; I will then labour to bring forth some work as worthy of your fame as my ambition therein is of your pardon.

> By the most true admirer of your highness' virtues,
> And most hearty celebrator of them,
> Ben Jonson

226

1 *third time*: after the masques of *Blackness* and *Beauty*.

6 *best artist*: 'Horace, in *Ars Poetica*' (J).

11 *I was careful to decline*: either: 'I was on my guard against a falling off from', or 'I took pains to deviate from'.

12 *last . . . boys*: in the *Haddington Masque*.

23 *quae . . . possit*: 'who, furnished with so many poisons, might seem to have come from the mouth of hell'.

25 *eleven*: the number symbolized evil and imperfection.

43 *anoint*: 'When they are to be transported from place to place they use to anoint themselves, and sometimes the things they ride on' (J).

51 *tree . . . die on*: gallows.

53 *strike . . . heat*: make another attempt.

55 *horse of wood*: 'that which our witches call so, is sometime a broom-staff, sometime a reed, sometime a distaff' (J).

57 *goat*: 'The goat is the devil himself' (J).

58 *green cock . . . thread*: based on 'a vulgar fable of a witch, that with a cock of that colour and a bottom of blue thread, would transport herself through the air; and so escaped, at the time of her being brought to execution, from the hand of Justice. It was a tale when I went to school' (J).

69 *The owl . . . a-turning*: 'All this is but a periphrasis of the night, in their charm, and their applying themselves to it with their instruments, whereof the spindle in antiquity was the chief' (J).

74 *pictures . . . quick*: waxen images into which needles are stuck to bewitch the victim. J cites Bodin, who 'reports a relation of a French Ambassador's out of England of certain pictures of wax, found in a dunghill near Islington, of our late Queen's; which rumour I myself (being then very young) can remember to have been current'.

77 *little Martin*: 'is he that calls them to their conventicles, which is done in a human voice, but coming forth, they find him in the shape of a great buck goat, upon whom they ride to their meetings' (J).

84 *Dame*: 'This Dame I make to bear the person of Ate, or mischief' (J). The subsequent description uses details from Homer and Horace.

96 *For to have . . . narrations*: an attack on an old-fashioned mode of presentation, where each stage of the masque was explained by a presenter. Jonson perhaps particularly had in mind Daniel's *The Vision of Twelve Goddesses* (1604).

113 *oblique look*: sidelong glance.

116 *First . . . Mischief*: 'In chaining of these vices I make as if one link produced another, and the Dame were born out of them all' (J).

126 *retrieve . . . gold*: see *Gold*, headnote.

130 *I hate . . . increase*: an allusion to James's pacific foreign policy, which was coupled to his interest in all matters religious. (James had as his motto '*Beati pacifici*', 'blessed are the peacemakers'.) There were many who did not share the King's aims, and it may be that Jonson glancingly satirizes them here.

133 *hinge of things*: axis of the earth.

140 *quarter*: dismembered body of executed criminal.

148 *mandrake*: mandragora; its root was supposed to emit a shriek when pulled up.

153 *charnel-houses . . . pits*: three kinds of burial place; stores for bones exhumed to make space for further burials, private tombs, and pits into which, for example, the bodies of plague victims were tipped.

161 *piper . . . ale*: a piper (possibly a bagpiper, conventionally associated with lechery) begat the child at a church festivity where ale was provided. (These traditional feasts were targets of Puritan hostility.)

162 *blow . . . tail*: 'The pun is both anal and phallic' (O).

170 *Sir Cranion*: a fly.

187 *basilisk*: fabulous reptile whose look and breath could kill.

193 *in his*: i.e. his *Eclogues*. For full references see O 479.

202 *These . . . untied*: 'The untying of their knots is when they are going to some fatal business' (J).

206 *Hecatè*: deity presiding over magic and spells; a malign version of the moon-goddess. (For l. 217 J cites Virgil, 'threefold Hecate, the three faces of the virgin Diana'.)

230 *Deep . . .*: 'Here they speak as if they were creating some new feature . . . by the pronouncing of words, and pouring out of liquors on the earth . . . All which are mere arts of Satan, when either himself will delude them with a false form, or troubling a dead body, makes them imagine these vanities the means; as in the ridiculous circumstances that follow, he doth daily' (J).

241 *drake*: dragon; blue was the colour of plagues and things hurtful.

247 *Ashes . . . west*: these rites 'are all used (and believed by them) to the raising of storm and tempest' (J).

254 *do it kind*: follow its nature.

256 *Rouncy . . . Robble*: sounds of thunder, imitated from Stanyhurst's translation of the *Aeneid* (H&S).

263 *Stay!*: 'This stop, or interruption, showed the better, by causing that

general silence, which made all the following noises, enforced in the next charm more direful' (J).

289 *Chaos*: here the void of the underworld rather than the prima materia (cf. *Aeneid* vi. 265).

320 *property*: characteristic nature.

332 *pyramid*: emblem of Fame.

341 *I . . . name*: when Perseus, the child of Zeus and Danaë, boasted he would bring back the head of the Gorgon Medusa, he was helped by Pallas Athena's shield which allowed him to see the reflected head of Medusa (to look on it directly would have transformed him to stone), by Mercury's bill-hook with which he beheaded her, and by the helmet of Pluto, which enabled him to escape.

344 *Erinyes*: the three Furies, who lived in the darkest pit of hell.

352 *sounding brass*: a detail from Ovid's description of the house of Rumour (*Metamorphoses* xii. 39–63).

361 *file*: string on which papers are placed for preservation and reference.

379 *'gainst . . . Time*: their good reputation has been preserved for history against all their detractors.

382 *Bel-Anna*: Jonson's coinage for Queen Anne (modelled, suggest H&S, on Spenser's 'Belphoebe' for Queen Elizabeth).

392 *She*: i.e. Queen Anne.

413 *machina versatilis*: turning machine, which revealed the new set.

415 *Iconologia . . . Ripa*: see note to *Barriers*, l. 61.

417 *Orus . . . Hieroglyphica*: Horapollo's work, of the second or fourth century AD, interpreted Hermetic (occult) symbolism.

419 *Virgil . . . her*: *Aeneid* iv. 176–7.

430 *in gears applied*: put in harness.

433 *griffins*: fabulous beasts with the head of an eagle and body of a lion.

444 *disposed . . . election*: suggests either that the ladies were randomly apportioned their roles, or possibly that they chose the roles they wanted rather than those they might in some way be fitted for.

451 *inter . . . extitere*: 'amongst the bravest men many examples of her courage stood out'.

457 *Aurea . . . virum*: 'After the golden helmet her brow did bare, | her dazzling beauty overcame the conquering hero.' *Elegies* II. xi. 15–16.

470 *Hos . . . plantas*: 'In addition to these there comes, of Volscian clan, Camilla, leading her contingent of horsemen and their troops shining bright with bronze, a warrior-woman she. Not to Minerva's distaff or wool basket her feminine hands are accustomed, but as a maiden hardened to endure battles and by speed of foot to outstrip the winds.

She either would have been flying over the uncut cornfield's topmost growths, and not bruising in her course the tender ears, or over the midst of the sea, upon swelling wave held aloft, she would have been speeding her way, not dipping her swift feet in the surface of the sea.' *Aeneid* vii. 803 ff.

488 *Quod . . . mortem*: 'Because in war she engaged the most powerful king of the Persians and despoiled him of both life and camp, in order justly to avenge her son's most undeserved death.'

490 *Artemisia*: J conflates two women of the same name (H&S).

496 *Viri . . . viri*: 'In truth as men have my women shown themselves, but as women my men.'

512 *ad . . . leonis*: 'linked to the tail of Leo'.

516 *even from*: even from the time when she was.

519 *Cognoram . . . magnanimam*: 'I knew you to be great of heart even from girlhood.'

526 *Tonsis . . . interesset*: 'For, having cut off her hair, she accustomed herself to horse and to arms, whereby the more easily to share in his toils and dangers.'

540 *maximi . . . appellatae*: 'a woman of the utmost courage and of such great service to her people that all the queens of the Ethiopians, thereafter, have been called by her name'.

552 *Bunduca . . . prevailed, etc.*: Spenser, 'The Ruins of Time', 108–12.

560 *Bunduica . . . severo, etc.*: 'Bunduica, a British woman, born of royal stock, who not only ruled over them with great dignity and authority but also conducted war in its every aspect, and her spirit was that of a man rather than of a woman . . . A woman of most distinguished appearance, austere expression, etc.'

570 *ea . . . conceptionibus*: 'of such appearance that to the Roman People nothing else seemed more possessed of triumphal splendour . . . that not even of her husband did she have carnal knowledge, except for attempted conception'.

585 *sine . . . viderentur*: 'nobody saw her without a feeling of veneration and to hear her speaking was held to be a marvellous thing. So great was the weight of her authority in delivering judgement, that those convicted of a crime, when they were being punished, seemed to experience nothing grievous to themselves.'

595 *inter . . . feminas*: 'amongst the most outstanding women'.

603 *hers proper*: her own name.

612 *Mezentius*: a tyrant who destroyed his victims by binding the living to the dead (*Aeneid* viii. 485–8).

631 *Chaucer*: in *The House of Fame*, 1184 ff.

633 *several-coloured lights*: produced by oil lamps shining through coloured glass.

666 *took out the men*: invited men in the audience to dance with them in the revels.

677 *numerous*: made up of numbers; referring metaphorically to the proportion of the dance and of the music, and specifically to the geometric 'figures' they traced.

679 *Charles*: James and Anne's second son, the future Charles I.

Tethys' Festival

This masque was Daniel's second and last for Queen Anne, for whom he was a groom of the Privy Chamber. It was her contribution to the festivities that surrounded the investiture of Prince Henry as Prince of Wales in 1610. Its interest lies first in the elaborate descriptions of settings and costumes (none of the scene designs survive). The attention paid to the 'body' of the performance is symptomatic of Daniel's attack on Jonson's view of the masque itself. The work is suffused with uncertainty about the power of performances such as these to stand against their own transitoriness, and insists upon the limitations of art in transcending the real world. Daniel lost the argument, and literary critics have tended to take Jonson's side ever since—but he has a real case to offer.

The work was issued in a 1610 quarto, but for some reason not in Daniel's posthumously collected works.

   Wake: holiday feast.

3 *magnificence*: princely virtue of generosity, richness, and moral worth.

8 *in regard to*: with purpose to.

13 *digito . . . est*: 'to be pointed at with the finger—that's the man'.

22 *affection . . . to do*: where both emotional and intellectual opposition were in control.

25 *ut . . . videatur*: '[may make it] so that our judgement appears as fear'.

30 *battery . . . ordnance*: metaphors from gunnery (with a pun on 'ordinance/ordnance').

32 *shadows*: see below, ll. 343–8.

35 *flying . . . authors*: the sense of the futility of arming oneself with literary authorities is a stand against Jonson's defence of the masque by an appeal to antiquarian scholarship.

38 *argument . . . imbecilities*: proof that we are all fools.

43 *low . . . abilities*: clearly aimed at Jonson's arrogance.

58 *only . . . Jones*: this does not necessarily imply that Jones actually wrote the descriptions.

59 *Tethys*: daughter of Uranus and Gaia, she personified the feminine fecundity of the sea, and by her husband Oceanus had more than 3,000 children who were all the rivers of the world; appropriate here to the queen as mother, honouring one son and performing with her other two children.

80 *Monmouthshire*: the ladies were all daughters of the fourth Earl of Worcester, whose estates were largely in the county.

86 *interset*: Q reads 'interser'.

89 *Nereus*: an Old Man of the Sea, a friend of fishermen and sailors.

91 *His . . . retinendo*: 'by these arts', 'by ruling and restraining'.

Hae . . . etc.: 'these will be your arts (of government)'; *Aeneid* vi. 852. The pacific emphasis of the passage from which the quotation is taken fits with James's political attitudes, and with the later advice to Henry in this masque.

93 *Triton*: minor deity in the retinue of Neptune.

104 *port or haven*: celebrating Prince Henry's interest in shipping and fortification.

110 *Zephyrus*: 'the figure of Zephyrus might aptly discharge this representation in respect that messages are of wind, and *verba dicunter alata* winged words: besides this a character of youth and of the spring' (Daniel).

eight: one contemporary account suggests that there were twelve attendants.

112 *antemasque*: Daniel's spelling retained; it is not an 'antimasque' in Jonson's terms.

Duke of York: Prince Charles.

114 *wing . . . labels*: the wings were made of a fine gauzy fabric in narrow bands (*labels*) hanging from a wire frame.

139 *new . . . state*: the new status of Prince Henry as Prince of Wales.

144 *Meliades*: a version of Moeliades, the name chosen by Prince Henry because it was an anagram of *Miles a Deo* ('Soldier from God'), combining chivalric and religious revivalism.

148 *trident*: appropriate to James's rule over the ocean, and also to his triple kingdom.

rich sword: said to have been worth 20,000 crowns.

150 *intelligence . . . sphere*: invoking the Platonic belief that the spheres were driven by spirits, or 'intelligences'.

156 *these*: i.e. the gifts, which are given to the good.

188 *Milford . . . that*: Henry VII landed at Milford Haven, unseated Richard III, and united the warring houses of York and Lancaster; James descended from Henry VII, and saw his union of the kingdoms as an extension of the earlier triumph (cf. *Lord Hay's Masque*).

191 *Oceanus*: the Atlantic.

195 *Lord . . . Isles*: Henry's Scottish title as eldest son of the monarch.

197 *Astraea*: goddess of justice. She was frequently associated with Queen Elizabeth, and Daniel may here be emphasizing the continuity from the previous reign.

203 *scarf . . . day*: the scarf which is embroidered with a map of Britain (his 'empery') is, significantly, a 'zone' or girdle to contain the sword, which itself must only be exercised in the cause of justice. The masque combats some of the more aggressively bellicose hopes being pinned upon Prince Henry.

207 *Alcides' pillars*: pillars of Hercules, or Straits of Gibraltar.

211 *Indies . . . brought*: the West Indies (or Americas) brought to Spain.

216 *Aurora*: the dawn.

222 *language . . . design*: implies that Daniel is using the technical language of Jones. 'Design', for Italian *disegno*, was still an unfamiliar term in English, here meaning perhaps 'graphic art'. *Mestier*, either French *métier*, or Italian *mestiere*.

226 *manner . . . scene*: the turning of the *machina versatilis*.

230 *pillars*: Q reads 'pillows'.

231 *modern . . . room*: meaning is obscure.

246 *jewel . . . like*: candles or oil lamps shining through coloured glass.

249 *cartouches*: tablets for an inscription made to represent a sheet of paper.

263 *equal*: to the same height.

269 *shell*: the profusion of shells associates Anne with Venus, who was born from sea-foam, and often depicted standing in a shell.

288 *Lady Elizabeth*: Princess Elizabeth, James and Anne's daughter, then aged 13.

293 *maritime invention*: marine designs.

299 *with the work of*: with the same needlework as.

    cypress: valuable satin cloth.

305 *Tree . . . bay*: the laurel; an Elizabethan medal had depicted a bay tree on a mount rising out of the sea.

338 *well-set parts*: both 'firmly based' and 'musically well arranged'.

342 *another song*: this song, with the preceding one, forms the core of Daniel's reflection upon the nature of the masque.

365 *confusion . . . shows*: both the 'real' confusion of the rush to the banquet,

and also the philosophical 'confusion' of performer and role, which Daniel assertively undoes by presenting his masquers as themselves.

388 *imaginary sight*: fictional spectacle.

411 *none . . . sort*: i.e. no professional actors of the kind employed in Jonson's antimasques.

422 *Pretulerim . . . ringi*: Horace, *Epistles* II. ii. 126–8, 'I should prefer to be thought a foolish and clumsy scribbler, if only my failings please, or at least escape me, rather than be wise and unhappy.'

Love Restored

The masque was performed on Twelfth Night, 1612. It is referred to in the Book of the Revels as 'the Princes Maske', so Prince Henry may have taken some part in it. But on this, as on everything else, the printed description is silent. We know little or nothing about performers, scenery, or music. O&S conjecturally ascribe one Inigo Jones costume design to the masque, and a partly decipherable letter by John Chamberlain suggests that the masquers were principally Scots; he gives three names, John Livingstone of Kinnaird, Groom of the Bedchamber, Abercrombie, and Sir Henry Bowyer. Clearly this was an economical masque—H&S suggest that it may have cost as little as £280. James's finances were in parlous condition, and the failure of the Great Contract in the 1610 Parliament, when in return for a regular income the King had offered to surrender certain rights, exacerbated matters further. It is in this context that the masque's discussion of the justification of expenditure on such entertainments has to be placed. Jonson attacks the objections of the 'Puritan' Plutus by satirizing his bourgeois values, and deploys the iconological overlap between this god and Cupid wittily to revise the audience's perception of wealth. The presence of the country spirit Robin Goodfellow enables the work to take a rather ambivalent view of courtly behaviour, but in the end the masque endorses James's right to financial support through the love of his subjects returned to a sovereign who himself frees love from bondage to mere riches.

   by . . . Servants: members of the theatrical company the King's Men (Shakespeare's company).

5 *speak . . . vizard*: a key sentence in establishing the masque's interest in disguise and truth.

9 *attire . . . attired*: the repetition seems meaningless; probably, as H&S suggest, a textual corruption.

11 *never paid . . . nothing*: a pointed joke by Jonson, who was very aware of his own financial interests.

   morris-dance: not just a dance, but a mummers' performance.

13 *no other*: H&S; Ff read 'neither'.

wild music: cf. *Pleasure Reconciled*, 1. 4.

16 *Enter Plutus*: there were two traditions in the representation of Plutus. In one (used by Jonson in his work for the King's 'passing to his coronation') he is a 'little boy, bare headed, his locks curled, and spangled with gold' (H&S vii. 97), hence easily mistaken for Cupid; in the other he is an old man, blind and decrepit. Masquerado is taken in by his disguise as Cupid.

34 *Robin Goodfellow*: cf. *Coleorton Masque*.

35 *no masque*: F1 punctuates the second cry 'no, masque', perhaps to indicate Robin's incredulous emphasis.

45 *England's Joy*: a play advertised in 1602, but the promoter vanished with the entrance money, and provided no performance.

47 *short service*: short-term employment.

shoeing . . . mare: literally, a difficult job; also the name of a Christmas game.

50 *recovered . . . you*: he has put off his disguises, and appears as himself.

52 *riddles . . . maids*: maids are puzzled by the way their chores are done.

53 *hot cockles*: 'a rustic game in which one player lay face downwards . . . with his eyes covered, and being struck on the back by the others in turn, guessed who struck him' (*OED*).

57 *shop . . . revels*: the whole repertory of masque devices.

58 *admit . . . feats*: he had hoped to demonstrate his tricks as part of a masque.

60 *rude*: rural, lower-class.

61 *admitty*: Jonsonian coinage (H&S suggest it is a misprint for 'activity').

65 *wood-yard*: yard outside palace, otherwise known as Scotland Yard.

76 *Coryat*: Thomas Coryat, famous traveller, who had himself smuggled into a masque in a trunk.

case o' catsos: (O following Ricks); Folio reads 'a case: vses'. Others have suggested 'case of asses' and 'case of aufs (oafs)'. The meaning is 'a pair of rogues' ('catso' was also slang for 'penis').

80 *engineer . . . motions*: Robin posed as one involved with the construction of the (moving) scenery.

84 *mark . . . mouth*: I was too old (a metaphor from horses, who with age lose the markings on teeth).

87 *feather . . . Blackfriars*: making feathers for court costume, a common employment in this Puritan district.

98 *too much*: i.e. to drink—with the unfortunate consequences that follow.

101 *cataract . . . stargazing*: literally, a waterfall (of urine) landing in the eye as he looked upward, but with subsidiary pun on cataract as near-blindness caused by looking up the skirts of the women on the steps.

104 *Black Guard*: ironic and derogatory term for the lowest of kitchen servants, dirty from tending fires.

vestry: a rare usage meaning 'dress', though with clear bawdy implication.

105 *Christmas cutpurse*: highly topical reference to one John Selman, who had picked pockets in the royal chapel and was executed the day after this masque.

107 *forgo my form*: discard my disguise.

112 *could not . . . example*: since it could not be handed over in total secrecy, the guards were afraid to take a bribe lest they be observed and punished as an example to others.

132 *I . . . states*: standard attack on the extravagance of masques, particularly pointed at this time.

136 *post . . . rich*: 'post and pair' and 'noddy' are card games, 'God make them rich' a kind of backgammon.

141 *draw-gloves . . . dreams*: various parlour games.

142 *wires and tires*: *wires* used to make ruffs stand out; *tires*: fine clothes.

143 *taken-up braveries*: fine clothes bought on credit (O).

144 *so ill*: such bad report.

147 *reformed*: carries also the suggestion of a member of a reformed religious sect.

151 *Anti-Cupid*: according to one mythological tradition there were two Cupids, Eros and Anteros, earthly and heavenly love. Jonson dramatized the myth in his *Challenge at Tilt* the following year, and in *Bolsover*.

160 *arbitrary from him*: depend upon his arbitrary whim.

165 *his . . . arms*: the forcibly stolen shape and weapons of Cupid.

205 *thou . . . shine*: the double iconography of Plutus (see above, l. 16) is employed in this speech.

210 *commandement*: Jonson's spelling retained for the metre.

222 *The majesty . . . slave*: King James is secured by the love of his people; he therefore does not need to sue for Plutus's help, but can compel it. (In the context of James's financial difficulties and the failure of the Great Contract with Parliament this is a highly charged, if ambiguous, suggestion.)

243 *Dances*: the specially choreographed dances of the masquers.

256 *Till greater . . . them*: until the ladies in the audience dance with them.

262 *The Revels*: the normal process of taking out the ladies in the audience was presumably intended here, with the last song acting as epilogue. Jonson probably omitted to mention the revels in his published account since, according to Chamberlain, the ladies (including Frances Howard, Countess of Essex, and her sister, wife to Lord Cranborne) turned their backs on the men, who then had to 'make court to one another'.

270 *morning . . . true*: a belief persisting from classical times (O).

The Memorable Masque

This masque was performed as part of the celebrations for the marriage of Frederick, Elector Palatine, to Princess Elizabeth, the King's daughter, who were married on St Valentine's Day 1613. Masques were provided on three consecutive nights, by Campion, Chapman, and Beaumont. The last two were presented by the Inns of Court at considerable expense. The total raised by the two Inns involved in this masque amounted to £2,255.

The choice of a Virginian subject was probably influenced by Prince Henry, Chapman's patron, who, before his death in 1612, was closely involved with the preparations for the marriage and was a noted supporter of exploration (and of Sir Walter Raleigh). The subject was topical, as strenuous efforts had been made in the previous three years to rekindle enthusiasm for the colonization of Virginia. It was frequently linked with anti-Spanish sentiment and Protestant religious enthusiasm, feelings that the marriage itself also generated. The work, therefore, accords with, even if it moderates, the atmosphere of religious revivalism which surrounded the marriage. Chapman draws on material from the literature of travel, including matter from his own earlier poem 'De Guiana', which had prefaced Keymis's account of the 1596 voyage and had sought to defend the reputation of his friend Raleigh, but he seems more interested in the symbolic ends his work might serve than in geographical accuracy.

Two major ideas underlie the work: the reconciliation of opposites, and the question of right perception. The former is seen in the deployment of the myth of the marriage of heaven and earth, love and beauty; the latter is evident from Chapman's angry defence of his work, and is explored in the relationship of Plutus and Capriccio in the antimasque, and in the central device of the 'conversion' of the Virginian priests' perceptions of the sun.

Two quartos were published in 1613; they have been carefully collated by G. Blakemore Evans, who also draws on MS emendations in one copy of the printed text. This edition is based on his text, collated with Q1.

White-Hall: in the Great Hall, not the Banqueting House, which had been used the previous night for Campion's *Lords' Masque*.

Master of the Rolls: the keeper of records in the Court of Chancery, and *ex officio* judge of the Court of Appeal.

architect: at this date Jones had not erected a single building, but was surveyor to Prince Henry.

Invented . . . Chapman: the respective roles of designer and poet are ambiguous, but the implication might be that Jones was responsible for the invention of the 'work' (i.e. scenery) alone.

19 *only ingenuous will*: open, free-hearted will alone.

30 *thus set forth*: the ensuing description has been re-paragraphed to aid clarity.

34 *baboons*: according to Chamberlain, they were played by 'little boys'. Baboons 'will imitate all humaine actions, loving wonderfully to wear garments' (E.Topsell, *The Historie of Four-Footed Beasts* (1607), 11). Those who imitated foreign fashions were frequently called 'apes'.

fantastical travellers: cf. Campion, *Caversham Entertainment*.

40 *These were . . . invention*: each one was completely different in design.

41 *musicians*: O&S note payments, amongst others, to Thomas Cutting, John Dowland, Thomas Ford, all of them composers as well as lutenists. Robert Johnson and Ford are recorded as the actual composers of the music for the masque.

42 *the sun is there adored*: probably derived from accounts of the Incas, rather than Virginians.

43 *Phoebades*: derived from 'Phoebus', god of the sun.

feathers: already firmly associated with representation of Amerindians.

78 *habits of themselves*: the dress of the masquers, though elaborate, was less of a departure from their 'ordinary' selves than that of the torch-bearers, which was more 'extravagantly' foreign.

90 *Capriccio*: the details of the costume are derived from Ripa's *Iconologia* (see note to *Barriers*, l. 61).

93 *Eunomia*: one of the Hours, the three daughters of Zeus and Themis, representing Law.

94 *Phemis*: Fame. Honour derives from public esteem as well as private virtue.

96 *pentacle*: garment in the shape of a pentangle, a magical symbol.

103 *Plutus*: god of wealth; often conflated with Pluto, god of the underworld. Chapman is consciously revising the figure presented in Jonson's *Love Restored*.

134 *All . . . colour*: an image of the upward aspiration which underlies the masque's myth. The image is based on descriptions of golden mountains in travel literature, especially in Raleigh's account of Guiana.

136 *composed order*: mixed classical orders.

139 *bastard order*: John Peacock informs me that Jones derived the term from Serlio; he suggests it is 'a dwarf order of pilasters relatively or completely unadorned, used in an upper storey in relation to a regular order in the principal storey'.

140 *HONORIS FANUM*: Temple of Honour.

143 *round stone . . . Fortune's*: these are the standard attributes of Fortune. Her presence here reflects a commonplace debate about whether Honour is achieved through Fortune or Virtue; in 'fixing' the symbols of mutability Chapman presents a reconciliation of the three.

147 *figuring this kingdom*: Britain is represented by the temple of Honour.

put off . . . fixed: Fortune has surrendered and immobilized the emblems of her fleeting inconstancy. He draws on Plutarch's *Moralia* 317F–318A where Fortune stays fixed at Rome.

155 *These following*: Chapman prints here stage directions he had intended to insert in their proper places later in the text, but the printer had proceeded too quickly with setting the copy for the additions to be made.

168 *Orphean virtue*: a charm with the power of Orpheus' music.

175 *state*: Evans (MS emendation). Qq 'seate'.

192 *To answer . . . necessary*: the speeches were necessary to make the action of the masque seem probable, and its relevance to participants and audiences clear.

212 *est . . . grave*: 'opportunity is a disease of the soul, when it strikes it gives the soul a grave wound'. Plutarch, *Morals*, Amatorius 763, b.

213 *some*: Parrott; Qq 'all'.

218 *insania . . . furor*: Chapman distinguishes mere madness (*insania*) from the divine fury (*divinus furor*) of inspiration. (The same distinction is made in Campion's *The Lords' Masque*, also performed to celebrate this wedding.)

224 *Emollit . . . feros*: 'It makes character gentle and is not permitted to be savage.' Ovid, *Pontic Epistles* II. ix. 48.

235 *Honour . . . virtue*: as in Roman temples to Honour, only reached after passing through the temple of Virtue.

245 *Non . . . fidem*: 'There is no certain trust which an injury does not overturn. And the haven itself betrays the trust.' Two lines from Propertius: III. viii. 19 and III. vii. 36.

252 *rocks . . . devices*: a joke at the expense of Jonson's *Oberon* and other masques.

257 *stony-hearted . . . masques*: an allusion to Campion's *Lords' Masque*, performed the previous night, which featured ladies transformed to statues.

266 *ut sequitur*: as follows.

269 *Sisyphus*: father of Ulysses, and a trickster; condemned perpetually to roll a rock uphill in Hades.

270 *Philosopher's Stone*: goal of the alchemists, believed capable of transmuting other metals to gold.

271 *Proteus*: god of the sea, and able incessantly to transform himself. All these comparisons emphasize the shape-changing trickery of Capriccio.

282 *Spruce*: Prussia; here used for land of Cockayne.

284 *no transformation*: not the conventional masque revelation promised by the splitting of the rocks.

295 *divisus . . . Britannus*: 'Britain divided from the world'—a frequently cited idea from Virgil, *Eclogues* i. 67.

302 *Paeans*: originally songs specifically to Apollo, god of the sun.

313 *will be shortly extant*: Chapman recognizes the fact that gold had not yet been found in Virginia, but suggests the oft-repeated hopes of its discovery.

342 *tobacco shop*: James was notoriously opposed to tobacco, ironically to become the main source of Virginian wealth.

344 *trencher-fools*: parasitic fools-at-table.

351 *shoemaker*: Simon Eyre, whose rise is charted in Dekker's *The Shoemakers' Holiday* (1599).

360 *courser in the field*: a charger on the field of battle.

361 *wizards*: philosophers or sages.

394 *encouragement . . . disgrace*: Capriccio makes some telling points (particularly in view of his later treatment); there is, perhaps, a covert allusion to the fate of Raleigh, at the time of the masque still imprisoned in the Tower.

428 *predecessor Ulysses*: in that he was a traveller and shape-changer.

431 *Go*: Evans (MS correction); Qq 'So'.

439 *Argus*: legendary figure depicted in a cloak with a hundred eyes.

440 *Pluto . . . Jupiter*: 'even Pluto gives way to Jupiter'.

453 *Law*: Evans (MS correction); 'Love' Qq.

481 *a plain*: meaning is ambiguous; suggestions are: 'strikes a full note' (Parrott); 'strikes a plainful note' (Dutton); or, as *a-plain*, 'strikes plainly'.

492 *Kiss, heaven and earth*: alluding to the myth of the coupling of Uranus (Heaven) and Gaia (Earth).

506 *stance*: stanza; here referring to the group of three verses, in imitation of the Pindaric Ode.

508 *Tethys*: personification of the sea; her dwelling in the far west where

the sun, represented as her lover, comes to rest. A poetical common-place.

522 *our clear Phoebus*: James, shining as the sun god.

523 *piety . . . deity*: recapitulating James's claims to the divine right of kings.

548 *Phoebe*: the moon; in legend sun and moon were twins born to Latona.

549 *songs dost set*: Apollo/Phoebus was also god of poetry; the line is a compliment to James as a writer of verse.

563 *mother*: Mary Queen of Scots.

576 *offered . . . region*: the Virginian enterprise, especially at the time of this masque, was represented as a missionary activity.

578 *Loud music*: Evans (MS addition to printed copy).

584 *Twins*: Chapman notes: 'bride and groom were figured in Love and Beauty. Twins of which Hippocrates speaks.' This favourite image of his derives from Cicero, and was appropriate on this occasion, as he also notes, because Frederick and Elizabeth were 'both of an age'.

598 *single*: as a solo, or accompanied by a single lute.

599 *Panthaea*: this seems to be a myth of Chapman's own invention.

609 *Doing . . . kindness*: each offering grace and kindness to the other.

622 *golden world*: the Americas were often invoked in paradisal terms.

625 *holy rage*: divine fury.

651 *Hercules*: Zeus lay two nights with Alcmene. The invocation of Hercules here refers back to the 'choice' of the antimasque, between the paths of virtue and vanity. It is also appropriate on the second night of Frederick and Elizabeth's marriage.

Chapman appended 'A Hymn to Hymen', an epithalamion, to the published masque.

The Caversham Entertainment

After bidding farewell to her newly married daughter, Princess Elizabeth, Queen Anne set out on her progress towards Bath, which she visited regularly for her gout. She stayed at Caversham, the house of Sir William Knollys, son-in-law of the Earl of Suffolk. The masquers were four of Suffolk's sons, with Richard Sackville, Earl of Dorset, Dudley Baron North, Sir Henry Carey, and Sir Henry Rich (later Earl of Holland). The Queen was accompanied by Alice Egerton and Anne Clifford.

The work revisits many of the pastoral topoi of the progress entertainments for Queen Elizabeth. It is gracefully arranged, as the various figures greet the Queen with increasing sophistication of language and music as she approaches nearer to the house. No music or designs survive.

5 *Caversham*: (spelt 'Cawsome' in Q). The house was rebuilt in the early eighteenth century, and later destroyed by fire.

9 *flight-shots*: about two-fifths of a mile.

10 *Cynic*: a follower of the philosophical school of which Diogenes was the most famous exponent, espousing absolute simplicity of life. Campion makes his character speak in the style of Seneca, whose Stoicism has some similarity with the doctrines of the Cynics. The figure may owe something to the surly Porter who opened the Kenilworth entertainment of Queen Elizabeth in 1575.

11 *skin coat*: a tight leather jerkin, but also, as becomes clear later, a garment suggesting nakedness.

31 *fantastic traveller*: cf. Chapman, *Memorable Masque*. Campion gestures towards the eccentric style of Thomas Coryat (see *Love Restored*, note to l. 76), for whose travel-book he had provided a prefatory epigram.

60 *go*: walk.

69 *Action . . . action*: echoes Cicero, *De Officiis* I. vi. 19, one of the most celebrated tags in the commonplace debate between the merits of the active and contemplative life.

81 *Monmouth-caps*: tall, round-crowned, brimless caps, worn by soldiers and Welshmen.

85 *farthingale-wise*: puffed out as if with hoops like a farthingale.

102 *feign*: the word is puzzling; it may imply that these grown men mimed the treble parts which were actually sung by boys who were concealed.

144 *trees . . . distance*: John Nichols (*The Progresses of James the First*, 4 vols. (London, 1828), ii. 634) says that one of three avenues was called Queen Anne's Walk in memory of this visit.

152 *codpiece*: the padded phallic protrusion was distinctly old-fashioned by this time.

160 *antique*: the form 'anticke' which appears in the copy-text can either mean 'grotesque' (as above, l. 105), or, as here, 'antique'. This fits with the Gardener's old-fashioned Euphuistic style.

186 *accept . . . desire*: accept our wish to please, even if the execution is less than perfect.

197 *division*: ornamentation of the melodic line. The singer is a virtuoso. Unfortunately we do not know what the 'unusual instruments' might be.

234 *two . . . pap*: her breasts ('pap' is 'infant food').

237 *travelled*: pun on 'travailed', which had the same spelling.

245 *Bacchus*: god of the vine and revelry.

246 *bravery*: fine clothes.

255 *à la . . . France*: 'in the French manner'; Davis suggests 'in pantomime'.

274 *Silvanus*: god of the woods, his depiction often blurred with that of Silenus, the satyrs, and Pan.

279 *Cyparissus*: beautiful youth beloved, in different versions, of Apollo or Sylvanus. In his grief at killing a stag he was turned into the cypress, tree of sadness.

306 *answerable . . . vizards*: the masks which the performers wore both concealed and declared their identities.

322 *mean presents*: according to Chamberlain, the Queen was given 'a dainty coverlet or quilt, a rich carcanet (necklace) and a curious cabinet to the value in all of £1,500' (cited in Davis, p. 234). Since these do not tally with the gifts specified in the preceding stage directions, there were probably additional presentations made.

The Golden Age Restored

Herford and Simpson's argument, followed by all subsequent commentators, that this masque was placed out of sequence in the Folio, and was performed in 1615, has been decisively overturned by John Orrell's discovery of a letter from the Florentine ambassador indicating that *The Golden Age Restored* was indeed the 1616 masque. The revision of the dating renders much of the comment on this masque in editions and critical works redundant.

The masque dramatizes one of the most frequently invoked classical myths, in which Saturn's age of gold was succeeded by the silver age of Jupiter, then the age of brass, and finally the iron age. During this last age of bloodshed the goddess of justice, Astraea, the last of the immortals on earth, fled back to heaven. Virgil's famous fourth Eclogue suggested that the reign of Augustus saw her return. The myth was invoked in religious and political contexts during the Renaissance, and had been a potent element in Elizabethan iconology. It is here being used to celebrate James's purging of the corruption of the court. The issue had particular topicality since the trials for the murder of Thomas Overbury were in process. Most of these took place in late 1615, but at the time of the masque the prosecution of Robert Carr, Earl of Somerset, James's former favourite, and his wife Frances Howard for their part in the murder was still awaited. The whole proceedings were presented as a triumph of James's love of justice over the claims of favouritism and high birth.

No designs survive for this masque, nor, though it would seem from the verse-form that much of it was sung, does any of the music.

    Gentlemen . . . Servants: the acting company, the King's Men.

1 *Pallas*: Athena (Minerva), goddess of wisdom.

5 *him . . . thunder*: Jove.

9 *Jove . . . stronger*: suggesting that James has decided to take action against the corruption of the court.

12 *golden chain*: from Homer, *Iliad* viii. 19; the idea of the golden chain was, as J says elsewhere, 'interpreted diversely'.

13 *mettle*: also 'metal'; both words were spelt the same.

17 *Time . . . father*: Jove's age (which followed that of Saturn, or Time) is golden too. A suggestion, perhaps, that James can make a golden age equal to that of his predecessor, Elizabeth/Astraea. (Jonson seems specifically to be countering the increasing prevalence of a restrospective idealization of her reign among James's opponents.)

25 *As*: as if.

30 *shield*: to which was attached the Gorgon's head (given to her by Perseus), and which therefore turned to stone anything that looked at it.

42 *stands*: offers itself as candidate.

43 *more*: greater.

48 *pyrrhic dance*: imitating battle in the steps.

66 *giants*: Titans, overthrown by Jove.

78 *metamorphosed*: they presumably 'froze' as if turned into stone.

97 *grace . . . due*: the restoration of justice is a matter of divine and kingly grace, and should be accepted as such.

114 *Egyptian . . . lyre*: in Plato, *Laws* vii. 799, the Egyptian consecration of music is a model for resistance to innovation; the Thracian lyre is that of Orpheus.

115 *Chaucer . . . Spenser*: the standard list of famous English poets.

118 *pressed*: oppressed; also an allusion to the palm tree, emblem of truth, which flourishes the more it is pressed.

123 *Elysian . . . keep*: the only indication of what kind of 'Scene of light' (l. 133) the masquers were presented in. Possibly an allusion to the maintenance of justice in the countryside by nobles established on their estates.

130 *put . . . be*: take on the character of.

138 *tumour . . . vein*: 'swelling' of passion (as in the iron age).

144 *genii . . . grounds*: the golden age is imagined in rural terms.

148 *quickening power*: power to give life.

152 *earth unploughed . . .*: many of the details in the following lines come from classical sources, esp. Hesiod, Ovid, Virgil.

162 *mandrake*: poisonous plant (mandragora).

168 *used to join . . .*: the ensuing picture of innocent sexual frankness— particularly pointed in the context of the revelations about Robert Carr

and his wife—owes something to Spenser's Garden of Adonis, *Faerie Queene* iii. 6.

171 *feature . . . advance*: Platonic terminology: individual shapes were perfected into their ideal ones (O).

200 *fear*: i.e. with fear.

201 *What change . . . give*: in some copies of F1 this speech forms the conclusion of the masque, following the speech of Pallas. Jonson may have felt that Astraea's celebration of James's Britain made a more fitting end to his volume. The most likely performance order is here restored.

206 *behold . . . retire*: in the absence of any description of the set it is impossible to know whither Pallas urges the masquers to retire.

Christmas His Masque

This work, performed at court perhaps on Christmas Day, 1616, is an oddity. A contemporary MS (Folger MS 2203.1) carries the title 'Christmas his Showe', which is in many ways more appropriate. The work draws on traditions of mumming and folk-play in a deliberately old-fashioned, uncourtly entertainment. It sets out to dramatize the love of the city towards the King, but in Cupid's failure to speak his lines at the end Leah Marcus has seen an ironic comment on the failure of Londoners to live up to old practices (*The Politics of Mirth*, 82). Clearly she is right to set the work in the context of religious controversy about the celebration of Christmas itself, seen by many stricter Protestants as an intolerable preservation of pagan and Popish rituals.

2 *brooch*: worn as ornament, and to hold the feather.

8 *Lord Chamberlain*: the person responsible for the organization of court entertainment (the Earl of Pembroke at the time of this masque).

14 *Gregory Christmas*: J is perhaps alluding to the fact that Gregory the Great had sanctioned the Christian taking over of old pagan festivals at the time of the conversion of England (Marcus).

Pope's Head Alley: in Cornhill by the tavern of the same name.

15 *as . . . Protestant*: the comment acts as a defence against the Puritan charge that the celebration of Christmas was a Popish survival.

19 *Curriers' Hall*: headquarters of the guild of leathermakers.

weather . . . open: free from frost.

28 *flat cap*: worn by London citizens.

30 *Misrule*: the Lord of Misrule was a figure of inversion and feasting

appointed to head the revels in great houses at Christmas time; the rope, and so on, are signs of his trade as a carrier.

38 *cowlstaff . . . cloth*: large stick and blindfold for Blind Man's Buff.

39 *Post and Pair*: a common card-game.

40 *pairs and purs*: packs of cards; jacks.

42 *New-Year's Gift*: presents were given then, rather than at Christmas.

43 *rosemary gilt*: customary practice on festive occasions.

47 *box*: Christmas collection box.

ringing it: either jingling the coins in the box, or, perhaps, ringing a bell.

54 *cake . . . peas*: 'a bean and pea were put in the Twelfth Night cake; whoever got the slice with the bean was king, and whoever got the pea was queen' (H&S).

58 *highness small*: Prince Charles, now heir to the throne after the death of his elder brother, Prince Henry.

64 *Noise outside*: (O).

65 *'A' peace*: 'have peace', be quiet.

66 *Friday Street*: in Cheapside, where fishmongers lived.

67 *Fish Streets*: north from London Bridge, where fish-markets were held.

69 *Fish . . . days*: legislation banned the eating of meat on Fridays, Saturdays, and other fast days.

72 *Milk Street*: centre of dairy trade.

99 *I was . . . beseech you*: these lines are found only in MS, where they follow l. 93. I follow O's placement of them here.

101 *Pudding Lane*: where butchers made black pudding, a sausage of pig's blood and fat.

102 *Love Lane*: 'so called of wantons' (John Stow, *A Survey of London*, 1598).

103 *bird-bolts*: arrows for shooting birds, here alluding to Cupid shooting ladies.

108 *smith*: Venus's husband, Vulcan, was a smith.

109 *Do-little Lane*: a passage with no dwellings, alluding also to Vulcan's sexual inadequacies.

111 *fishmonger's daughter*: literally the daughter of a lecher (Jupiter), but also alluding to Venus's birth from the sea.

112 *house*: her astrological house is Pisces (the fishes).

118 *Burbage . . . Hemminges*: actors and sharers in the King's Men (the company actually performing the masque).

125 *pur-chops . . . pur-dogs*: meaning uncertain.

126 *groom-porter*: court official in charge of cards and dice.

159 *cony*: literally a rabbit; but also a dupe or a prostitute.

246

161 *stake*: pole around which they are to dance.

164 *roll and farthingale*: the roll was a framework to support the upswept hair-style; the farthingale the wire structure that underpropped the skirt.

167 *'what you lack'*: a characteristic cry of street vendors.

173 *Bosoms Inn*: a noted inn for travellers and carriers.

182 *Philpot*: named after fourteenth-century mayor; pun on 'fill-pot'.

186 *Scalding Alley*: where poulterers scorched their birds.

189 *Hercules . . . Lane*: Hercules was made to spin with Omphale's distaff.

194 *cardmakers*: either of playing cards, or of maps.

Pur-alley: not a street, but punning reference to the legal term 'purlieu' (or 'puralee').

195 *box and his dice*: for the game of mum-chance.

196 *Mac-pippin*: most London costermongers were Irish.

198 *a'*: he.

202 *Honey Lane*: a narrow, dark lane, so named for 'the often washing and sweeping it to keep it clean' (Stow).

204 *most*: MS; F reads 'more'.

207 *tree*: i.e. the withe of l. 50.

210 *Penny-rich Street*: Peneritch Street in Cheap.

213 *child Rowlan*: heroic nephew of Charlemagne, celebrated in the ballad 'Childe Roland', as well as *The Song of Roland* and other works.

217 *Log*: the Yule log.

229 *Cupid, etc.*: presumably implying that Cupid continues to stammer out the same three words.

236 *warmol 'quest*: inquest carried out by the wardmote, the meeting of guild members of a city ward.

237 *hench-boys*: pages who ran on foot beside officials.

241 *eight pence a day*: twopence more than the usual rate for a boy actor.

243 *out enough*: nonplussed, put out of his part.

252 *artillery-garden*: where shooting practice was revived in 1610, according to Stow, *Annales* (1631).

256 *gi' . . . fires*: shoot blanks.

Pleasure Reconciled to Virtue

This has been a masque much praised by modern critics for the complexity of its moral allegory and its unity of design. Its first performance, however, was not a success. Since the Queen was ill, a second performance was called

247

for the following month, and Jonson completely rewrote the antimasque, producing in effect a new work, *For the Honour of Wales*. The reasons for this failure are hard to recover (though the flat performance of the masquers provoked the King's anger, a situation only rescued by the Marquis of Buckingham executing some nimble capers). It would seem that either the content or the performance of the antimasque was particularly to blame.

The controlling myth of the masque is the legend of the choice Hercules confronted at the outset of his heroic career between the siren Pleasure and heroic Virtue. The accommodation made between these two qualities in the masque itself, defining acceptable and limited Pleasure as a holiday under the control of Virtue, reflects the King's policy on the question of rural pastimes enshrined in the declaration published in Lancashire in 1617 and reissued nationally later in 1618, known as *The Book of Sports*. The spectacle of excessive feasting at the opening of the masque may also reflect the efforts at financial retrenchment at court being made by Lionel Cranfield, which included curbs upon excessive hospitality.

An account of the masque's performance by Orazio Busino, chaplain to the Venetian ambassador (reprinted in *BoMasques* and O&S, in Italian in H&S) contains many details about its visual effect, the most significant of which are recorded in the notes. From contemporary records the masquers seem to have been Prince Charles, the marquesses of Buckingham and Hamilton, the Earl of Montgomery, Sir Thomas and Sir Charles Howard with a younger brother, Sir Gilbert Haughton, John Auchmouty, Roger Palmer, Abraham Abercrombie, 'Carr' (probably Robert Carr, Earl of Ancrum), and Sir William Erwin.

The work was not published until the 1640 Folio, though an earlier MS survives in the collection of the Duke of Devonshire.

1 *Atlas*: according to Busino the hill's head 'rolled its eyes and moved itself with wonderful cunning'. The figure is significant in a number of ways. First, the Libyan Mount Atlas is an appropriate geographical setting for Hercules' battle with Antaeus. Secondly, the masque engages with two conflicting legends about Atlas, both of which are relevant to the masque's subject. In Ovid he was turned into a mountain for failing in hospitality, but there is a different tradition of a hospitable Atlas, friendly to Hercules. Thirdly, towards the end of the masque itself the mountain becomes the hill of Virtue, thus taking on a specifically Christian resonance.

5 *Comus*: not the classical representation of Comus as a beautiful youth (as in Milton). This Bacchic figure owes its conception and a number of details to Rabelais's Gaster, the god of the belly, in *The Fourth Book of . . . Pantagruel*.

8 *Hercules . . . bowl*: Hercules was said to have obtained a bowl from the sun to sail to Libya in.

10 *Room, room*: the usual opening of mummers' plays (O).

17 *dog . . . wheel*: a dog walked inside a wheel to turn the spit in front of the fire.

19 *gimlet and vice*: the former bored a hole in the cask, the latter was the tap.

20 *an*: MS; F reads 'and'.

Hippocras bag: cloth funnel used as a strainer; Hippocras was spiced wine.

21 *cries swag*: declares himself a swag-belly.

23 *weezle*: F's 'weesell' might be modernized as 'weasel', as in Dutton and Orgel, so that the meaning of ll. 22–4 might be: 'Though the pleasure result only in an increase in girth, yet the gullet will not forgo any delight or make it in any way easier for the back to support the great belly.' But perhaps more probable is *BoMasques'* reading as 'weezle', or 'throat'. The point then is to continue the image of the funnel, the constricted throat leading to the great belly, acting as a huge sack for the drink.

29 *even or odd*: however many; alluding to classical superstition that to consume an even number of drinks was unlucky (O).

31 *scarce . . . laced*: punning on 'pudding' as rope tied to support mast of ship, and 'laced' meaning 'add' as well as 'tie up'. Comus can neither be tied up because he's too big; nor could he take any more pudding.

38 *saturnals*: the Roman licentious festival of Saturnalia is paralleled to the Twelfth Night feast at which the masque is being performed.

39 *stands . . . hat*: i.e. keeps his hat on where he should normally go bareheaded out of respect (*BoMasques*).

43 *tripe*: intestines; *OED* gives 1676 as first date for modern sense 'rubbish'.

50 *teaching . . . jackdaws*: from *Fourth Book of . . . Pantagruel*, ch. 63.

53 *Venter*: (Lat.) belly.

66 *Jovial . . . Kindred*: O's suggestion that these are tavern names seems more likely than H&S's conjecture that they are ballad tunes.

74 *Here . . . Hercules*: the antimasquers were boys dressed as bottles and a cask; Busino reports that after or during this antimasque Hercules was seen wrestling with Antaeus before his next speech.

76 *Antaeus*: son of Poseidon and Gaia (the Earth), who made all travellers fight with him and killed them. He was invulnerable so long as he kept touch with the earth, his mother. Hercules lifted him off the ground and crushed him to death in the air.

77 *such . . . her*: such monsters on earth (O).

79 *his*: Antaeus'.

81 *Hopes . . . first*: does earth hope to redeem Antaeus' crime of inhospitality by being hospitable to vice?

118 *pygmies*: Busino saw twelve boys dressed like frogs.

122 *brother*: 'like Antaeus, the pygmies are "contraries" begotten on the earth goddess' (O). The two episodes draw on Philostratus, *Icones* II. xxi–xxii. 374K–376K.

124 *many . . . yields*: there were a number of classical heroes named Hercules.

140 *poplar*: especially associated with Hercules.

147 *grandsire Atlas*: according to one legend Mercury was born of Maia, one of Atlas' daughters.

151 *he that did . . . way*: the less familiar form of the legend of the Hesperides, in which Hercules rescues Atlas' daughters, the Hesperides, from Busiris, King of Egypt, and is rewarded with apples or sheep (the same word in Greek).

152 *learning of the sphere*: astronomy or astrology.

153 *like him*: Hercules briefly assumed Atlas' burden.

166 *Hesperus*: Atlas' brother, the evening (western) star, representing King James.

169 *pillars, Hercules*: straits of Gibraltar, entrance to the Mediterranean.

173 *such another*: the same idea of Britain as a world apart as in *Blackness*, l. 219.

175 *reconciled*: a subsidiary meaning of the word is 'to bring into a state of acquiescence or submission' (*OED*), and this is reflected in Virtue's always prior role.

176 *twelve*: appropriate perhaps to the twelve labours of Hercules.

178 *one, and chief*: Prince Charles, dancing in his first masque.

184 *Hesperides . . . garden*: J seems to be using 'Hesperides' of the paradisal garden, rather than the maidens who lived there.

185 *grow . . . effeminate*: over-indulgence in sexual pleasure was often represented as making men effeminate.

188 *masquers*: according to Busino, they were dressed in white and crimson (perhaps symbolizing the joining of virtue and pleasure), and wore black masks. It is not clear whether Virtue led them out (as implied in l. 176), or whether Pleasure brought them forward (l. 200). Busino reports seeing a goddess in white amongst twelve musicians clad in red with mitres on their heads, but it is not clear whether the goddess was Pleasure or Virtue. Marcus has suggested that the mitres are part of a religious allegory in the masque.

208 *Daedalus*: in Greek legend an artist and inventor who built the labyrinth of Minos.

216 *in form*: Busino's comments suggest that the first dance was begun in the figure of a pyramid.

218 *curious knot*: allusion to the *nodus Herculaneus*, a complex knot which only such as the heroic Hercules could untie; also a pattern of crossing lines (as in 'knot-garden').

221 *figure . . . way*: this and the following lines allude to the choice of Hercules between the paths of Virtue and Pleasure. The dance must have been choreographed to represent ('figure out') the nature of that choice, and the hesitation implied in the word 'doubtful' ('uncertain').

229 *numerous*: made up of 'numbers' or rhythmical units (the term was used for poetic metres and music as well as dance).

230 *you*: MS; 'they' F.

236 *measured . . . rise to it*: an exposition of the Neoplatonic view of dance's potential, by its imitation of divine harmony and number, to affect the mind of those who watched it; it is not merely a demonstration of the skill of the dancer.

246 *ground*: foundation, basis; also background to painting and musical ground-bass.

278 *him*: presumably Daedalus, though the lines are addressed to the masquers.

The Coleorton Masque

This entertainment was given by Sir Thomas Beaumont of Coleorton (Coleoverton) in Leicestershire to Sir William Seymour and his recent bride, Frances Devereux, sister of the Earl of Essex, who also performed in the masque. The date of the masque is indicated by the fact that Seymour married in 1617 and was known as Lord Beauchamp after 1619. Sir Thomas was a significant figure in his area, not least as a mine-owner. He was also a friend of Essex; he had acted as the nobleman's second when a duel was provoked with Henry Howard who had taunted the Earl with the claims of his impotence made in the hearings to annul his marriage to Frances Howard.

It is not known who wrote this masque, though Philip J. Finkelpearl makes a strong claim for Thomas Pestell, poet and rector of Coleorton (see Select Bibliography).

Underlying the masque is a celebration of the values of hospitality, perceived as under threat by many in the early seventeenth century, including both the king and those, like the performers here, less attached to the court. It is a significant masque in this volume as representative of a domestic, private entertainment well away from court. Many households (and many of them households which would be classed as 'Puritan') enjoyed masques.

Notable, too, is its presentation of female and male virtues in competition one with the other.

Though the staging must have been fairly straightforward, it was yet possible to arrange for descents, and for clouds to be opened.

The masque survives in one nineteenth-century transcript, MS Dyce 36, at the Victoria and Albert Museum.

> *Candlemas*: feast of the Purification of the Blessed Virgin, 2 February. One of the old Catholic feast-days which survived the Reformation.
>
> *Coleorton*: MS 'Coleoverton', in Leicestershire, the seat of one branch of the Beaumont family
>
> *Earl of Essex . . . Seymour*: not all the participants can be identified (see Index of Performers below). One puzzle attends the figure of 'Lord Willoughby'; this might well have been Robert Bertie (the only available lord of that name at the time), but equally likely participants would be the local Willoughby family of Wollaton Hall—but they were not ennobled. A mistake in the MS transcript is possible.

1   *buttery spirit*: the antimasque is based on conventional fairy lore; the spirits are hobgoblins, often associated with specific domestic spheres, here with the 'buttery', or store-room for provisions.

4   *Tom*: a common name for a hobgoblin, but here, perhaps, a jocular reference to Sir Thomas, who has raided the buttery for the night's entertainment.

10   *pinching*: a characteristic fairy punishment, but also here 'miserliness'.

13   *O ho ho!*: as much the trademark of Puck as subsequently of Father Christmas.

15   *thee*: MS has 'té', which may be an attempt to indicate a regional accent.

     Robin: Robin Goodfellow, another name for Puck.

16   *flax*: wick of a candle (Bob pretends it is a fuse for an 'explosion').

18   *Buzz . . . bee, etc.*: this charm is apparently unique to Jonson's *Alchemist* and *Oberon*, to which, therefore, the writer of this masque must be referring.

26   *Down . . . shall*: from John Dowland's *Second Book of Airs* (1600), iii.

27   *downfall . . . dairy*: alluding to enclosure of land and conversion from agricultural use, frequently seen as inhibiting the practice of hospitality.

29   *rag of Rome*: relic of Catholicism; the speech parodies characteristic Puritan rhetoric.

32   *Pauncius . . . buried*: the spelling is presumably intended to indicate a pun, being pronounced 'Paunch-us'. The remark may represent a jocular misquotation of the words of the Apostles' Creed in the Prayer Book: 'suffered under Pontius Pilate, was crucified, dead and buried'. It alludes to the Puritan attempts to suppress traditional pastimes

('country mirth') which King James defended in the *Book of Sports* later in 1618.

34 *three . . . old way*: even those who do live in the country do not maintain the old traditions of open hospitality.

38 *lantitantical*: from 'lant', meaning 'urine'; this seems to be a nonce coinage.

43 *baronets*: the jibe against upward mobility is somewhat weakened since Sir Thomas was to be made baronet in 1619.

46 *Phoebus*: according to Ovid (*Metamorphoses* ii. 154) Phoebus had four horses—the point is not clear.

51 *This wood . . . petticoats*: the complaint that women's mercenary ambition wasted fortunes was commonplace in contemporary dramatic and controversial literature.

52 *dittymouse*: titmouse (the spelling may be a dialectal form and is retained), a small bird of the tit family.

55 *soaked in piss . . . gilding*: urine was indeed apparently used in this way—Brotanek cites Wilson, *Inconstant Lady*.

56 *committing . . . justice*: as a bribe for favourable judgement.

61 *gone*: MS 'gene', possibly a dialect form.

65 *Little Britain*: a subsidiary allusion to a London street inhabited especially by booksellers may be intended here.

66 *white money*: silver money; small change.

69 *Harry of Ashby*: Henry Hastings, Earl of Huntingdon, patron of John Fletcher, something of a Puritan, and staunch defender of 'old' values of open-house hospitality.

Bob of Lichfield: Robert, Earl of Essex, whose house was at Chartley in Staffordshire.

70 *a brace . . . Beaumonts*: there were Beaumonts at Gracedieu and Stoughton, as well as Coleorton. Presumably it is to the last two families, performing in the masque, that allusion is made.

76 *Tom's Egyptians*: miners, black through their work. ('Egyptians', or gypsies, were tawny-skinned.) Both Beaumont and Willoughby families derived their wealth from substantial mining interests.

78 *keep . . . candles*: keep their candles burning in the mine.

sough: a drainage channel for a mine; here perhaps a specific reference to one of the mines, known as 'Sough Pit'.

91 *Aberience*: Brotanek takes this as a variant of 'abearance', but, though pre-dating *OED*, 'Aberrance' seems more likely.

94 *boy*: MS 'boys'. Puck may be speaking to the boys, but since they continue with their dance ('*dance it out*'), the instruction seems to be to Bob to watch what is happening.

95 *Iris*: the rainbow, messenger of Juno.

97 *distractly*: in different directions.

99 *close again*: Iris, having frightened off the spirits, disappears again from view, until she surprises Favonius.

100 *Favonius*: west wind (Latin form of Zephyrus).

102 *Jovi . . . Sacrum*: sacred to Jove, god of hospitality. This was one of the many attributes of Jupiter/Jove.

110 *this beauteous hill*: the house was in fact set high on a hill.

135 *thy sake*: 'Lady Francis' (MS marginal note).

138 *And . . . fair*: MS 'And (what's true . . . rare) | Thou'. This punctuation, repeated below ll. 318–9, obscures the syntax here, where the 'ruler of the sky' is the subject of the verb 'sends'.

149 *Sir Vere Dux*: an anagram of Devereux, the Earl of Essex's family name; as the highest-ranking masquer he is identified, and given the first role. ('Vere' must be pronounced as a disyllable, perhaps 'Veré' to reflect Latin meaning 'true knight'.)

153 *in the touch*: when it comes to the test.

157 *Heroës*: trisyllabic form (imitating Greek).

158 *Sir Arthur*: the presiding representative of male virtue in Spenser's *The Faerie Queene*.

161 *Sapient and Artegall*: the latter is hero of *Faerie Queene*, Bk. V; the former is not a Spenserian figure. The choice of names associates these masquers with oppositional figures and poets for whom the decay of an Elizabethan chivalry which had been represented in Spenser's poem was a sign of the times.

165 *old confusion*: formless chaos out of which it was made.

166 *Guyon*: hero of *Faerie Queene*, Bk. II.

170 *Does relish them*: imparts savour to them.

171 *Calidore*: hero of *Faerie Queene*, Bk. VI. (The last completed book of Spenser's work, in which courtesy is represented as a virtue including all the others.)

178 *This age . . . contrary*: not clear; but seems to be referring to the controversy about cross-dressing and gender roles which raged in the later Jacobean period. The debate which follows between male and female virtues has many precedents.

Mistress Rainbow: Iris appears with the masquers.

Juno: queen of the gods.

186 *Sir Puffin*: i.e. Favonius, with a pun on the wind that 'puffs'.

199 *is*: Brotanek. MS reads 'This meekness'.

202 *Meekness . . . Chastity*: however 'radical' the later speeches, this is an entirely conventional litany of female virtues.

213 *middle region*: the air (between earth and heaven).

217 *masque*: 'masques' MS.

227 *Song*: presumably sung by Iris.

231 *list to prove*: want to put it to the test.

254 *them*: MS 'him'.

255 *pace*: dancing.

Song: presumably sung by Favonius.

279 *not . . . Valentine*: looking ahead from Candlemas (2 Feb.) to St Valentine's day on the 14th.

295 *Mad Bob . . . late*: MS has line-break after 'buttery' (and analogously after 'here', 'then', 'run'). Relineation makes the structure of the stanza clearer.

298 *When . . . plate*: when the drinking vessel of skin was stolen, the vessels of plate were fortunately left.

328 *used*: which are accustomed.

338 *whose*: MS 'who'.

340 *things . . . befell thee*: an allusion to the controversy which attended Essex's divorce from Frances Howard in 1613.

343 *Consigning*: Brotanek emends to 'conciling'. But the emendation is unnecessary; though the phrase is elliptical, it implies 'assigning to their fate' those who are malicious.

361 *God*: MS 'Gods'.

Neptune's Triumph

Despite the title-page, this masque was in fact never performed. The official reason given was that the King was unwell, but the real reason probably had to do with the impossibility of accommodating both French and Spanish ambassadors at a performance. The diplomatic problems were great because the work responded, albeit belatedly, to the return of Prince Charles and Buckingham from Spain in October 1623. They had left secretly in February of that year to prosecute the marriage of Charles to the Spanish princess. This match had long been sought after by the King, though he seems not to have known of his son's madcap project. It was deeply unpopular with many in England, especially in the heightened political and religious tensions that attended the beginning of the Thirty Years War, involving James's daughter Elizabeth and her husband Frederick, Elector Palatine. Whatever their motives for going to Spain, the return of Charles and Buckingham without a Spanish bride provoked unparalleled popular rejoicing, and Jonson was faced with the problem of celebrating what could only be seen as a failure of the King's policy. He responded by obfuscating the reasons for the journey (and the disgrace of the return) and by denigrating the popular rejoicings of a few months before.

The masque was published in quarto in 1625, and again in the 1640 Folio.

Omnis . . . Deum: 'And every altar now makes sacrifice for the God returned.'

3 *NEP. RED.*: *Neptuno reduci*—'to Neptune, the guide home'.

SEC. IOV.: *secundo Iove*—'the second Jupiter'; 'for so Neptune is called by Statius in *Achilleis* I' (J).

4 *disperse the argument*: give out the playbill or argument of the masque.

7 *pluck for*: term from the card-game primero, as are 'colour for', 'encounter with', 'what went you upon' below. (The players drew ('plucked') four cards in turn with the object of obtaining either one of each suit ('colour') or four in one suit.)

50 *oracle of the bottle*: from Rabelais, *The Fifth Book of . . . Pantagruel*.

51 *Hogshead Trismegistus*: 'a thrice-great barrel'; parodic form of Hermes Trismegistus, credited with mystical writing in antiquity.

52 *Pegasus . . . hoof*: the winged horse struck Mount Helicon with his hoof, producing the sacred spring of the Muses.

76 *chemists . . . Cross*: alchemists and Rosicrucians, supposed members of a mystical religious brotherhood. The implication of 'bare-breeched' may simply be that they were poor, or may possibly imply sexual perversion.

82 *this fury . . . divine*: this outburst demonstrates the Cook to be possessed by the divine fury of poetry.

83 *device*: plan for the masque.

90 *chief . . . riding*: Neptune was the creator of the horse.

91 *Albion*: Prince Charles. What follows is an allegorized (and sanitized) version of the events of the previous year. Hippius is Buckingham, the King's favourite and Master of Horse, Proteus Sir Francis Cottingham. They journeyed through France ('Celtiberia') to Spain ('the Hesperian shores'). Tactfully little is said about the reasons for their return—the failure of the mission.

104 *How near . . . lost*: they nearly drowned on the journey home.

113 *her . . . snakes*: i.e. Envy's; snakes are traditionally associated with her. J is here explicitly defending Buckingham, whose unpopularity before and during the Spanish adventure was enormous.

115 *But . . . now*: a pertinent question, since the court made no celebration of the return. This ingenious justification turns scorn for popular celebration into good reason for the delay.

119 *Minerva*: goddess of wisdom.

120 *tumultuous verse or prose*: many popular and satirical (therefore 'tumultuous') works were indeed produced.

126 *Archy*: the court dwarf, Archibald Armstrong, who had accompanied Charles.

133 *Delos . . . emergent*: when Latona (Leto) was about to produce her twins, Apollo and Artemis (sun and moon), Juno, angry at her husband's having fathered them, forbade anywhere on earth to offer shelter. Neptune fixed the island of Ortygia, renamed Delos after the birth, for her.

137 *sirens*: sea-demons, half-woman, half-bird, who lured sailors to destruction.

138 *Arion*: musician whose singing charmed a dolphin to save him from drowning.

142 *tree*: the banyan, which 'grows as Jonson says. The story that it was first planted by the sun in Musicanus on the river Indus, is told by Strabo, *Geography*, xv. i. 21' (O).

160 *heterogene . . . by-works*: antimasques are only accessories to the 'device' of the masque, being things so mixed in kind.

outlandish: bizarre; with secondary sense 'foreign'.

174 *persons*: the Cook uses the term to mean actors ('personators'), while the Poet reacts with surprise at the idea of people representing a stew.

176 *relish . . . di stato*: enjoy nothing but affairs of state. The ensuing passage is characteristically dismissive of newsmongers of all kinds; the difficult political situation had made this a time of increased censorship.

179 *clouds . . . mysteries*: the dominant meaning is simply 'the masques and their accoutrements', but 'mysteries' also carries the suggestion of arcane rituals.

181 *master . . . camels*: fictitious officials, guying the claimed 'sources' of the gossips.

185 *therein . . . says*: the proverb is 'Had I fish was never good with garlic' (O). O repunctuates the lines, with a comma after 'fishes', to produce the sense 'they are silent as fish about their own business, but their breath fills the air as the smell of garlic does'. But retaining the F punctuation gives H&S's sense (which I prefer): 'Of the real business of state they know nothing, and they are as mute as fishes about it. But this does not prevent their talking . . . and poisoning the news as the breath of the eater of garlic poisons the air.'

189 *Amphibian Archy*: see l. 126 above.

195 *gallimaufry*: both 'hash, ragout' and 'ridiculous medley'.

201 *laced mutton*: whore.

204 *Grave . . . Paul's*: the nave of old St Paul's Cathedral was the centre of gossip.

208 *Grace's Street*: now Gracechurch Street.

223 *Nam . . . amat*: 'for even a triumph loves a joke' (Martial VIII. viii. 10).

230 *shepherd . . . seas*: Proteus.

231 *ports . . . keys*: Portunus, god of ports.

247 *such a wisdom . . . worth*: suggests, contrary to reality, that it was the King who dispatched Charles abroad.

249 *Saron*: god of navigation.

257 *No intermitted blocks*: obscure; blocks of wood are contrasted with the 'odorous stocks'.

261 *as*: as if.

265 *silver-footed*: 'An Epithet frequent in Homer and others' (J).

270 *Galatea*: daughter of Nereus (one of the sea-gods), who turned her lover Acis into a stream after he was killed by the cyclops Polyphemus.

271 *Doris*: the daughter of Oceanus and wife of Nereus; mother of the Nereids (sea-nymphs).

272 *Haliclyon*: Buckingham as Lord High Admiral. (H&S say the name is Jonson's construction, meaning 'famous at sea'.)

279 *mad of men*: mad for men?

290 *figure*: dance; masque dances were often in the form of successive shapes or figures.

297 *salts*: with a pun on 'leaps' (O).

300 *Oceanus*: originally the river flowing round the flat disk of the Earth, then associated with the Atlantic Ocean, the western boundary of the ancient world.

319 *Pallas . . . arts*: the mortal Arachne challenged the goddess Pallas Athene to a weaving contest and was turned into a spider by the goddess.

353 *Castor . . . Pollux*: sons of Zeus and Leda, known as the Dioscuri, which name was applied to twin-pointed forms of St Elmo's fire, regarded by seafarers as a favourable omen.

354 *Leucothe*: the white goddess of the spray, guide of sailors in storms.

365 *fifty girls*: the Nereids.

372 *gifts of peace*: the return of Charles and Buckingham in fact precipitated the disastrous move to war against Spain.

Chloridia

This, Jonson's last masque at court, is a companion piece to the King's masque, *Love's Triumph through Callipolis*, which was performed on Twelfth Night. These are the first of the Caroline entertainments that have survived, and indicate clearly the new direction and new thematic preoccupations of the masques of the period, with their celebration and idealization of the royal marriage. But they also mark the end of the Jonsonian era. Jonson's omission of Inigo Jones's name from the title-page provoked the final rift between them, and henceforward Jones was the dominant figure in Caroline entertainments.

The masque was published in quarto in 1631, and again in the 1640 Folio.

 Unius . . . erat: Ovid, *Fasti* v. 222. 'The earth was of a single colour before [the transformation of Chloris into Flora by Zephyrus].'

3 *like number*: the same as in the King's masque, *Love's Triumph* (see above).

5 *Chloris*: in Ovid, *Fasti* v, was transformed into Flora.

7 *Arbitrium . . . habe*: 'you, goddess, have dominion over the flowers' (v. 213).

25 *Zephyrus*: the west wind.

38 *heaven . . . odds*: heaven will not be superior to earth.

53 *humour*: here means 'moisture'.

59 *Napaeae*: nymphs of the dells.

70 *argument*: the story of the masque to follow.

78 *his mother*: Venus.

82 *forced . . . away*: removed his bow and arrows.

97 *expatiate*: both 'wander at will' and 'speak at length'.

100 *news*: Jonson consistently, in plays and masques, deplored the circulation of newsletters.

102 *Pluto and Proserpine*: Pluto, god of the underworld, abducted Proserpina as his queen. She was supposed to spend half the year with him, and half the year on earth, associating her with the regeneration of the spring.

104 *Tantalus*: tormented by water and fruit just out of reach.

107 *Ixion*: bound to a burning wheel.

109 *caprioles . . . friskals . . . lavoltas*: lively capers and dances.
 Lamiae: female spirits who sucked the blood of children.

109 *Sisyphus*: as soon as he rolled the stone to the top of the hill it fell back.

111 *Tityus*: a giant, son of Gaia, who for assault on Leto was condemned to have his liver perpetually ripped out; his nine-acre body is from *Odyssey* xi. 576.

116 *Danaus' daughters*: obeyed their father's instructions to murder their husbands on their wedding night, and were punished by endlessly filling leaking vessels.

119 *strictness . . . tonight*: Charles had tightened up on admission to the masques.

124 *Spanish . . . passage*: the needles of steel were made in London, but there seems to be some political reference here (and a bawdy *double entendre*).

135 *Queen's dwarf*: Jeffrey Hudson.

149 *Juno*: queen of the gods, patroness of marriage, but also in myth made pregnant after consulting Chloris, by a touch from a herb.

159 *sprigs of egrets*: heron feathers.

167 *Hours*: the guardians of the seasons.

168 *Iris*: the rainbow.

186 *she . . . root*: in Ovid's *Fasti* Chloris is the first to sow seed on earth.

201 *your birds*: peacocks.

207 *Fame . . . Sculpture*: it is to this concluding tableau that Jonson angrily alludes in his attack on Jones, 'An Expostulation with Inigo Jones', ll. 35–40.

231 *the seven*: the Pleiades.

Tempe Restored

The masque was performed on 14 February 1632 in the Banqueting House at Whitehall, as a return offering for the King's *Albion's Triumph* (also by Townshend) some five weeks earlier. It derives from perhaps the most famous of French court entertainments, Baltazar de Beaujoyeulx's *Balet Comique de la Reine* of 1581, but, apart from the opening entry of the Fugitive and the closing allegory, is not close to it in detail. It is clear that Inigo Jones had a crucial part in the design of the whole, consciously reflecting the Queen's French tastes in his designs and costumes, and taking every opportunity to emphasize the importance of spectacle.

The theme of the masque, the replacement of Circe's charms by the purer (but not asexual) Divine Beauty of the Queen, is typical of its period, as is the Neoplatonic philosophy of love to which it alludes. The masque is remarkable for the presence of female singers/actresses, apparently for the first time on a British stage.

The Quarto in which the work was published exists in a number of different states, incorporating major revisions. I have leaned heavily on the collation in Cedric Brown's edition.

1 *Circe*: the story of the witch who transformed men to beasts originates in the *Odyssey*, but she is here a rather more ambiguous figure than is customary.

13 *voluntary*: they have chosen to be subject to Circe.

15 *Influences*: in astrology the ethereal fluid supposed to flow from the stars and act upon human affairs.

18 *interview*: meeting of King and Queen.

20 *Tempe*: a valley between mounts Olympus and Ossa, famed for its beauty in classical literature, and connected with the worship of Apollo.

29 *Invention . . . Knowledge*: based on Ripa, *Iconologia* (see note to *Barriers*, l. 61). The wings signify 'the elevation of all the intellectual parts'.

31 *wreathen trumps*: twisted or curled trumpets.

40 *Curious Ignorance*: fuses the figures of *Ignoranza* and *Curiosità* from Ripa; poppy and bat signify sleepiness and nocturnal darkness; the frog is a figure for curiosity because of its large eyes.

43 *nothing . . . motion*: Jones's triumphant answer to Jonson's attack on him in 'An Expostulation with Inigo Jones', where he belittled 'shows, mighty shows'.

54 *verdures . . . types*: sprigs of leafage decorate the cupolas that top some of the bays.

58 *gentleman*: played by Thomas Killigrew.

61 *Out of . . . speaks*: this opening speech is close to the *Balet Comique*, even down to the handkerchief.

68 *Promethean fire*: Prometheus, the mortal who first brought fire from heaven, is a type of human aspiration to the divine.

88 *'He finds . . . own'*: proverbial, see Tilley H412.

90 *lies . . . seats*: where presumably he remains for the performance.

95 *naiades and dryads*: water and wood nymphs.

98 *Madame Coniack*: it is ironic that nothing seems to be known of her, or her colleague Mrs Shepherd, despite their historical importance.

122 *antimasques*: in the designs reproduced in O&S animals have elaborate masks and skin coats; the Indians have feathered skirts and headdresses, whereas the Barbarians have eastern dress; the pagoda, or idol, has a beehive of a hat, wings, animal mask, and extended fingers.

151 *rites*: Q reads 'rights'.

157 *descant . . . ground*: song fitted to the ground-bass of the music of the spheres (imagined as endless repetition of particular tones, as a ground-bass repeats).

177 *chain*: the golden chain let down from heaven (cf. *Gold*).

219 *that ye see*: this song elevates the principle of the dominance of sight at the expense of other senses.

233 *Janus*: the two-faced god of boundaries and the new year. The Spheres look both ways, at the King in the audience and the Queen among the masquers.

236 *he . . . slept*: hundred-eyed Argus.

239 *old Saturn's reign*: the age of gold (cf. *LRest, Gold*).

260 *hecatombs*: a sacrificial tribute of many victims (i.e. the antimasquers).

261 *deduced . . . spoil*: derived from plunder.

267 *gods . . . cloud*: Circe reminds Jupiter of one of his former amatory exploits, which Pallas (Minerva), the chaste, armour-clad goddess of wisdom, tries to excuse. In the iconology of the masque the quieting of Pallas at one extreme balances the submission of the unchaste aspect of Circe at the other, symbolizing the marital chastity of Charles and Henrietta Maria.

268 *Man-maid*: the rebuke is particularly loaded since, exceptionally, Circe is played by a woman, whereas, presumably, Pallas is played by a male actor.

269 *turn . . . stone*: with the face of Medusa on her shield (cf. *Gold*).

290 *intermedium*: part of the entertainment (from Italian *intermedio*, a musical entertainment between the acts of a play).

Allegory: closely based on that by 'Lord Gordon, a Scotsman, chamberlain to the King', which was appended to the *Balet Comique* alongside other allegories.

308 *desire . . . beauty*: the core of Neoplatonic love, represented as essentially the desire for beauty.

Coelum Britannicum

This, Carew's only masque, was the King's return offering for the Queen's performance of Beaumont and Fletcher's *The Faithful Shepherdess* on Twelfth Night, and followed the Inns of Court masque, Shirley's *Triumph of Peace*, which had been twice staged in the previous fortnight. That masque had voiced oblique criticism of aspects of Charles's policies, which Carew's masque perhaps sets out to answer. Carew drew the central idea of a reformation of the heavens, and verbal detail for a number of speeches, from

Giordano Bruno's *Spaccio de la Bestia Trionfante* (1584). This masque is ostensibly the most complete celebration of the court of Charles and Henrietta Maria, with its praise of the moral purity encouraged by the royal couple envisaged as a model for the whole society. But critical discussion has focused on the degree to which Momus's satirical comments on that reformation, his parody of official styles, and his gestures towards abuses can or should be taken as a serious questioning of aspects of royal policy in the period of Charles's personal rule.

The elaborate setting by Inigo Jones was much admired at the time. Though in the 1640 edition of Carew's poems the music was attributed to Henry Lawes, none survives, and the attribution has been questioned.

The masque was published, anonymously, in 1634 and reprinted in the posthumous edition of Carew's poems in 1640.

> *Non . . . putat*: 'I have not the inborn talent; but because Caesar has commanded it, I shall have it. Why should I deny myself to possess the ability which he thinks me to possess?'
>
> 1 *ornament*: the elaborate proscenium.
>
> 5 *harpies*: half-women, half-animal; seen by Peacham (*Minerva Britanna* (1612), 115) as types of the greedy courtier. Here perhaps tamed by their vegetative lower halves.
>
> 8 *COELUM BRITANNICUM*: the British Heaven.
>
> 15 *Mansuetude*: gentleness; insisting on a picture of Charles as combining authority and mildness.
>
>   *their . . . arms*: i.e. of the women, not the youths.
>
> 17 *Animum . . . forti*: courage beneath a stalwart breast.
>
> 20 *lily*: flower of France, appropriate to the French queen.
>
> 22 *Semper . . . virtus*: 'ever-renowned virtue'.
>
> 26 *the scene*: Jones had designed an analogous setting of decay for Jonson's *Prince Henry's Barriers* (1610). His source for this scene is Parigi, though his own experience of the decayed monuments of Rome no doubt contributed. It sets in motion the link between reformation of morals and reformation of building which is part of the work's design—and makes reference to Charles's own interest in building.
>
> 45 *Cyllenius*: Mercury was born on Mount Cyllene.
>
> 50 *Styx*: river and god of the underworld, upon whom the gods swore oaths.
>
> 52 *exemplar life*: the commonest topos of praise for Charles and his queen.
>
> 75 *When . . . stains*: compare ll. 177–8 below.
>
> 79 *Lethean flood*: the underworld river of forgetfulness.
>
> 86 *Ariadne's diadem*: jewel given by Dionysus on his wedding to Ariadne, earlier deserted by Theseus.

93 *influence*: in astrological sense (see *Tempe Restored*, note to l. 15).

94 *Momus*: the son of Night, god of ridicule, banished from the heavens for finding fault with the gods.

96 *parti-coloured*: derived from Ripa's description of Discordia in his *Iconologia*, signifying the diversity of opinion.

109 *god . . . larceny*: Mercury was patron of thieves.

118 *privilege . . . courts*: during the period of feasting the deities are frequently encountered in masques.

123 *Momus . . . Eternity*: *ap* is Welsh for 'son of'. In this mock ancestry he claims descent, amongst others, from Somnus (Sleep) and Erebus (god of the underworld).

124 *Theomastix*: scourge of the gods; alluding to William Prynne's attack on the court in *Histriomastix* (1633).

Protonotary: principal notary, clerk or recorder of a court, used specifically of the clerk to the Court of Chancery.

125 *Arch-Informer*: informers reported offenders to the ecclesiastical courts.

131 *perdu*: applied to a sentinel in a dangerous position, here a look-out for someone engaged in illicit love.

133 *woolsack god*: the Woolsack is a seat for judges summoned to the House of Lords, especially used of the Lord Chancellor. Here a pointed suggestion of the complicity of judges in the personal rule of Charles.

142 *father*: Uranus, whom Saturn castrated ('gelt' = gelded).

Smith: Vulcan, who trapped Venus his wife and Mars her lover in a net.

143 *Hebe*: servant to the gods, cupbearer to Jove, goddess of youth. She lost her place to Ganymede after the incident here described, a late mythological addition.

146 *Puteolum*: modern Pozzoli near Naples; a place of resort for Roman nobility, where Cicero had a villa. I can find no record of a grotto there—but Carew's bawdy joke scarcely needs accurate foundation.

148 *Aretine*: Pietro Aretino (1492–1556), Italian writer best known for his satiric and erotic writings.

150 *Rabelais*: François (*c.*1495–1553), author of *Gargantua* and *Pantagruel*.

151 *French . . . oratory*: Dunlap suggests that the reference here is to François Malherbe (1555–1628), poet, critic, and translator.

156 *dog in a doublet*: proverbial (Tilley D452) for pride and vanity.

166 *countenance legatine*: official status as an ambassador or legate.

168 *treble key*: an allusion to the three keys to the bedchamber of the king, and symbol, therefore, of access to his private apartments and secret thoughts. (The triple keys are depicted hanging from the belt of William, Earl of Pembroke, Lord Chamberlain, in Van Dyck's portrait of him.)

178 *decay . . . abilities*: Momus supplies an alternative motivation to that given by Mercury (one taken from Bruno).

182 *two-leaved book*: female genitals.

196 *inquisition erected*: Archbishop Laud was particularly keen to control dissenting writing.

209 *Titanian line*: the lineage of the Titans, whom Jupiter had defeated.

210 *new orders*: this speech converts Bruno's account into allusions to many recent proclamations for the reform of abuses, for example, the order that those selling drink could not sell tobacco, and the repeated proclamations for the repair of gentlemen to their country houses.

212 *sophistication of wares*: adulteration of commodities.

222 *Amazonian . . . hospitality*: that it was wives who, for delight in fashion, urged London residence on their husbands was a common complaint of moralists.

225 *Ganymede*: cupbearer to, and lover of, Jupiter. A perhaps rather dangerous reference to the male favourites of James, and even to Buckingham, the favourite of Charles until his assassination in 1628. Those who served in the bedchamber had closest access to the king; Charles seems to have made a point of not allowing those serving him in private function to have a great deal of public political power.

230 *ore tenus*: literally 'by word of mouth', here an oral legal proceeding.

232 *fifth of November*: anniversary of the thwarting of the Gunpowder Plot in 1605, kept as a public holiday.

234 *Gigantomachy*: the celebration of the victory of the gods over the giants, the mythical occasion of Bruno's dialogue; here applied to the Gunpowder Plot.

238 *deformities*: Vulcan was lame.

243 *milky way*: the sexual/astronomical pun is buttressed by the legend that the Milky Way was created from milk spilt from the breast of Jupiter's wife, Juno.

267 *Lernean Hydra*: a many-headed monster killed by Hercules.

unlicked Bear: baby bears were supposed to be formless until licked into shape by their mothers.

269 *goatfish Capricorn*: Capricornus was traditionally represented with foreparts like a goat, and with a fish's tail.

294 *stamp . . . impression*: imagery of coining given sexual application.

307 *On the right . . . Capricorn*: the highest point the sun reaches in the sky is at the Tropic of Cancer (the Crab), at which it seems to pause, before moving towards the Tropic of Capricorn.

308 *lofty*: Q reads 'laughty'; possible misprint for 'haughty'.

317 *another*: an unexplained topical reference.

354 *plantation . . . England*: the opportunity that colonization offered to rid the country of its riff-raff (or here, religious dissenters) forms a constant thread in the discussion of the new American colonies.

369 *eighth sphere*: the sphere of the fixed stars.

370 *Booker, Allestree*: compilers of almanacs.

371 *Tycho*: Tycho Brahe, Danish astronomer (1546–1601).

377 *Germans . . . lately*: Germany, whose emblem is the eagle, had suffered during the Thirty Years War.

Dolphin: both a constellation and an alternative spelling of the French 'Dauphin'.

381 *Perseus . . . nation*: Momus argues that if diverse constellations, each derived from different myths, were combined together, then there would be an appropriate emblem for England's St George. *Perseus* was the slayer of the Gorgons, *Pegasus* the winged horse born at the time of Perseus' adventure, and subsequently aiding Bellerophon to kill the Chimaera. *Python* was a dragon killed by Apollo.

385 *Oyez*: Momus parodies the manner and style of royal proclamations.

392 *hangings*: ten tapestries made for Lord Howard of Effingham and bought by James in 1616.

393 *victory of '88*: the defeat of the Spanish Armada in 1588.

397 *Star Chamber*: both referring back to Jupiter's star-covered bedroom, and to the Court of Star Chamber.

402 *inscrutable bosom*: alluding to Charles's personal rule—with what satiric intent is open to question.

445 *pretenders . . . desert*: Plutus suggests that because he has descended to take up the challenge, then all other claimants must make their claim only on the basis of their own merit, putting to one side ('waiving') any favouritism (or 'partial grace').

502 *Danaë*: locked away, she was yet seduced by Jupiter appearing as a shower of gold.

509 *Ida . . . show*: Paris was asked to judge which of Venus, Minerva, or Juno should win the golden apple.

535 *Poenia*: the description of poverty is modelled on Ripa.

543 *buckets . . . another*: proverbial; see Tilley B695, 'Like two buckets in a well: if one go up the other must go down', and N17 'One nail drives out another'.

598 *tub*: reference to Diogenes, Cynic philosopher, who lived in a tub.

623 *Tiche*: Greek name for Fortune. The qualities described mix the wheel of Fortuna with the head of Occasio, bald behind to symbolize the need to grasp opportunity by the forelock.

640 *Astraea*: figure of justice, who fled the earth after the ending of the age of gold (see *Gold*).

672 *cross-bill*: legal term for a filed counter-claim.

707 *Hedone*: the only one of the interlocutors not present in Bruno.

725 *wisest . . . philosophers*: Epicureans.

749 *Lysimachus . . . Scythians*: story from Plutarch, *Moralia* 126 E–F.

774 *Circean*: Circe's charms transformed lustful men to beasts.

792 *Exit Momus*: who has acted as co-presenter with Mercury, the realist by the side of the idealist; the fact that he slips away has led to suggestions that his criticisms are never truly countered by the masque itself.

831 *Pyrrhica*: war-dance of the ancient Greeks.

833 *grew . . . mountain*: probably a series of jointed flats were pulled up. The image suggests the ascent to civilization through history.

881 *Hesperian . . . dragon*: the fabled gardens of the Hesperides were guarded by dragons.

939 *Eridanus*: the river was transformed into a constellation after Phaëton fell into it while attempting to drive the horses of the Sun.

970 *A Guy, a Bevis*: Guy of Warwick and Bevis of Hampton, heroes of popular knightly romances.

1014 *Garter*: Charles renewed the importance of the Order of the Garter, and celebrated St George's day with new pomp.

1015 *Eusebia . . . Euphemia*: classical versions of the names Religion . . . Reputation given in the stage direction.

Love's Welcome at Bolsover

This, Jonson's last entertainment, was written for William Cavendish, Earl of Newcastle (as was the *King's Entertainment at Welbeck* the previous year) to entertain the King and Queen on their progress. It represents part of the Earl's attempt to gain favour with the sovereign, and on both entertainments he spent lavishly. The entertainment's theme of the power of love is conventional enough, but the piece is noteworthy for its inclusion of Jonson's last attack on Inigo Jones, and, like all progress entertainments, for the way it uses the specific nature of the place where it was performed (though the house-bound Jonson could not have visited Bolsover for many years). The castle was still being constructed, so the royal couple went back to Welbeck for the night—and this gives point to the antimasque of Coronell Vitruvius and his builders.

The text exists in a MS version, from which the Folio of 1640 took its text. There are significant differences in the stage directions between the two versions.

3 *If . . . residence*: sets the Neoplatonic theory of love as aspiration to perfection firmly at the beginning of the masque.

4 *senses . . . placed*: the Neoplatonic hierarchy of the senses; perhaps suggested by their depiction on the walls of the pillar chamber in the Little Castle at Bolsover.

9 *Love . . . Love*: the mutual love of the royal couple and the love of the sponsor of the feast for them both.

29 *retired*: stage direction in MS has 'retired into a garden and are entertained'. The circular Fountain Garden with a statue of Venus in the centre would have made an ideal spot for the performance.

30 *Vitruvius*: a classical architectural authority (first century AD); Inigo Jones was influenced by him, and here Jonson uses the name to signify his great rival.

39 *the poet*: Chaucer, in *The Canterbury Tales*, 'General Prologue' 321–2, describing the Man of Law.

41 *hammer-armed*: F; MS reads 'neighbour'.

sledges: blacksmith's hammers, producing the music by beating on anvils. Jonson's marginal note says that Captain Smith (Vulcan was a smith in legend) was accompanied by three Cyclops.

43 *polt-foot*: club foot.

47 *Chesil . . . man*: all names of builder's tools; chisel, hammer, carpenter's square, and axe.

50 *Dresser . . . Beater*: plumber's mallet, pane of glass, carved ornament in ceilings, and tool used for stirring mortar.

51 *finishers . . . footing*: punning on building and balletic meanings.

59 *number . . . proportion*: the replication in dance of God's making of the world by 'number, weight, and measure' is the standard claim for the moral seriousness of dancing; here it perhaps ironizes the extravagant claims being made by Vitruvius/Jones for the significance of his artisan performers.

62 *Iniquo*: MS reads 'Cor'nell'. At some point Jonson must have decided to make the identification with Inigo Jones unmistakable.

63 *lily . . . rose*: emblems of the kingdoms of France and England.

65 *The king . . . Loves*: stage direction in MS reads 'The King and Queen, having reposed themselves. At their departure in a fit place, selected for the purpose, two Cupids present themselves.' Though the 'clouds' might suggest that the audience returned inside for this last part of the masque, Cedric Brown, in an unpublished essay, argues that a simulated banquet might have been lowered from walks on top of the garden wall. The contest between the two loves is a reworking of material used in the *Challenge at Tilt* of 1613.

89 *struck a tally*: the notched tally-stick recording debts was split in two, and a piece given to debtor and creditor.

96 *Themis*: the mother of the Horae, and a prophetic divinity—the oracle before Apollo.

118 *will . . . thing*: both to wish and not to wish for the same things.

121 *which is circular*: as was the Fountain Garden where the performance probably took place.

124 *Philalethes*: 'lover of truth'.

133 *rhyme*: what follows expresses Jonson's bitterness at his exclusion from court and at the triumph of Jones's spectacle over his poetry.

137 *it is done of*: it is the end of.

139 *case of canters*: pair of thieves using rogues' slang.

148 *whitest wool*: sign of good fortune.

160 *descended . . . warlike*: from the pacific King James and the bellicose Henri IV, King of France, grandfather of the Queen.

161 *peace . . . sweetness*: 'alluding to the holy riddle' (J); Judges 14: 14.

Salmacida Spolia

This, the last of Davenant's masques, and the last to be performed at court before the Civil War, was performed twice in 1640. Set against the increasingly troubled political situation, as Charles's need for money to deal with the rebellion of the Scots forced him to recall parliament after the period of personal rule, it sets out the King's desire for co-operation, and the terms of his wish for peace. Unusual in that both the King and Queen performed, it makes one last effort to reassert their role as model of the love that should infuse the whole of society.

Critics have disagreed about the political tendency of the masque, but consideration of the fact that many of the masquers were courtiers known to be discontented with the King's policies suggests that conciliation was its purpose. At the same time its advocacy of peace takes a stand against those, perhaps including the King, who wished to use further force against the Scots.

10 *dispersed harmony*: groups of musicians placed about the hall.

17 *Pallas*: Athene, martial goddess of wisdom.

23 *Reason*: derived from Ripa's *Iconologia* (see note to *Barriers*, l. 6). There she bridles a lion, an image here transplanted to the winged child.

26 *riding . . . lion*: in Ripa the figure is named as *Dominio di se stesso* ('rule of oneself').

31 *Counsel*: Ripa's 'Consiglio'; the purple cloak signifies a senator, the heart the source of true counsel.

36 *bird of Pallas*: the owl.

46 *Riches*: Ripa's 'Abondanza'.

51 *grasshopper*: Dinet, *Cinq Livres des Hieroglyphiques* (1614), refers to Thucydides speaking of Athenians wearing grasshopper pins in their hair 'because grasshoppers are not travellers, and never come from elsewhere, but are born, live, and die in the same place'.

60 *Salmacida . . . opprimit*: 'Salmacian spoils, achieved without bloodshed or sweat, rather than a Cadmian victory when destruction falls upon the victors themselves.'

100 *Fury*: details derived from description of Allecto in Virgil, *Aeneid* vii. 324.

110 *winds . . . birth*: Pliny II. xliv. 115.

120 *stir . . . body*: to unbalance the four humours whose concord in the body ensures good health.

133 *religion . . . vice*: attack on Charles's Puritan opponents and perhaps particularly the Scottish Kirk, whose opposition to the prayer-book the King and his archbishop, Laud, tried to impose upon them had led to the so-called 'Bishops' Wars' in 1639/40.

137 *antimasque . . . past*: music must have been played here (see l. 258)

146 *scarf*: hanging down from one shoulder across the body.

147 *descent*: Q reads 'dissent'.

173 *honest . . . nation*: those activities commended in the *Book of Sports*, reissued by Charles in 1633.

180 *Invisible . . . Rosicross*: the point of this joke about the secretive Protestant cult of the Rosicrucians is obscure.

193 *first matter*: the original chaos from which all things come.

194 *Medea*: classical sorceress (see Ovid, *Metamorphoses* vii).

198 *Menippus*: Cynic philosopher who committed suicide after losing his wealth.

hemp: of which the hangman's noose is made.

202 *Gallo-belgicus*: a half-yearly newspaper published on the Continent.

204 *disprovu*: conjecturally 'one not provided for, a needy man' (*BoMasques*).

206 *Florio . . . Montemayor*: the first a dictionary of Italian, the second a pastoral romance.

211 *Frankfurt dryfat*: a vessel for holding dry things—alluding to Frankfurt as centre of the book trade (*BoMasques*).

230 *Tartaglia . . . Francolin*: obscure; Tartaglia was a mathematician with a speech impediment.

242 *roaring boys*: term used to characterize arrogant, noisy youths.

249 *Jeffrey Hudson*: the Queen's dwarf.

250 *antic*: both 'grotesque' and 'antique'; their costume was of medieval design.

262 *Pausilipo . . . Naples*: Roman tunnel under Mount Posilipo.

268 *Queen Mother*: Maria de' Medici (1573–1642), widow of Henri IV, mother of Henrietta Maria.

273 *growing comforts*: the Queen's children, Charles, James, and Elizabeth (aged 9, 6, and 3)—and possibly alluding to the Queen's four-month pregnant state.

280 *rites*: Q reads 'rights'.

283 *chief . . . victors*: Henri IV, murdered in 1610.

286 *Tuscan*: she was born in Florence.

288 *printed . . . sung*: perhaps circulated in print before the masque; its sentiments were perhaps at odds with the King's view of his situation, stressing as they do the urgency of action.

294 *travail*: also means 'travel', the preferred modernization of spelling in *BoMasques* and O&S.

299 *priests*: ambiguous; alluding either to the Covenanters or to Archbishop Laud.

311 *captives . . . postures*: stressing the King's power and determination, rather than conciliation.

332 *imperial . . . sin*: in statute merely to imagine the death of the monarch is construed as treason; the idea that treasonous ideas are contagious is a commonplace.

339 *rule alone*: a contentious phrase when the 'personal rule' was coming to an end.

369 *lost . . . art*: the star-gazer wrapped in his difficult science.

371 *optic*: both 'eye' and 'telescope'.

378 *mind . . . out*: standard Neoplatonic theory, that the beauty of the mind is figured in external beauty, and that the soul shines out through the eyes. 'Casements of her eyes' means eyelids.

422 *music of the spheres*: the perfect music which, it was believed, the heavenly spheres made in their movement round the earth (though humans could not hear it).

441 *strangers*: foreigners.

Lanark/Limerick: Q reads 'Lanerick'. *BoMasques* suggests William Hamilton, Earl of Lanark in 1639; O&S suggest William Villiers, Viscount Grandison of Limerick.

INDEX OF PERFORMERS

This list represents no more than a very basic identification of most of the masquers and performers. Where biographical data have not been found names are not included.

Abercrombie (Abraham): Chamberlain called him 'a Scottish dancing courtier'. (*LRest, PlRec*)

Andover, Lady: see Savage, Dorothy.

Arabella, Lady (1575–1615): only daughter of 1st Duke of Lennox, cousin of the King; married William Seymour, July 1610, in contravention of restrictions placed on her, and was imprisoned in the Tower until her death. (*Teth*)

Arundel, Countess of (Alathea Talbot, d. 1654): third daughter of 7th Earl of Shrewsbury; married Thomas Howard, Earl of Arundel, 1606. (*Qu, Teth*)

Astley (Ashley), Sir John (d. 1639): Master of Queen Elizabeth's Jewels; Master of the Revels to James and Charles I. (*Hay*)

Auchmouty, John: Scot who came to England with James, and profited by it; Groom of the Bedchamber. (*PlRec*)

Badger, Sir Thomas (d. 1638): Master of the Harriers for life, 1605; said to have the finest breed of bulldogs in England. (*Bar, Hay*)

Beaumont, Elizabeth: Sir Thomas of Coleorton's wife, who outlived him. (*Cole*)

Beaumont, Katherine(?): the wife of Sir Thomas Beaumont of Stoughton, uncle to the Coleorton Sir Thomas (d. 1621). (*Cole*)

Beaumont, Sir Thomas: of Coleorton (d. 1625); MP for Leicestershire; mine-owner; created Viscount Beaumont of Swords, 1622. (*Cole*)

Bedford, Countess (Lucy Harrington, 1581–1627): married 3rd Earl of Bedford in 1594; patron of writers and collector of pictures; Jonson, Donne, Daniel, and Drayton were all patronized by her. Lady of the Bedchamber and close friend of Queen Anne, she largely left the court after a serious illness in 1612. (*Bla, Qu*)

Berkshire, Countess of (Elizabeth Cecil, d. 1672): daughter of William, 2nd Earl of Exeter; married Thomas Howard, Earl of Berkshire, 1614. (*Chlo*)

Bevill, Lady (Frances Knevyt, d. 1605): widow of Sir William Bevill; married Francis Manners, 6th Earl of Rutland, 1602. (*Bla*)

Bowyer, Sir Henry (d. 1613/14): according to Chamberlain this excellent dancer died after overheating himself practising to dance at the wedding of Frances Howard. (*LRest*)

Brackley, Lord (John Egerton, 1623–86): also Lord Ellesmere; son of Earl of Bridgewater; Elder Brother in Milton's *Comus*; married daughter of Earl of Newcastle, 1642; a royalist. (*TempR, CBrit*)

Buckingham, Duke of (George Villiers, 1592–1628): favourite of King James and of King Charles; successively Viscount, Earl, Marquis, and Duke of Buckingham; achieved massive political power and influence before he was assassinated. (*PlRec*)

Carey, Sir Henry: Master of the Jewel House. (*Hay, Cav*)

Carey, Sir Robert (1560?–1639): tenth son of Henry, Lord Hunsdon; famous for riding post-haste to Scotland on the death of Elizabeth, for which he was (briefly) rewarded by becoming Groom of the Bedchamber; Earl of Monmouth, 1626. (*Bar*)

Car(e)y, Mistress Victoria (Victory) (b. 1620): daughter of the writer Lady Falkland, Maid of Honour to Henrietta Maria and frequent performer in court revels; married Sir William Uvedale, 1640. (*TempR, Salm*)

Carlisle, Countess (Lucy Percy, 1599–1660): daughter of Henry, Earl of Northumberland, married (against her father's wishes) James Hay, Earl of Carlisle, 1617; a notable (and somewhat scandalous) figure in Henrietta Maria's circle. (*Chlo, TempR*)

Carlisle, Earl of (James Hay, 1612–60): 2nd Earl; son of James Hay; a royalist in the Civil War. (*Salm*)

Carnarvon, Countess (Anna Sophia Herbert, d. 1695 'at a great age'): daughter of Philip, 4th Earl of Pembroke; married Robert Dormer, Earl of Carnarvon, 1625 (he was a Catholic). (*Chlo, TempR, Salm*)

Carr, Robert (1578–1654): Captain of the King's Body Guard to James I; Gentleman of the Prince's Bedchamber, 1625; Earl of Ancram (Ancrum), 1633. (*PlRec*)

Cavendish, Lady Anne (d. 1638): daughter of William, 2nd Earl of Devonshire; married Robert, Baron Rich, second son of Robert, Earl of Warwick, 1632. Patroness of literature. (*Chlo, TempR*)

Cavendish, Mr Charles (1620–43): brother to Earl of Devonshire; killed at Gainsborough, fighting for the King. (*TempR, CBrit*)

Cecil, Lady Elizabeth (*c.*1620–89): daughter of William, 2nd Earl of Salisbury; married William Cavendish, 3rd Earl of Devonshire, 1638. (*TempR*)

Chandos, Lord (George Brydges, 1620–55): royalist in Civil War. (*CBrit*)

Clifford, Anne (d. 1676): daughter of George, 3rd Earl of Cumberland, tutored by Samuel Daniel; married (1) Richard Sackville, Earl of Dorset, 1609; (2) Philip Herbert, 4th Earl of Pembroke, 1630. A doughty battler for her rights, she left a well-known diary. (*Qu, Cav*)

Constable, Sir William (of Flamborough, d. 1655): knighted by 2nd Earl of Essex, 1599, and involved in his rebellion, though pardoned; baronet in 1611; a parliamentarian and regicide. (*Bar*)

Cranborne, Lord (1619–60): son of William Cecil, 2nd Earl of Salisbury; a parliamentarian in the Civil War. (*CBrit*)

Cromwell, Sir Oliver of Hinchinbrook (*c*.1566–1655): knighted, 1598; involved in Essex rebellion 1601; Knight of the Bath, 1603; High Sheriff of Huntingdon and Cambridge; friend of Earl of Suffolk; uncle of the Protector, but fought for the King in Civil War. (*Bar*)

Dalison, Sir Roger (of Laughton, Lincs., d. *c*.1622): High Sheriff of Lincoln, 1601; Master of the Ordnance; client of Earl of Suffolk; created baronet, 1611. (*Bar*)

Derby, Countess of (Elizabeth de Vere, 1575–1627): daughter of 17th Earl of Oxford; married William, 6th Earl of Derby, 1594. (*Bla, Qu*)

Devereux, Frances (1599–1674): sister of the 3rd Earl of Essex. (*Cole*)

Devereux, Sir Walter: either the natural brother of 3rd Earl of Essex, knighted in 1617, or his cousin, later Viscount Hereford. (*Cole*)

Devonshire, Earl of (William Cavendish, 1617–84): 3rd Earl; he travelled abroad, 1634–7, with Thomas Hobbes; a royalist during the Civil War. (*CBrit*)

Digby, Lord (George, 1612–77): son of Earl of Bristol; a royalist in the Civil War. (*CBrit*)

Digby, Sir (Mr) John (1580–1653): knighted, 1607; Earl of Bristol, 1622; Gentleman of the Privy Chamber; Carver to the King, Gentleman of the Bedchamber to Charles; Vice-Chamberlain of the Household; ambassador at Madrid; shifted allegiance from parliament to the King in Civil War. (*Bar, Hay*)

Dorset, Countess of: see Clifford, Anne.

Dorset, Earl of (Richard Sackville, 1589–1624): married to Anne Clifford; something of a wastrel. (*Cav*)

Drury, Sir Robert (d. 1615): of Hawsted, knighted by 2nd Earl of Essex, 1592; patron of John Donne, who travelled with him and lived at Drury House. (*Bar*)

Dudley, Baron North (1581–1666): a musician and poet in his own right; parliamentarian in Civil War. (*Cav*)

Dungarvan, Lord (Richard Boyle, 1612–97): 2nd Earl of Cork, 1643. (*CBrit*)

Dunluce, Lord (Randal MacDonnell, 1609–82): Earl of Antrim, 1636; a royalist. (*CBrit*)

Dutton, Sir Thomas (d. 1614): sheriff of Cheshire, 1611. (*Bar*)

Effingham, Lady (Anne, d. 1638): married William Howard, 1596. (*Bla*)

Effingham, Lord (William Howard, 1577–1615): eldest son of Earl of Nottingham. (*Bar*)

Egerton, Alice (1619–89): daughter of Earl of Bridgewater, married Richard Vaughan, Earl of Carbery, 1652; the Lady in Milton's *Comus*. (*TempR*)

Egerton, Lady Katherine (b. 1611): daughter of Earl of Bridgewater; married Sir William Courten, *c*.1633. (*TempR*)

Egerton, Lady Penelope (b. 1610): daughter of Earl of Bridgewater; married Sir Robert Napier of Luton, Beds., *c*.1633. (*Chlo*)

Egerton, Thomas (1625–48): second son of Earl of Bridgewater; the Younger Brother in Milton's *Comus*. (*CBrit*)

Elgin, Earl of (Thomas Bruce, 1599–1663). (*CBrit*)

Ellesmere, Lord (*TempR*): see Brackley, Lord.

Erwin, Sir William: Gentleman Usher of the Prince's Privy Chamber, described as a dancing tutor to Prince Henry. (*PlRec*)

Essex, Countess of (Frances Howard, *c*.1593–1632): married Robert, 3rd Earl of Essex, 1606; after annulment in 1613, married Robert Carr, Earl of Somerset; convicted in 1616 of the murder of Thomas Overbury; imprisoned in the Tower. (*Teth*)

Essex, Earl of (Robert Devereux, 1591–1646): 3rd Earl; Lord Lieutenant of Staffordshire, 1612–46; Captain General of the parliamentary forces in the Civil War. (*Cole*)

Feilding, Lady Anne (d. 1635): daughter of Richard Weston, Earl of Portland; married Basil Feilding, later 2nd Earl of Denbigh. (*TempR*)

Feilding, Lady Elizabeth (b. 1619): sister of Basil; married Lewis Boyle, Lord Kynalmeaky (Kellymekin), son of Earl of Cork. (*Salm*)

Feilding, Lord (Basil Feilding, *c*.1608–75): son of Earl of Denbigh; ambassador to Venice, 1634–8; in opposition to his father he joined parliamentary forces in the Civil War. (*CBrit, Salm*)

Ferrabosco, Alfonso (?1572–1628): instructor to Princes Henry and Charles, Master of the King's Music in 1626; contributed music to a number of Jonson's masques.

Ger(r)ard, Lord (Thomas, Baron Gerard of Gerard's Bromley, *c*.1564–1618): soldier, courtier, and follower of 2nd Earl of Essex; friend of Robert Cecil; Knight Marshal of the Household. (*Bar*)

Gerrard (Jarret), Sir Thomas (*c*.1560–1621): of Bryan; MP for Liverpool and Lancashire; the cost of his baronetage was refunded in recognizance of his father's sufferings in the cause of Mary Queen of Scots. (*Bar, Hay*)

Giles, Thomas: organist of St Paul's and dancing master. (*Hay, Qu*)

Goodyere, Sir Henry (*c*.1571–1628): of Polesworth, Gentleman of the Privy Chamber to James I; intimate friend of Donne. (*Bar*)

Goring, Master George (*c*.1583–1663): cousin to Honora Denny; Earl of Norwich, 1644; Gentleman of the Privy Chamber to Prince of Wales and James; Knight Marshal of the Household; Vice-Chamberlain to Henrietta Maria and her Master of Horse; royalist in Civil War. (*Hay*)

Grandison, Viscount (William Villiers, 1614–43): nephew of Buckingham; killed in the siege of Bristol fighting for the King. (*CBrit*)

Gray, Sir John (d. 1611): a follower of 2nd Earl of Essex, knighted by him at Cadiz, 1596. (*Bar*)

Grey, Lady Elizabeth (Talbot, *c*.1587–1651): daughter of 7th Earl of Shrewsbury; married Henry Grey, Earl of Kent. (*Teth*)

Grey, Lady Elizabeth of Stamford (?): sister to next. (*TempR*)

Grey, Lord, of Stamford (Thomas, 1622–57): later a parliamentarian and regicide. (*TempR*)

Guildford, Lady Elizabeth (Elizabeth Somerset): daughter of 4th Earl of Worcester, married Sir Henry Guildford of Hemsted Place in Kent in 1596 (celebrated by Spenser's *Prothalamion*). (*Qu, Teth*)

Gunteret, Mr: a German, knighted 1608. (*Bar*)

Haddington, Viscountess (Elizabeth Radcliffe, d. 1618): daughter of 5th Earl of Sussex, her marriage was celebrated with Jonson's *Haddington Masque* in 1608; a great beauty. (*Teth*)

Hamilton, Marquis of (James, 2nd Marquis, 1589–1625): Gentleman of the King's Bedchamber; Lord Steward of the Household; Earl of Cambridge, 1619. (*PlRec*)

Hay, James (*c.*1580–1636): Scottish favourite of James and Charles, Viscount Doncaster, 1618; Earl of Carlisle, 1622. Gentleman of the Bedchamber; Master of the Great Wardrobe; Groom of the Stool; employed on diplomatic missions; conspicuous spender; married (1) Honora Denny, 1607; (2) Lucy Percy, 1617. (*Hay*)

Herbert, Lady (Anne, 1583–1606): daughter of Henry, 2nd Earl of Pembroke. (*Bla*)

Herbert, Lord (Charles, 1619–35): son of 4th Earl of Pembroke and Montgomery. (*TempR*)

Herbert, Mr Philip (1621–69): son of 4th Earl of Pembroke and Montgomery; styled Lord Herbert after 1635; a strong parliamentarian. (*TempR, Salm*)

Herbert, Sir William (1572–1655): son and heir of Edward, second son of William, Earl of Pembroke; Baron Powys, 1639. (*Bar*)

Herbert, William (1622–*c.*1649): son of 4th Earl of Pembroke; MP for Monmouth in 1640; royalist. (*CBrit*)

Hobart, Sir Henry (*c.*1554–1625): Attorney-General, 1606–13; Chief Justice of Common Pleas, 1613–25; Chancellor to Prince Henry and later to Charles. (*MemM*)

Holland, Earl of (Henry Rich, 1590–1649): Captain of the Yeomen of the Guard; Chancellor of Cambridge University; High Steward to the Queen; Groom of the Stool; a side-changer in the Civil War, executed in 1649. (*Cav, TempR, CBrit*)

Houghton, Sir Gilbert (1591?–1647): son of Sir Richard; MP for Lancashire and High Sheriff in 1643; royalist in Civil War. (*PlRec*)

Houghton, Sir Richard (1570–1630): sheriff of Lancashire, 1598, knighted by 2nd Earl of Essex, 1599; baronet, 1611; entertained James on his journey south in 1603, and visited by him in 1617. (*Bar*)

Howard, Lady (?): H&S suggest 'the wife of the Sir William Howard who danced in *Love's Triumph*'. There is considerable doubt who this might be. (*Chlo*)

Howard, Sir Charles: either (1579–1642) second son of Earl of Nottingham, whom he succeeded in 1624; MP for various places; Lord-Lieutenant of Surrey; or the son of Earl of Suffolk, below; or Charles Howard of Bookham (d. 1652), whose brother(s) were performers. (*Bar*)

Howard, Sir Charles (d. 1622): fourth son of Earl of Suffolk; married Mary Fitz of Fitzford, Devon. (*?Bar, Cav, PlRec*)

Howard, Sir Edward: either (of Great Bookham, 1580–1620) cupbearer to James; or seventh son of Thomas, Earl of Suffolk (d. 1675), who seems rather young. (*Bar*)

Howard, Lady Elizabeth (1586–1658): daughter of Earl of Suffolk; married Sir William Knollys (see below), 1605 (his second wife). (*Bla*)

Howard, Frances: see Essex, Countess of.

Howard, Lady Frances: daughter of 2nd Earl of Suffolk. (*Salm*)

Howard, Lady Frances of Berkshire (d. 1658): Maid of Honour to Henrietta Maria. (*TempR*)

Howard, Sir Francis (d. 1651): of Great Bookham, knighted 1604. (*Bar*)

Howard, Henry: third son of Earl of Suffolk; married Elizabeth Basset of Blore. (*Cav*)

Howard, Mr Henry, of Berkshire: presumably brother to Frances of Berkshire. (*TempR*)

Howard, Lady Margaret (1623–89): daughter of 2nd Earl of Suffolk; married Robert Boyle, Lord Broghill, 1641. (*Salm*)

Howard, Theophilus: see Walden, Lord.

Howard, Master Thomas ?(1619–1706): younger brother of Charles, Viscount Andover; later 3rd Earl of Berkshire. (*Salm*)

Howard, Sir Thomas (d. 1669): second son of Earl of Suffolk; Viscount Andover, 1622; Earl of Berkshire, 1626. (*Hay, Cav, PlRec*)

Huntingdon, Countess (Elizabeth Stanley, 1587–1633): daughter of 5th Earl of Derby; married Henry Hastings, 5th Earl of Huntingdon, 1601. (*Qu*)

Jarret, Sir Thomas: see Gerrard.

Kellymekin, Lady: see Feilding, Elizabeth.

Killigrew, Sir Robert (1580–1633): father of Thomas; MP for various Cornish boroughs. (*Bar*)

Killigrew, Thomas (1612–83): servant of the Queen in exile; playwright and theatre manager at the Restoration. (*TempR*)

Knollys, Sir William (c.1545–1632): Treasurer of the Household, 1602–16; Master of Court of Wards, 1614–19; originally a client of 2nd Earl of Essex; married Elizabeth Howard, daughter of Earl of Suffolk, 1605. (*Cav*)

Lanier, Nicholas (1588–1666): singer, composer, and painter; first holder of the title 'Master of the King's Music'; innovator in declamatory songs, from Campion's *Somerset Masque* of 1613 onwards. (*TempR*)

Leigh, Sir John, of Coldrey, Hants (*c.*1575–1612): knighted by 2nd Earl of Essex at Cadiz, 1597; MP for Cornish boroughs. (*Bar*)

Lennox, Duchess of (Mary Villiers, 1622–85): daughter of Duke of Buckingham; married 4th Duke, 1637 (her second marriage). (*Salm*)

Lennox, Duke of (Ludovic Stuart, 3rd Duke, 1574–1624): accompanied James to England; later Baron Settrington and Earl of Richmond, Earl of Newcastle, and Duke of Richmond. Gentleman of the Bedchamber; Lord Steward of the Household, 1621. (*Bar*)

Lennox, Duke of (James Stuart, 4th Duke, 1612–55): later Duke of Richmond; Privy Councillor and Gentleman of the Bedchamber; royalist in Civil War. (*CBrit, Salm*)

Livingstone, John, of Kinnaird (d. 1628): Groom of the Bedchamber to James. (*LRest*)

Lupo, Thomas (d. 1628): violinist in the King's Music, composer of songs and, especially, of music for strings. (*Hay*)

Ma(u)nsell, Sir Lewis (*c.*1584–1638): son of Sir Thomas of Margam, Glam.; baronet, 1611; succeeded to title in 1626. (*Bar*)

Ma(u)nsell, Sir Robert (*c.*1569–1656): of Pentney and Norwich. MP for various constituencies; knighted by 2nd Earl of Essex at Cadiz, 1596; Vice-Admiral of the Narrow Seas, 1603; Treasurer of the Navy; Vice-Admiral of England, 1618; married Elizabeth Roper, maid of honour to Queen Anne. (*Bar*)

Monson, Sir Thomas (1564–1641): master falconer and master of the armoury at the Tower; client of the Howards, patron of Campion; later implicated in the Overbury murder trials, imprisoned though never found guilty. (*Bar*)

Montgomery, Countess of (Susan Vere, 1587–1629): daughter of 17th Earl of Oxford; married Sir Philip Herbert, Earl of Montgomery (later 4th Earl of Pembroke), 1604. (*Bla, Qu*)

Montgomery, Earl of (Philip Herbert, 1584–1650): younger brother of William, 3rd Earl of Pembroke; Earl of Montgomery, 1605; 4th Earl of Pembroke, 1630; Lord Chamberlain, 1626–41; parliamentarian in the Civil War; married (1) Susan Vere, (2) Anne Clifford. (*PlRec*)

Mounteagle, Lord (William Parker, 1575–1622): Catholic peer, famous for the letter he received giving a clue to the Gunpowder Plot. (*Bar*)

Newcastle, Earl of (William Cavendish, 1593–1676): Gentleman of the Bedchamber and Governor to Prince of Wales, 1637; playwright and pre-eminent horseman; royalist in Civil War; his second wife was the writer Margaret Cavendish. (*Bols*)

Newport, Countess of (Anne Boteler, d. 1669): daughter of Sir John Boteler and Buckingham's half-sister Elizabeth; married Mountjoy Blount, 1627; became a Catholic, 1637. (*Chlo, LRest, Salm*)

Newport, Earl of (Mountjoy Blount, 1597–1666): illegitimate son of Penelope Devereux/Rich and Earl of Devonshire; Privy Councillor; Master of the Ordnance. Sympathetic to parliamentary grievances, he yet fought for the King. (*CBrit, Salm*)

Nottingham, Lord (Charles, Lord Howard of Effingham, 1536–1624): Lord High Admiral; Lord Steward of the Household; victor over the Armada. (*Bar*)

Oxford, Countess (Beatrice van Hemmema, d. 1653/7): married 19th Earl of Oxford before 1626. (*Chlo, TempR*)

Paget, Lord (William, 1609–78): married to Earl of Holland's daughter; a waverer during the Civil War. (*CBrit, Salm*)

Palmer, Roger: cupbearer to Prince Henry and Prince Charles; master of Charles's household; a fine dancer. (*PlRec*)

Petre, Lady Katharine (Catherine Somerset, d. 1624): daughter of 4th Earl of Worcester; married William, Baron Petre of Writtle, in a joint ceremony with her sister Elizabeth (see Guildford). (*Teth*)

Philips (Phelips), Sir Edward (1560?–1614): Speaker of House of Commons, 1604; Chancellor to Prince Henry. (*MemM*)

Porter, Mrs (Olivia Boteler, d. 1663): niece of Buckingham; sister of Countess of Newport; married Endymion Porter, *c.*1620; a Catholic. (*Chlo*)

Portland, Countess (Frances Stuart, 1617–94): sister of Duke of Lennox, married Richard Weston, Earl of Portland. (*Salm*)

Preston, Sir Richard (d. 1628): later Lord Dingwall; Gentleman of the Privy Chamber to James; instructor in arms to Prince Henry. (*Hay*)

Reynolds, Sir Carey (Carew Reynell) (*c.*1563–1624): knighted by 2nd Earl of Essex, 1599; closely involved with him and his son; Gentleman Pensioner to Elizabeth and James. (*Bar*)

Rich, Lady (Penelope Devereux, d. 1607): daughter of 1st Earl of Essex, the 'Stella' of Sidney's sonnets; married Robert, Lord Rich, 1581, but lived openly with Charles Blount, Lord Mountjoy, by whom she had five children. Divorced 1605. (*Bla*)

Rich, Lord (Robert, 1611–59): son of the Earl of Warwick; married the daughter of the Earl of Devonshire; switched from king to parliament in the Civil War. (*CBrit*)

Rich, Lord, of Holland (1620–75): son of Earl of Holland.

Richard, Lewis (d. 1658): composer of music for *Salm*, none of which survives.

Russell, Lady Anne (d. 1696): second daughter of 4th Earl of Bedford; married George Digby, 2nd Earl of Bristol. (*TempR*)

Russell, Lord (William, 1616–1700): 5th Earl of Bedford, 1641; married daughter of Robert Carr/Frances Howard; parliamentarian in Civil War. (*Salm*)

Russell, Master (Francis, d. 1641): younger brother of Lord Russell. (*Salm*)

Saltoun, Lord (Alexander Abernethy, 1611–70). (*CBrit*)

Savage, Mrs Dorothy (*c*.1611–91): daughter of Viscount Savage, married Charles Howard, Viscount Andover, son of Earl of Berkshire, 1637. (*Chlo, Salm*)

Savage, Mrs Elizabeth: sister of the above; married Sir John Thimbelly of Irnham, Lincs. (*Chlo*)

Seymour, Sir William (1587–1660): styled Lord Beauchamp from Sept. 1618; Lord Hertford, 1640; Duke of Somerset, 1660; married (1) Lady Arabella Stuart, 1610; (2) Frances Devereux, 1617. (*Cole*)

Somerset, Sir Thomas (1579–*c*.1650): third son of 4th Earl of Worcester, went to Scotland to bring news of Elizabeth's death to James; Queen Anne's Master of Horse; Viscount Somerset of Cashel, 1626. (*Bar*)

Spencer, Mr Henry (1620–43): Earl of Sunderland, 1643; killed at Newbury fighting for the King. (*CBrit*)

Strange, Lady (Charlotte, d. 1663): daughter of Claude de la Trémoille; married James, Lord Strange, 7th Earl of Derby, 1626; defended Latham Castle in 1644. (*Chlo*)

Suffolk, Countess (Catherine Knyvett): married second husband, Sir Thomas Howard, 1st Earl of Suffolk, 1583; Keeper of the Queen's Jewels; Lady-in-Waiting to Queen Anne. (*Bla*)

Sussex, Earl of (Robert Radcliffe, 1573–1629): 5th Earl, 1593; knighted by 2nd Earl of Essex at Cadiz, 1596; imprisoned on suspicion of complicity with his rebellion; Lord-Lieutenant of Essex. (*Bar*)

Vere, Lady Susan: see Montgomery, Countess.

Villiers, Lady Mary (b. 1621): daughter of the Duke of Buckingham. (*TempR*)

Walden, Lord (Theophilus Howard, 1584–1640): eldest son of Thomas Howard, Earl of Suffolk; 2nd Earl of Suffolk, 1626; married Elizabeth, daughter of Earl of Dunbar in 1612. (*Bar, Hay*)

Walden, Lord (James Howard, 1620–81): son of Theophilus, 2nd Earl of Suffolk. (*CBrit*)

Walsingham, Lady (Ethelreda or Audrey Shelton): wife to Sir Thomas Walsingham; accompanied Queen Anne from Scotland; with her husband Chief Keeper of the Queen's Wardrobe. (*Bla*)

Weston, Mrs (Anne): daughter of Richard, Earl of Portland; married Basil Feilding, heir to 1st Earl of Denbigh. (*Chlo, TempR*)

Wharton, Lord (Philip, 1613–96): reputed to be one of the handsomest of courtiers in his youth; a parliamentarian, holding office during the Commonwealth and Protectorate. (*CBrit*)

Willoughby, (Lord): possibly Sir Percival Willoughby of Wollaton Hall (d. 1643), or his son Sir Francis (1591–1662). (?*Cole*)

Willoughby, Lord (Robert Bertie, Lord Willoughby de Eresby, 1582–1642): Earl of Lindsey, 1626; Lord High Admiral, 1636; General of the King's forces, 1642; killed at Edgehill. (*Bar ?Cole*)

Windsor, Lady (Catherine Somerset, 1590–1641): seventh daughter of 4th Earl of Worcester; married Thomas, 6th Lord Windsor. (*Qu, Teth*)

Winter, Lady (Anne Somerset): third daughter of Lord Worcester; married Sir Edward Winter of Lydney, Glos., ?1595/?1597. (*Qu, Teth*)

Woodhouse, Sir William: knighted by 2nd Earl of Essex, 1591. (*Bar*)

Worcester, Earl of (Edward Somerset, 1553–1628): 4th Earl; Master of the Horse; Lord Privy Seal. (*Bar*)

Wroth, Lady (Mary Sidney, *c.*1586/7–*c.*1651/3): daughter of Robert and niece to Philip Sidney; married Sir Robert Wroth, 1604; mistress of 3rd Earl of Pembroke; perhaps the most important woman writer of the period, with poetry and the long prose romance *Urania* to her credit. (*Bla*).

GLOSSARY

a-cross crossed (*Qu*)
absolute perfect, noble (*Bla*)
accessions additions (*Qu*)
accited summoned (*Bla*)
adventure, at recklessly (*LRest*)
an if
anadem wreath, garland (*Bar*)
antic grotesque (*MemM, Cav*)
apprehensive ready to seize (*MemM*)
approved demonstrated (*Bar*)
artificial skilfully made or crafted
    (non-pejorative) (*Bla, Hay, Teth*)
aspire breathe (*Gold*)
assisted jointly produced(?) (*MemM*)
attend, attending (a)wait, waiting
    (*Bar, CBrit*)
aversed turned aside (*Qu*)

baffled publicly disgraced (*MemM*)
baldric shoulder-belt
balneo bain-marie (*Salm*)
bandora flat-backed, wire-strung
    instrument, used as bass instrument
    in lute consort (*Hay*)
barb mow (*CBrit*)
bases pleated skirts after the pattern of
    Roman armour (*Teth, MemM, Chlo,
    CBrit*)
battle battalion (*Teth*)
bavin bundle of brushwood (*PlRec*)
behoof benefit (*CBrit*)
belie fake (*LRest*)
belly (of costume) stiffened, padded
    front to doublet (*Cav*)
bewray betray, reveal (*Teth*)
bidet pony (*Chlo*)
biggin(s) child's cap (*Chr, Salm*)
birth offspring (*Qu*)
blown in bloom (*Hay*)
bobs earrings (*Chr*)
boisterous rough, violent (*LRest*)
bolter sieve (*PlRec*)
bombard large drinking-vessel (*LRest*)
bottom spool (*Qu*)

bouge court-rations (*LRest*)
brack flaw in cloth (*Bols*)
bugle glass bead (*Chr*)
bully (adj.) jolly (*Chr*)
buskins long boots (*Hay, Teth,
    MemM, Bols*)

cacodemon evil spirit (*CBrit*)
caduce, caduceus staff twined with
    two serpents (*CBrit*)
Camber Wales (*Teth*)
Cambria Wales (*Teth*)
Cantus treble part (*Hay*)
caparisons ornamental covering of
    horses (*MemM*)
card map (*Nept*)
caroche carriage (*Cav*)
casque helmet (*Qu*)
cassock long, loose gown (*Bols*)
cat-a-mountain wild cat (*Qu*)
catholic universal (*LRest*)
cavallerizzo riding-master (*Salm*)
cavils quibbles (*CBrit*)
chandry candle-makers (*LRest*)
charger large flat dish (*Nept*)
check(s) rebuff(s), restraint(s) (*Bar*)
chemic alchemical (*Teth*)
chevron inverted 'v' shape (*Teth*)
church-ale festival feast (*Qu*)
cithara lyre (*CBrit*)
clinquant sparkling, glistering (*MemM*)
close (music) cadential figure, final
    phrase (*Chlo*)
cockle-demois ?shells representing
    money (*MemM*)
collied soot-darkened (*CBrit*)
complement ceremony, formality
    (*Teth, MemM, Bols*)
conceitful witty, ingenious (*MemM*)
confederacy conspiracy (*Salm*)
congee bow (*Cav*)
conger eel (*Nept*)
conspicuous striking to the eye (*Bla*)
cony rabbit (*Chr*)

282

coranto (1) lively dance in triple time (*passim*); (2) news-sheet ('courant') (*Nept*, *Salm*)

cornetts curved wooden instruments with brass-type mouthpiece, and finger-holes like a recorder; thought of as particularly suitable for accompanying voices (*Hay*, *Qu*, *Cav*, *Nept*)

costard-mongers apple-sellers (*Chlo*)

counter-tenor male voice singing alto part in falsetto (*Cav*)

country county (*Cole*)

courage sexual appetite (*Salm*)

credence credentials, mark of good faith (*Hay*)

cuirass breastplate (*MemM*)

curtal small horse (*Chlo*)

curvet leap about (*Chlo*)

degrees seats on scaffolds, steps (*MemM*, *PlRec*, *TempR*)

design (v.) indicate (*Bar*, *Qu*)

desinent terminal (*Bla*)

device masque invention (*LRest*)

diameter, in diametrically (*CBrit*)

diapason octave (*Hay*)

discoloured of various colours (*Chlo*)

displays opens (*Bar*)

dissolve explain (*MemM*)

dizzards idiots (*MemM*)

doublet worn over the shirt, usually with padded and stiffened 'belly piece'

drake dragon (*Qu*)

draughts bow-shots (*MemM*)

dressed (1) purified (*Bar*)
(2) prepared, ready (*Nept*)

electuary medicine (*Salm*)

ell measure of length of about 45 inches (*Chr*)

elogy poem of praise (*Qu*)

enchase engrave (*MemM*); set in (*Bla*)

encounter oppose, contest (*MemM*)

entertain support, maintain (*Teth*)

epicene having characteristics of both sexes (*Nept*)

errors wanderings (*Bla*)

estrangeful foreign in appearance (*MemM*)

event outcome (*LRest*)

exhalation vapour (*Salm*)

expect await (*Gold*); ?pay attention (*Nept*)

expense (v.) disburse (*Cole*)

expostulate reason with (*Bar*)

extols raises (*Bar*)

fabulous fond of fictions (*Bla*)

facile affable, courteous (*Hay*)

fain (adv.) willingly, eagerly (*Hay*)

fardel burden (*MemM*)

feat neat, well-turned-out (*Cav*)

feature form, shape (*Bla*)

fell savage (*Chlo*)

fetch trick (*MemM*)

figuring representing

finèd refined, cleared (*Teth*)

fisling fussing, fidgeting (*Chris*)

flamed ardent (*LRest*)

forwardness preparedness (*LRest*)

fotive warming (*CBrit*)

frolic make merry (*Hay*)

front forehead (*Bla*)

frontispiece proscenium (*Teth*, *CBrit*, *Salm*)

furniture costume, equipment (*Qu*)

galliard (n.) triple-time dance (*passim*); (adj.) lively, sturdy (*Bols*)

gamachios leggings (*Cav*)

gargarism a gargle (*Salm*)

gear harness (*Chr*)

gears riding equipment (*Qu*)

genial nuptial (*Bar*)

genii guardian spirits (*Gold*)

glory aureole or nimbus (*TempR*)

good den good evening (*CBrit*)

gramercy thank you (*MemM*)

gratis free (*Bols*)

greaves leg-armour (*MemM*)

greces steps (*Bla*, *LRest*, *MemM*)

guaiacum resin from the West Indian tree used in medicine (*CBrit*)

guidon flag, pennant (*Teth*)

hability ability (*LRest*)

habit(s) costume(s)

hales hauls (*Nept*)

halfpace step upon which throne is placed (*CBrit*)

head-tire head-dress (*Teth*)

high-palmed having lofty antlers (*MemM*)

hight are named (archaic) (*Gold*)

hind farm servant (*Cole, CBrit*)

hoboy predecessor of the modern oboe; louder and coarser in tone, used especially for processions (*Hay*)

honest (v.) honour (*Qu*)

honour, to make an to bow

horn drinking-vessel (*Cole*)

hose breeches

humour caprice, fantasy (*MemM*); elsewhere one of the four fundamental elements

hutch box into which flour was sifted (*PlRec*)

imprese emblems with motto (*Bla, CBrit*)

incline make obeisance (*Bar*)

induced brought in (*Bla*)

ingenious wise (*Teth, MemM*)

ingenuously freely, generously (*Qu*)

insociate solitary (*Bar*)

intendment intention (*Teth*)

invade violate the rights of (*Gold*)

invention design, plan, idea

jagged (of garment) cut or slashed to reveal contrasting fabric beneath (*Cav*)

jars arguments (*Hay*)

julep sweet drink (*Salm*)

just exactly (*Hay*)

kill-pot heavy drinker (*Chr*)

knap break (*Cole*)

labels narrow bands of fabric (*MemM, Teth*)

laborious hard-working (*Mem*)

lantitantical from 'lant', meaning 'urine'; this seems to be a nonce coinage (*Cole*)

late recent (*Qu*)

lavolta active triple-time dance including leaps (*Hay, CBrit*)

livery members of a guild (*Chr*)

lout bow (*Cav*)

lubricity slipperiness (with secondary sexual sense) (*CBrit*)

luciferously proudly, like Satan (also known as 'Lucifer') (*Mem*)

lutes standard instrument for accompanying the voice, strung like guitar, but with pear-shaped back; there were different sizes.

luxuries lustful actions (*CBrit*)

luxurious lecherous (*CBrit*)

main large, solid (*MemM*)

make mate (*Bar*)

manage exercise of horses in dressage (*Salm*)

mandril miner's pick (*Cole*)

marchpain marzipan (*Chr*)

mawkin mop (*PlRec*)

mazarded knocked on the head (*LRest*)

mazer wooden drinking-bowl (*Hay*)

mean space in the meantime (*MemM*)

measures dances

mention trace, vestige (*Bar*)

metheglin spiced mead (*Bar*)

mew shed feathers (*CBrit*)

miching skulking (*MemM*)

motet polyphonic piece, often sacred in content (*Hay*)

motley a fool's particoloured costume (*CBrit*)

muckenders handkerchief, napkin (*Salm*)

muscadine muscatel wine (*Salm*)

music in addition to the standard meaning (1) band of musicians, (2) musical instruments (*Teth*)

neat (of dress) elegant, trim (*Chr*)

neophyte novice (*Salm*)

object (v.) place before (*Bar*)

oblation solemn offering (*TempR*)

obnoxious subject (*Gold*)

observant servant (*MemM*)

offer at try (*LRest*)

olla podrida stew (*Nept*)

or ... or either ... or (*passim*)

orcs sea monsters (*Nept*)
ordnance cannons (*Qu*)
orgies secret rites (*Qu*)
orient lustrous (*Bar*)

pace dancing (*Cole*)
pack worthless fellow (*MemM*)
paled in fenced, enclosed (*Cav*)
paper-rush papyrus (*Bla*)
parsons personages (*Chlo*)
parterre ornamental flower-bed (*CBrit*)
participate share in (*Cav*)
particle small part (*MemM*)
pawn pledge (*Nept*)
peculiar particular, special (*CBrit*)
peel baker's shovel (*PlRec*)
pelf wealth (*Chr*)
period ending (*Bla*)
perpetuana glossy cloth like serge (*Cav*)
personated acted (*Bla*)
personator actor (*Bar*)
perspectives telescopes (*Salm*)
perspicuity clarity (*Qu*)
pervert (v.) subvert (*Chlo*)
pester overcrowd (*Teth*)
piebaldly in various colours (*Cav*)
piece cask (*PlRec*)
pikes difficulties (*Chr*)
pinching miserliness (*Cole*)
platan plane tree (*Salm*)
podrida rotten (Spanish) (*Nept*)
pomado scented ointment (*Salm*)
pompously in magnificent splendour (*MemM*)
poniard dagger (*CBrit*)
ported having gates (*Bar*)
post messenger (*Chlo, Teth*)
postilion swift messenger (*Chlo*)
pot it drink (*Cole*)
powdered (of meat) salted or spiced (*PlRec*)
prefer proffer (*MemM*)
preferrer promoter (*MemM*)
preposterous in inverted order; absurd (*Qu*)
present, presently immediate, immediately
president presiding deity, guardian (*Qu*)

pretend claim (*CBrit, Chlo*)
prevent anticipate, forestall
prick-song song from printed music (*TempR*)
proper to belonging to (*Salm*)
prospect view (*Teth*)
prospective perspective scene (*Nept*)
prove test, try (*Qu*)
pumps light dancing shoes (*Bols*)
purfle profile (*Bla*)
purl thread of twisted gold (*MemM*); pleat (*Bols*)
purset little purse (*Qu*)

quadrature square (*TempR*)

ranged classified (*Bla*)
rare thin (*Bla*)
rather, the the more readily (*Gold*)
reach fathom, understand (*CBrit*)
reality integrity, loyalty (*LRest*)
receipt receptacle (*Teth*)
record sing of (*Cav*)
redargutory confutatory (*CBrit*)
redoubts fortifications (*CBrit*)
reflex reflection (*Qu, CBrit*)
relievo relief-work (*Teth*)
repair return (*Cole, MemM, CBrit*)
reverberate reflecting (*Bla*)
review see again (*Nept*)
rosmarine sea-dew (*Teth*)
roundelays simple songs with refrain (*CBrit*)
rustic (architectural) rough-hewn (*Teth*)

sable gloomy, funereal (*Salm*)
sack a white wine (*Cole*)
sackbut narrow-bored trombone, quieter than modern instrument (of different sizes, the 'double' being the bass) (*Hay*)
sans without (*Cole*)
saraband triple-time dance (*TempR*)
scaffolds the temporary construction for seating spectators (*Hay, Cav*)
scarfing bands of cloth (*MemM*)
scene painted curtain (*Bla*)
sciental endowed with knowledge (*Bla*)
sconces fortifications (*CBrit*)
sedulous diligent (*CBrit*)

seeled blinded (*CBrit*)
seem think fit (*Teth*)
sempster seamstress (*Chr*)
sessions judicial trial (*CBrit*)
several, severally separate(ly), individual(ly)
shadowed concealed (*Hay, Cav*)
shift change (*Teth*)
shifts devices, tricks (*LRest*)
sieges seats (*Nept*)
silly lowly (*Cav*)
skirts (of male dress) tabs of varying lengths depending below the waistline of the doublet (*Teth, Cav, Salm*)
skirts (of night) the end (*Nept*)
slops very wide, baggy knee-breeches (*Cav*)
socks long boots (buskins) (*Bar*)
sod boiled (*PlRec*)
spagyric alchemist (*Salm*)
spurging excretion (*Qu*)
stale decoy, stalking-horse (*CBrit*)
state (chair of) king's throne
states nobles (*Hay*)
still always (*Bar, Gold*)
store plenty (*Qu*)
strangers foreigners (*LRest*)
stravagant extraordinary (*MemM*)
styles titles (*Nept*)
subject (v.) attribute to (*Bar*)
subtle pervasive (*Bla*)
surquidry presumption (*LRest*)
sustained bore up (*MemM*)
swabber low, vulgar person (*Cole*)
swarth black, dusky (*Bla*)

tabor small drum, usually accompanying a pipe (*PlRec*)
taking superficially charming (*Bar*)
tall fine, elegant (*CBrit*)
term statue of head and upper body merging into pedestal (*Chlo, TempR*)
thermae baths(?) (*CBrit*)
tiffany transparent fabric (*MemM*)
timbrels tambourines (*Qu*)
tirewoman ladies' maid, dresser; costumier (*LRest*)

toys trifles (*MemM, Cav*)
trace line (*Chr*)
translation transformation (*LRest*)
treacle medicinal compound (*Salm*)
trencher platter (*Bar*)
trencher-fools parasitic fools at a meal (*MemM*)
trestles legs (*Bols*)
turn-served experienced (*MemM*)
type a small dome (*MemM, TempR*)

undergone undertaken, performed (*Bar*)
undertake rebuke (*Cav*)
unrude uncouth (*Chr*)
use interest (*TempR*)

vail doff a hat (*Cav*)
venifical associated with witchcraft (*Qu*)
verge (1) brim (*CBrit*); (2) precincts of the court (*LRest, Bols*)
virgin wax fine, purified white wax (*MemM*)
vomit emetic (*Salm*)
votes prayers (*Nept*)

wantonly playfully (*MemM*)
watch await expectantly (*Hay*)
watchet blue (*MemM*)
water-gall a secondary or imperfect rainbow (*Cole*)
whimlens miserable wretches (*LRest*)
wights people (*Chr*)
wings (of costume) stiffened flaps at the shoulder
withe willow wand (*Chr*)
without outside (*Cav*)
witty wise (*Bar*)
wonted customary (*Qu*)
work scenery (*MemM*)
wreathed twisted (*Bla*)
writhen coiled (*Teth*)

Lightning Source UK Ltd.
Milton Keynes UK
UKOW08n0114250417
299836UK00006B/69/P